M000087870

Brother Joe

Brother Joe

A 20th Century Apostle

Biography
of
Joseph Wesley Mathews

by
James K. Mathews

resurgence publishing

COPYRIGHT ©2006 James K. Mathews

Brother Joe: A 20th Century Apostle. All rights reserved. No part of this book may be used or reproduced in any manner whatsoever without permission, except in the case of brief quotations in critical articles and reviews. Contact Resurgence Publishing Corporation.

Published with Permission: The original materials used in this publication are provided by James K. Mathews and surviving members of the family of Joseph Wesley Mathews (1911-1977). All editing of those materials is the responsibility of the editors of this publication and in no way is intended to represent the views or opinions of those who contributed originals or copies of the materials.

Info@ResurgencePublishing.com
www.ResurgencePublishing.com

Front cover sketch by Rudolph Wendelin, 1971

Cover design by Tara McDermott, Dubuque, Iowa

Printed on recycled paper

ISBN 0-9763892-1-5

Printed in the United States of America

Dedication

to

Joe's wife

Evelyn Johnston Mathews

and
their sons

Joseph, James, and John

and
Joe's siblings

Daisy, Margaret, Elizabeth, Donald, Alice, and Alleene

and to
our parents

James Davenport Mathews
Laura Wilson Mathews

Books by Bishop James K. Mathews

A Church Truly Catholic
A Global Odyssey: The Autobiography of James K. Mathews
Church Strategy in Alcohol Problems
Eternal Values in a World of Change
Selections from E. Stanley Jones: Christ and Human Need
     [with Eunice Jones Mathews]
Set Apart to Serve: The Meaning and Role of Episcopacy in the
     Wesleyan Tradition
South of the Himalayas: One Hundred Years of Methodism in
     India and Pakistan
The Matchless Weapon: Satyagraha (about M. K. Gandhi)
To the End of the Earth: A Study in Luke-Acts on the Life and
     Mission of the Church
Vision and Supervision (a compilation of the Council of Bishops,
     UMC, 2003) [co-editors, Bishop J. K. M. and Bishop
     William B. Oden]

Acknowledgements

It has often occurred to me that the writing of a book – particularly a biography or autobiography – is a collective enterprise. One speaks to many people in search for helpful recollections. Add to this the stacks of books consulted or the reams of lecture notes and correspondence. In sum, an immense debt of gratitude accumulates, which at the very least must be acknowledged.

One may begin with family. Once again, how do I thank my long-suffering and tireless wife, Eunice? I write everything in longhand and she is one of the few persons who can decipher my scrawl. She has seen the book through several drafts. This is spousal devotion of a high order.

Other relatives have made their contributions. My sister Alice Mathews Neill has provided an appropriate Foreword. My sister Alleene also was of help up to the time of her death in 2005. My brother's sons, Joseph, Jr., and James, were of considerable assistance. My daughters Anne Younes and Janice Stromsem gave freely of their memories of their uncle. They were present at his funeral. Our son Stanley provided a poem of tribute which appears in the first chapter. He also was a part of the trio who circumnavigated the globe, as recounted in Chapter 9.

Great appreciation needs to be expressed to Betty C. (Mrs. Martin) Pesek of Chicago, for years Joe's "secretary" and devoted guardian of the extensive files housed in the Kemper Building in Chicago. She went to very great lengths to assure access to these indispensable documents. Our colleague Carol (Mrs. Joseph) Pierce gave aid as well.

Then there exists an array of former associates of my brother. The list is long and should include in most instances their spouses as well. These include John Epps, John Cock, Joseph Slicker, Justin Morrill, Charles Lingo, Fred Buss, Don Cramer, Joseph and Marilyn Crocker, Don Clark, Frank and Aimee Hilliard, David Scott (paper of his late wife, Patricia), Kay Townley, Mary Warren Moffett, George Walters, George Holcombe, Raymond Spencer,

David McCleskey, Charles and Doris Hahn, and William and Nancy Grow.

In connection with the Christian Faith and Life Community in Austin, Texas, information was supplied by a number of the persons mentioned above. W. Jack Lewis, founder of that community, was helpful both in conversation and through documents before his death. Former colleagues at Perkins School of Theology were generous in providing recollections. Among these were Dr. Schubert Ogden, Dr. Victor Furnish, and a former dean, Dr. Joseph D. Quillian, Jr. To this may be added information from the current dean, William Lawrence. Former students who recalled experiences with Joe were William Holmes and his wife Nancy, Harry C. Kiely, James T. Clemons, and Roberto Escamilla.

Details about battles in the Pacific were provided by the Department of Defense. More facts came from the Rev. Dr. John M. Vayhinger, a former chaplain and colleague in ministry. Dr. John Godsey of Wesley Seminary, Washington, D.C., also helped.

Particular mention must be made of evaluations of Joe's work coming from Dr. John Silber, President of Boston University and a former dean at the University of Texas. The same is true of extensive content from Dr. John L. Epps, and letters from Gene W. Marshall, John P. Cock, and F. Nelson Stover, all colleagues of my brother from the Ecumenical Institute/the Institute of Cultural Affairs (EI/ICA). I greatly appreciate the information from my colleague, now deceased, Bishop Eugene Slater. And I consulted freely with Joe's sister-in-law, Eleanore Peterson of Lancaster, Pennsylvania.

There were the readers: Betty Pesek, John Cock, Alan Geyer, Alice Neill, and Joseph Mathews, Jr. To this group should be added the name of Dr. Edward C. Hobbs, once an associate of Joe Mathews while both were at Perkins. Now Professor Hobbs is at Wellesley College.

Much of Joe's earlier life and my own are practically identical. Therefore, Abingdon Press/Cokesbury granted permission for the reuse of some material which appeared in my autobiography, *A Global Odyssey* (2000). Some lengthy passages about the programs and processes of EI/ICA appear in the pages, which was often the product of "corporate writing" of which I myself was frequently a participant over the years.

Dr. Maynard Moore, a former student of Professor Joseph Mathews at Perkins, has undertaken the task of making this manuscript print-ready for the Resurgence Publishing editorial guild. For this I am very grateful. Many thanks!

On the front cover of this book appears a profile of my brother in pen-sketch style. It captures its subject in a remarkable way. It is signed simply "Wendelin '71," under Joe's signature. The artist, Rudolph Wendelin, was the person who originated the well-known representation of "Smokey the Bear." Diligent search was made only to discover that the artist is now deceased. He gave the sketch to Joe to use any way he wished. We gratefully acknowledge this picture.

If I have failed to mention others who have participated, it is unintentional and we do thank you.

~*James K. Mathews*

Contents

Foreword

By Alice Mathews Neill, Joe's Sister

When my brother Ken [the biographer, James K. Mathews] told me he was writing a book about our brother Joe, I was excited, and when asked to be one of his manuscript readers, I readily agreed. In response to the possibility of writing its Foreword, I was less certain. But, in considering what to write, it came to me that I could share some of my experiences with Joe, experiences which profoundly changed the course of my life, while pointing to that which would loom large later in his life.

My two brothers, Joe and Ken, often collaborated, and one summer between seminary years, they traveled the area surrounding our home, Mansfield, Ohio, teaching the Bible and giving sermons. In my teen years, as a member of the Methodist Church Epworth League, I asked them to speak to our group, anticipating that they would be well received. Yet, when they announced their topic, a study of the Book of Luke, my spirits sank. This would not interest the group, I felt. My fear, though, was unwarranted. Their presentation interested everyone, and they were asked to speak again. This was my introduction to the new method which Joe and Ken had learned and mastered. I recall the evening well, still remembering their charting of the twenty-four chapters of the third gospel. Later, I would find this method highly effective in classes I attended and classes I taught.

Joe's early interest in acting I remember well. He would ask me to cue him as he memorized his lines. I loved doing that, especially when he would encourage me to act out one of the parts. I saw him perform on stage and heard people comment on his excellent ability as an actor. I was thrilled when he took me to see the play "Hamlet." These experiences awakened in me a strong interest in the theater. On several occasions while I was in college, Joe saw me perform on stage. He indicated that I had done well and could become a fine actress. Later, he wrote to me saying that he hoped I would find a way to use this talent in serving others. This he surely did, and, in my own way, I followed his advice in teaching.

"Presume Not That I Am What I Was": this was the title of the sermon Joe gave the first time I heard him speak from a pulpit. Though I do not recall all of the content, I do remember I listened in rapt attention, and that his sermon opened for me a lifelong fascination with Shakespeare. I came to consider this great playwright a friend. During my teaching career I would explain to students that I had many friends whom I had never met – writers, playwrights, poets, filmmakers. I told students that I considered it "mighty friendly" when I learned much that enabled me to live life more effectively than I might have without the insights of these artists. I gleaned this response to literature, in no small part, from Joe.

Between college years I spent a summer with Joe at a Methodist parsonage in a small New England town. Taking care of the house, cooking, typing for Joe, working with a youth group, getting to know people in the church and community, and doing whatever I could to be of help made me feel quite useful. Only later did I realize that, yes, I had been helpful, but, oh, what I had gained from that summer! In discussing Joe's sermons with him I learned much from their content, how to listen effectively, and how to be engaged in another's thinking while evaluating my own response. From time to time he would talk about his beliefs. That interested me. Although once I recall telling Joe that I did not want him to tell me any more about what he believed unless I asked. I was concerned that I would not discover for myself what I believed. I can picture his wry smile as he replied, "Oh, is that what you want? All right." He honored my request. Before long, however, I did ask, and he took time to explain further what he believed, and he inquired about my thinking. Then, too, I observed him with other people, noting how he cared for those in the church and the community, how he listened to them, how they responded to him, how the church became filled on Sunday mornings – all this had a powerful impact on me. At the time, I sensed that I had

had a special experience that summer. How special became clear to me as I began to use what I had learned!

Joe was an Army chaplain in the Pacific during World War II, while I was in college. He wrote frequently, asking about my classes, social life, jobs, outside activities, ever encouraging me to do my best – I recall he was not pleased if I did not respond.

Recently, I came across a letter written by Joe in 1943, where he chides me in a playful way: "Alice, you must consider it your duty to supply me with much information which will enable me to form concrete opinions of you as I was ever wont to do when I annoyed you in person! These demands are made on the basis of my being your only brother by the name of Joseph!" He never spoke of what he had done for me during those years. Only later did I appreciate more fully the attention, guidance, and care he gave to me while he was encountering horrendous life-and-death events. This taught me more about caring for others than words can convey.

Our family was very special to me, particularly my two brothers with whom I had shared closeness since childhood. I had observed their progress through schooling and on into their careers, recognizing that they were interested not only in their own lives but, increasingly, in making contributions toward empowering others to live their lives more fully.

As the years passed, I had finished college, married, and become involved in raising my family. Joe, Ken, and I saw each other occasionally, kept in touch, and then they "came back" for me. I remember vividly their visit, inviting me to attend a ten-day session on "Intentionality" in Boston in 1964. Actually, it was a seminar for the clergy, their spouses, and officers in the Methodist Church of New England. Listening to their enthusiastic description of the seminar intrigued me, but I told them that there was no way I could attend. I had my husband and four children to care for plus involvement with many community activities. I can still see Joe looking at me very intently, with his wry smile as he said, "I am not sure that I heard you correctly, Alice, but I think you said, 'I cannot attend.'"

Of course I did go to Boston. What a meaningful experience! The talks. The study papers. The methodologies. The stroll. A life-changing event, the extent of which I would come to appreciate more and more in the years ahead. Joe and I were strolling through the Boston Commons during free time. Suddenly Joe stepped in front of me, took me by the shoulders and said, "Alice, although I am only nine years older than you, I am at least twenty years ahead of you." These words surprised, even shocked, me as I had never heard him say something so egotistical. Then, quickly, his voice changed, becoming more gentle as he said, "But, in a flash, you could change all that. You could catch up with, even surpass, me with one simple word. YES! You could say YES! YES to life!" The impact of this experience was powerful in that moment, and, as you can imagine, it became more so in the hours, days, weeks, even years ahead. This happening changed my life, resulting in my going to graduate school for a master's degree and becoming involved in a profession which became a lifelong passion – teaching.

Yes, that session in Boston profoundly influenced my life. How life is changed when you know that it matters what you do with your life, and know, also, that this is true for every human being. What an awakening! It took me back to the first time that I had heard Joe preach "Presume not that I am what I was," this time with a much deeper understanding.

Writing this Foreword has proven to be a great gift. It has enabled me at this very moment to understand and appreciate more than ever who my brother Joe was as a young man and how he evolved into a human being whose scope of caring became the whole world. More importantly, along with many other colleagues, Joe helped thousands to become awakened, sensitive, lucid, and caring human beings. These individuals, too, came to know the truth about life that it matters what each human being does with his or her life. It matters that each one calls out with a resounding YES!

1
THE END IS A BEGINNING

It is said that we live life forward, but we understand life backward. So we begin with the ending. For the Christian, the end is a beginning.

Joe Mathews died on October 16, 1977, just over a week after his sixty-sixth birthday. He would have recalled with some delight that it was on the eve of the two-hundredth anniversary of the British "surrender" at Saratoga, the turning point in the American Revolutionary War.

Some foreboding of his death was given when he embarked on what was to be his final trip around the world. In June of 1977, while visiting in Rome, he was seized with severe back pains. They did not go away. He proceeded to India where a Sikh specialist in Delhi advised him of serious indications. His trip was cut short as symptoms continued in Hong Kong, and he returned directly to Chicago.

It was evident that he was seriously ill. Jaundiced, he entered the hospital repeatedly – twice for surgery, followed by chemotherapy. No treatment was effective, and on October 10 he returned home to the Kemper Building for his last days, finally succumbing to cancer of the pancreas.

Meanwhile, friends and family traveled to Chicago. Colleagues gathered from around the world. As his younger brother, I interrupted a Mediterranean tour where I was serving as a chaplain for a visit to Pauline sites. Joe's sisters came from Texas and New York.

At exactly high noon on October 16, family and close associates gathered round his bed to sing a favorite song of the Order:Ecumenical from Isaiah 40, "Those that wait on the Lord." With his last strength Joe made an effort to join in to sing with them! Not a bad way to die! Not a bad way to live!

Three days later the cremated remains of Joe were returned to Kemper Building. To the ashes a handful of the soil of Fifth City – his favorite project – was added. Messages of condolence, from high and low, had poured in from all over the globe.

Funeral rites which the Order:Ecumenical had developed were celebrated. In a strange way, dignity and triumph melded as we rejoiced in one who had lived life to its fullness, who had died his death, and had now gone on before to explore the final mystery of life beyond death.

Indeed, the title of the witness I delivered at the funeral, October 20, 1977, was "The Final Mystery" and it is given here in its entirety.

The Final Mystery

Grace is yours and peace from God our Father and the Lord Jesus Christ. *Amen.*

We are gathered here to celebrate the life and death of Joseph Wesley Mathews. His unique and unrepeatable involvement in the human adventure has been marked by an unusual degree of awakenment, engagement, and fulfillment. Having lived his life and died his death, for him that adventure is now complete. By the community of faith, his life and death, and that of every person, is received in gratitude and humility.

What I declare here today is not spoken as from Joe's brother, though each of us long ago understood that we might have to "speak words" over the other as God should purpose. We who are his family have known with increasing certainty that his caring for us was finally under the rubric of that caring for all to which he was so relentlessly committed. Because that universal love was with him so strong, we who are bound to Joe with ties of marriage and blood have experienced love in very full measure. For this we are grateful.

Rather, I speak for the community of faith, for the historic church of which he is always profoundly a part. The Church has ever found ways to embrace and celebrate the life and death of its members. This is articulated in a great variety of ways but nowhere more specifically than in words St. Paul addressed to the earliest church in Rome when he said: "No one of us lives to himself and no one of us dies to himself. If we live, we live unto the Lord; and if we die, we die unto the Lord; so that whether we live or whether we die, we are the Lord's. For to this end Christ died and lived again, that he might be Lord both of the dead and of the living" (Romans 14:7-9). Let us hear these words as the very word of God.

I. Here is realism in pronounced degree. There is no attempt at avoidance of death – as if that were open to us! Death is a part of life and may not be explained away. All of us, without any exception, must die. Death is a gift of God and therefore affirmed as good. Though it involves grief and sorrow and experience of loss, Christianly, it is not seen as tragedy but as triumph; not as defeat but as victory.

Death intrudes into life and life intrudes into death. This insistence upon the linking of life and death bears in upon us throughout scripture with startling consistency. Whether the witness be psalmist or prophet or apostle or evangelist, all have testified to this truth and that within our hearing during this very service.

This final mystery, this wholly other, this "not-me-ness," this one we are up against when we are "up against it": Jesus, the Anointed One, called that final mystery "Father." There is in the Gospels a startling directness and immediacy about this relationship of Father and Son. Moreover, Jesus, the Christ, authorizes and empowers us to call God "Father," too – the One who is that terrifying reality we discern at the very heart of life. This mysterious One invites and warrants our utter confidence. In Him we live and move and die and have our being. In John 20, Mary Magdalene is confronted by one whom she thought was a gardener but finally recognized as the Lord. She tried to cling to him, to hold him in the past. It is as if he told her: "Don't try to interrupt this dynamic process. I *must* go to my Father and *your* Father and to my God and *your* God." The Lord of all is Lord of the Church, Lord of history, Lord of our lives, and Lord of our fathers and mothers. Our life and our death are in His being – and so, as Joe himself often stated so compellingly, we are participants in His endlessness.

Yet this truth is not operative in any automatic or autonomous sense. As we do not live unto ourselves, so we do not die unto ourselves. We are not in isolation, but in relationship, not merely with one another but with the One who placed us here and before whom we are finally accountable. But we do not belong to one another; we belong to the Lord in life and death. The whole story of the people of God shouts this out to all who will hear it. As if to make this unmistakably clear, it is in our text stated four different times in four different ways that living and dying we are the Lord's. This is the way thing are. There is no other way to make sense of human existence. This *is* eternal life. This is the reality of the resurrection symbol and story. He, the Lord, is the final Mysterious One. The Church is concerned from first to last with God.

II. During his last days Joe observed that he was prepared for death and had been for a long time. What he was not adequately prepared for, he said, was what lies "this side of death." These were pain, suffering, and loneliness: "In that order. And they are not the same," he insisted.

Few people have reflected more often or more penetratingly on death than Joe did. Here is a brief mosaic of his brooding: "Death comes to you as just sheer mystery. Death is all about mystery, and freedom, and love, and fulfillment. Death is a very lively part of a person's life and no life is finished without the experience of death. Death is a crucial part in the human experience which somehow transposes to every other aspect of life. Death is a happening to the Church, to the family, to society, and to the individual."

But, for Joe, death was not just a coherent, theological reflection, much less an ideological one. It was existential. "Each one of us has only one death to die," he repeatedly emphasized. The fact is that he died a long time ago, so for him life was a kind of resurrectional life. Among the papers of Samuel Miller, late dean of Harvard Divinity School, was the note: "I would die – if I had not already died." This is the fundamental point!

As for *pain*, Joe used to like to say that he simply could not stand it. But he did. Pain is physical, is solitary, is likely to be immediate and intermittent. It can be suppressed and even rather easily forgotten. Nevertheless, pain, though sometimes a danger signal, is an intruder, an offence, an affront, a threat to one's well-being.

Suffering is deeper. It may have physical marks (heartbreak) but it is mainly spiritual and affects the whole person. It is not as sharply focused as pain. It may be social as well as personal. There is such a thing as fellowship in suffering. Suffering cannot readily be suppressed nor easily forgotten. It addresses the deeps; it may even be unspeakable so that we must "suffer in silence." Suffering threatens not just our well-being but our very being itself. It poses the question, "Why me?" Its elements are both rational and irrational. Suffering therefore must be patiently endured.

So must *loneliness*, especially loneliness in death to which it is a prelude. It is to be distinguished from "lonesomeness" or merely being alone. It is a solitariness that is imposed by life and circumstance and not by an individual, self-chosen. It is experienced progressively as isolation, separation, desertion, being forgotten, overlooked, lost. It is finally the loneliness of the cross, of forsakenness. Psalm 22 wrestles with this experience so that it is no wonder that Jesus quoted this Psalm from the cross. "The monads have no windows." From the outside one can only wonder what one goes through from the inside of loneliness. As Joe said, "We are all alone before the Final Reality. We have to learn for ourselves, as unrepeatable individuals, to walk in The Way; to live in the Other World in the presence of this world. That can only be done in total and absolute solitude. In anything else we can assist each other. But in the profound deeps of consciousness we walk alone." When we do, we get a taste of effulgence and glory.

For pain, for suffering, for loneliness, Joe said that he was not fully prepared. But indeed he was prepared for these. It is the Church's business to prepare people for these strangers *before* they appear. The Gospel is, in one guise, a preparation for the vicissitudes of life. Jesus endured pain, experienced suffering, and so may we. Jesus "walked that lonesome valley" and so must we. A long time ago Joe was heard to say: "The greatest venture of all is the venture of death. The only sad thing is, you cannot share it."

Søren Kierkegaard said, "No one can go to school for you. No one can take a bath for you. No one can die for you."

III. What are we to say of this one man's journey into consciousness? The journey began in Breezewood, Pennsylvania. What an out-of-the-way place! It led to Ada in Ohio, an insignificant town it might seem, and yet one must experience awareness in a particular locality. The trek led from Ada through the blood-soaked beaches of the Pacific in World War II and to the "groves of academe" – Yale, Colgate, Perkins – to Austin; from Austin to Fifth City; from Fifth City to the *Oikoumene*, to the whole inhabited world. When one responds to destiny's summons, there is no turning back. What a *long march* it is for a follower of the Way!

In the course of his journey, Joe was always actor, always dancer, always practical visionary and theologian, always explorer; and above all, always evangelist – a conveyor of the Good News. All along the way he was also a merry man of God – in Luther's sense of being merry even when there is nothing to be merry about. Have we not seen him bring dramatically alive a multitude of valleys of dry bones? Have not some of us seen him performing an ecstatic Zorba's dance on the very brink of Victoria Falls on the roaring Zambesi, and do not all of us experience the sheer awe-filling wonder of such a moment? Have we not seen Joe plan a hundred campaigns with all the commitment and passion of a Chinese general? Have we not seen him set up a base camp at about the point of Rudolf Otto's elucidation of *The Idea of the Holy* and then lead an expedition into the depths of human consciousness, inventing a new vocabulary for states of being, meaningful to modern man and woman? (He helped to update the topographical signs of the Other World in the midst of this world.) Have we not seen him clarify the Gospel for his contemporaries and enable others to enter into fuller human consciousness? Our forebears would have called this conversion, for Joe was always a herald of Glad Tidings, a pilgrim and colleague along the cruciform way. All of his emphases were intended to lead to the realm of action and not to mere ideology.

This is not to say that one would always agree with Joe; but you could not ignore him! I confess that every time I heard such

words as "doed" and "be'd" I would cringe and feel that I was at-
tending yet another grammarian's funeral. You either loved him or
hated him. But he did perform the Christian's job of constantly
turning matter into spirit!

All this he did in deep commitment to the Church and in total
expenditure of himself for his neighbor, near at hand and throughout the globe. The Gospel authorizes the nobodies of this world to
become somebodies, and then it requires of those who know they
have become somebodies intentionally to become nobodies. However hard and prolonged the struggle, Joe was prepared to be a
nobody for the sake of the Gospel and all humanity.

IV. Finally, we come back to the Word, from which we have
not in fact greatly strayed. The same apostle Paul who gave us our
text in his letter to the Christians at Rome gives us this similar
word from his letter to God's people in Corinth when he wrote:
"Everything belongs to you – Paul, Apollos and Cephas, the world,
life and death, the present and the future, all of them belong to you
– yet you belong to Christ and Christ belongs to God" (I Corin-
thians 3:21-23).

These words I read in a little service with the Order just before
Joe's death. How much they speak to the condition of us all! Apollos suggests the Eastern tradition, Cephas, or Peter, the Roman
tradition, and Protestants like to think Paul is altogether theirs. But
the apostle says that we don't belong to any of them. They all belong to us. And we belong to Christ. And Christ belongs to God.

Or take the world, the whole wide world, the entire temporal
order. We do not belong to it. It belongs to us. Yet, we belong to
Christ and Christ belongs to God.

Or what of life and death? We do not belong to them. They belong to us; and we belong to Christ and Christ belongs to God.

Or what of the present and the future? We do not belong to
them. Rather, they belong to us. We belong to Christ and Christ
belongs to God! So our ownership is once more placed in its appropriate perspective. The event of the death of one of our
members brings these matters to sharpest focus.

Last Sunday, in the presence of members of the Or-
der:Ecumenical, I pronounced absolution for Joe in the name of the

Triune God. Last summer, he acknowledged his sin in a public confessional in this very room. For then he said in his last plenary address: "I am extremely grateful to all of my colleagues over the last twenty-five years, who have, with patience that in my solemn moments astounds me, put up with all my stupidities, my personal flaws, my personal mistakes, my wickednesses, my stumblings, my down-right sinfulness." And I add that this we know of a certainty: "If we confess our sins, God is faithful and just to forgive us our sins and to cleanse us from all unrighteousness."

Now, therefore, in this presence and on your behalf and on behalf of the whole Church, I declare the completed life of Joseph Wesley Mathews to be significant in history and entirely acceptable to God, into whose merciful hands we now commend him. In the name of the Father and of the Son and of the Holy Spirit. *Amen.*

*****

My son, Stanley Mathews, could not attend the memorial service, as did his two sisters. He did send this poem as a tribute to his uncle. I feel it warrants a place here.

Wage Life!

Wage life, he said,
As a general wages war.
On guard, always knowing death will win.
I nodded, not seeing how I could take hope in this.
You are sure of your death, it is all you have,
And the time until then: make the most of it.
Stalk life
Be shrewd with life
Be the hunter-warrior of time.
He told me I must read Don Juan,
The *Journey to Ixtlan.* It's all there, as code.
He, nearly 70, his hair silvered, though tarnished now and again
By relentless youth.
Surely a shaman, I thought.

But for the suit and moustache and Western bearing,
He could be.
I remember at Victoria's brim, vast across,
The Zambezi plunges down far into the chasm
The river simply ends,
Drops into violent anarchy, thunders with a roar
And explodes half a mile into the sky.
There was no sun, only wind-lashed clouds
And rain pelting in torrents.
I, terrified as a boy of twelve,
Awed, yet cautious as a pig on ice,
I remained back.
But lo, my uncle crouched low, stalking.
Pulled himself, as if upwards, to the cauldron's edge
And there saw sights I do not know.
It was power, I know now,
Power that he drew from Victoria.
Life-force, there in the chasm, the churning crucible,
For none but the human,
No animal but for the hunter-warrior
Would escape the bonds of self-preservation,
Free to face his own death, and know that he was in life.

We parted that day, we did not see each other again,
We spoke once, on the telephone,
I had called the Institute for the Paris number
And asked to speak to him.
We talked, he excitedly, wanting to know how my life was.
And I promised that indeed I would be in Chicago again, and would visit.
But I did not see him
Passing through on interstate, quickly, not stopping then,
It was jaundice, he must not be seen.
I did not see him then, and returned South,
I would see him, I would go again, there would be time.
It was not jaundice,
It was cancer, so vast that the surgeons, respectfully,
Closed him again,
Knowing their doing could not subvert the growing legions within.
Calls multiplying without and, without reason,
Life without death, unmindful at death,
Yet rushing into death,

This was no mere parasite.
My father came back early from Egypt, I did not know,
He had relapsed,
He was conscious, lucid,
He was dying,
He met his death, eyes open, at high noon.
Yes, like the hunter-warrior,
He had caught me,
I did not know time,
I had missed his death,
But he had been there.

> ~*J. Stanley Mathews*
> October 16, 1977

The Portent and this Book

That afternoon Joe's ashes were placed in a wall-crypt at Wood-lawn Cemetery, Forest Park, Illinois. As some of us left the last rites, we observed a strange sight in the skies above Chicago. We have not made too much of it, but we cannot fail to mention it: THREE SUNS appeared in the sky! I have seen this phenomenon before, and have seen it since – never so clearly as on that occasion. Astronomers call such an occurrence "sun dogs," a peculiar refraction of light through icy crystals in which an image of the sun is reflected on either side of itself. Of course the ancients saw this as a weighty portent and assigned great significance to it. There came to my mind the idea of the Trinity. It spoke also to me that Heaven cares! More than that need not be said.

That evening members of Joe's immediate family and a few close friends met for dinner. We reflected on the meaning of the day and the meaning of Joe and his contribution to the Church and to history.

What follows in this book is an account of that contribution.

2
BEGINNINGS

Breezewood, Pennsylvania, is a village nestled in the Tuscarora Mountains, a part of the Allegheny chain. It is a part of Appalachia. With the change of leaves during the early fall, the hillsides are painted in gold and crimson colors which rival the autumnal display in New England. The town was like thousands of others whose hiddenness makes them easily forgotten.

It was in this out-of-the-way place that my brother Joseph Wesley Mathews, on the morning of October 8, 1911, made his entrance into the world. He was the fifth child and second son of James Davenport Mathews and Laura Mae Wilson Mathews. (Joe's father wanted to name him "John" Wesley, but his mother insisted upon "Joseph.") His birth took place in a downstairs room of the parsonage of the Methodist Episcopal Church, since his father was a supply pastor there at the time. As it happened, I was also born some eighteen months later in the same house. We two brothers, years later, visited this rather humble abode, which now, alas, is no more.

Breezewood is now an interchange on the Pennsylvania Turnpike, from which a spur runs to Washington, D.C. It is a place at present marked by service stations, motels, and fast-food establishments. In 1911, it was virtually a hamlet with not so much as an inn of any kind. One born in Breezewood has no cause for airs.

As a supply pastor our father served not only the Breezewood church but also four other small congregations. In addition, he was in charge of a summer camp meeting at nearby Crystal Spring. His hands must have been very full indeed. With her growing brood, our mother's hands were also full indeed.

Joe's background was marked by a strong religious bias that had been in the family blood for generations. Of his great-grandmother, Rebecca Donaldson Mathews, it was said that she walked with God for more than seventy years and never missed a step. She was a shouting Methodist, though originally a reserved, pious Presbyterian.

The Mathews family was of Scotch-Irish extraction. They had roots also in England and in Wales. Preachers seem to have been abundant in their ancestry. Also, in keeping with other Scots-Irish ancestors, the Mathews family could lay claim to stalwart and sturdy stock. An examination of family annals reveals that "stern," "self-reliant," and "adventurous" were adjectives they were accustomed to apply to themselves. They showed great force of character, considerable leadership talent, together with great energy and ambition. In fact, they did not seem to have been endowed with excessive modesty, nor were they given to understatement.

They prized education for their children, and like many of their neighbors in Ulster, they opposed oppression and sought freedom, self-government, and new opportunity. Like many other Scots-Irish, they became immigrants to America, arriving in successive waves beginning in the 1730s. They settled in Virginia and Maryland.

The Mathews over decades inter-married with the MacDonalds (or the Donaldsons – the anglicized equivalent) stemming from the Clan Donald of Scotland. Joe's forebears made their way up the fertile river valleys of Pennsylvania. His more immediate ancestor was Moses Donaldson, whose first wife and two of their three children were killed in a British-inspired Indian raid. He married again and his son William moved to Ohio. From this family came Joe's great grandmother, Rebecca Donaldson Mathews. Another immediate ancestor, William Mathews, enlisted in the Continental Army and served under George Washington. His military pension as of 1820 was eight dollars a month! One of his sons, Isaac, married a Nancy Hamilton. They were early settlers in the then very wild Hardin County and became founders of the First Methodist Episcopal Church in Ada, Ohio. This couple was Joe's great, great grandparents. This all may seem a bit complicated but will show that Joe did have ancestors – essential, to say the least.

This is to tell only part of the story – that of the paternal line. Joe's mother was a Wilson. Her forebears also came from Ulster, apparently during the late 1700s. Her father, Hugh Wilson, was born in Sunbury, Ohio, in 1836. His grandmother was a Cadwallader from the vicinity of Philadelphia. This grandfather and his brothers were big and powerful men. He married Mary Ellen Algire (of German or Dutch descent) of Marysville, Ohio. She was the only grandparent Joe ever saw. They lived in Delphos, Ohio, where Joe's mother and her siblings were born. Hugh Wilson was a maker of staves and barrels and also a boatman on the canal, which ran through Delphos, linking Lake Erie and the Ohio River. He was strong of limb, a man to be reckoned with. He was one of Lincoln's first 75,000 volunteers and served throughout the Civil War in the 25th Ohio Volunteer Infantry, and one year beyond on garrison duty in the South. Twice he was wounded in the conflict, once at Gettysburg and once at Honeyville, S.C. Wartime deprivations undermined his health and undoubtedly contributed to his fairly early death. During the last two years of his life he was blind, the result of severe diabetes, from which he died in 1887.

Our father's father, Joseph by name, was blind too, as it happened. In 1860 he volunteered for the Union Army. He was a Second Lieutenant in the 135th Regiment of the Ohio National Guard. During a battle on a hot day he jumped over a small stream but tripped over his sword. He was pitched onto stubble, which put out one eye. Developing sympathetic ophthalmia, he subsequently lost the sight of his other eye. He could no longer practice as a pharmacist, but he did own a drugstore and also farmed. More about him later.

It is frequently observed that one form of immortality is this: parents continue to occupy a vital role in one's thoughts, which is certainly true in the experience of Joe and his siblings. His father was particularly lively fathering Joe's thoughts. Both of his parents, however, were present daily in his mind, and he would join with William Faulkner in observing that for him "the past is not dead; it is not even past." In Joe's family the parents were called Mama and Papa and the children would have thought it stilted to address them more formally.

Our father was a kind of walking genealogical table. He used to refer constantly to such ancestors, as I have mentioned, as if they were present – this reaching back several generations. Our mother could do much the same for her side. We their children have later wished that we had paid fuller attention to these recollections.

James Davenport Mathews, our father, was born at Huntersville, Ohio, on November 16, 1869, the same year that Mahatma Gandhi was born. Huntersville was a tiny settlement established mostly by various branches of the Mathews family. The small cemetery there is filled with ancestors' graves.

Papa was born in a log cabin. When they were young boys he took his three sons once to his birthplace. There were still a few logs lying around. We were deeply impressed and used to joke about why he had not gone from this log cabin to the White House, as American lore would suggest!

Soon after his birth, Papa's mother, Margaret Davenport Mathews, died of what was called childbirth fever. It always seemed to us children that Papa somehow blamed himself for his mother's death, occasioned by his birth. Those were insensitive days, and one gathers that some family members also blamed him. He was deeply scarred by this circumstance.

In 1871, our grandfather married a second time to a woman named Rosa Sparks, referred to as Aunt Rosie. She proved to be a shrew and a tyrannical stepmother after the classic mode, relentlessly abusing her two stepsons and Joe's father in particular. On one occasion she threw a block of wood at Papa, knocking him unconscious. The abuse became so pronounced that the brothers ran away, making their way to Iowa to live for a period with an aunt. Later, they bummed their way by freight train back to Ada, Ohio, where they lived with their grandmother, the saintly Rebecca Donaldson Mathews. She was very kindly and, doubtless, overly indulgent.

Meanwhile, Aunt Rosie deserted her husband after taking advantage of his blindness and relieving him of most of his assets. The wonder is that her stepson was not traumatized more than he was by these experiences.

James apparently had an adventuresome youth. During one period he raced on the old-fashioned bicycle – with big wheel in front and the little wheel behind. He came to be quite proficient at this sport, but suffered a concussion from one accident. On pot-marked dirt roads it was a dangerous diversion.

He and his elder brother, Finley, went through a period of being what were called dandies. They showed up one time during pregame practice on the playing field of one of the Chicago big-league baseball teams, James wearing a brown derby. One of the players hit a fly ball that landed squarely on the top of the derby, causing it to crumble. This did not dampen his ardor for baseball, and he instructed his sons in some of the refinements of the sport.

There is more than a suggestion that for a time Papa lived a little on the wild side. But then as a teenager he had what he called an educational "awakening," after which he displayed a great knack for learning and excellence. Later still, he had a striking religious conversion that must have surprised the community and pleased his grandmother immensely.

Our father excelled in English and mathematics. At what was called "mental arithmetic" he was nothing less than a marvel. He could compute the most abstruse problems in his head and endeavored to train his children in the same discipline, although it never really "took" with us. He loved grammar and rhetoric, an interest that he pursued until the very end of his life. A lot of this rubbed off on Joe.

Papa was far better educated than most of his contemporaries. For example, one of the Ohio congressmen determined to make appointments to the United States Military Academy based on a statewide competition. As a Civil War veteran, Papa's father insisted that his son James sit for the examination, although Papa had no particular interest in the military. He came out first and received an appointment to West Point. This was in the late 1880s.

He used to talk about his experience at the Academy. For the "plebes" – the first year students – there was some mild hazing. For instance, upper classmen could call a plebe to attention at any time or place. They were asked to mark time in place and to "fin out," which meant they were to assume a fish-like posture and look generally stupid. Then they would be questioned about their names, place of origin, and "previous condition of servitude." In those days, the academic standards were demanding, the socializing pleasant, and the discipline strict. Papa liked the higher math he was exposed to there. But he did not like the severe discipline of West Point and resigned after a year. Late in life he attended class reunions and was well treated by his erstwhile classmates, most of whom by that time were high officers in the army.

He continued his higher education and was graduated from Ohio Northern University in Ada. Later he did postgraduate work at Taylor University, Upland, Indiana, and at Valparaiso University, also in Indiana (now an institution of the Missouri Synod Lutheran Church). Papa did not go to seminary. Rather he took an annual conference ministerial reading course; nevertheless, he had about the equivalent of a master's degree level of training, unusual for his period.

Having stressed our father's intellectual endowments and training, the fact remains that professionally he never fully realized his potential, which mystified us children. Now it is clear to us that he suffered from major depressive disorder – severe, debilitating, and recurring episodes of depression that nowadays, alas, can be controlled by rather simple medical means.

He could not continue in the ministry, for his health broke. The doctors advised that he seek outdoors work. He eventually became a conductor on the railway, which was respectable but beneath his abilities. He must have thought himself a failure. We sons could never bring ourselves to talk to our father about this. We thought he must have suffered considerable inner hurt by the realization that he had somehow not made the fullest use of his abilities and did not attain success as this world might count it. On the other hand, he did instill great ideals into his children, and maybe in some final reckoning that might count more than what this world would consider to be successful. He had a fine sense of humor and was pleasant company. He held himself straight and could turn himself out well – even into his nineties.

In 1899, while still a college student in Ada, Papa married a young woman who, tragically, died a short time later. This was devastating for him. After two years, J. D. Mathews (Papa) began noticing another young woman also studying at Ohio Northern University while she worked in a boarding house for students kept by her sister and husband, the Rev. Franklin and Ida Ernsberger. On October 1, 1902, our parents were married.

Laura Mae Wilson was born July 7, 1878, in Delphos, Ohio, a town located on the Ohio River-Lake Erie Canal. Mama was devoted to her father and deeply mourned his death, which occurred when she was nine years old. She had two sisters and two brothers, and the family was close. They lived on a Civil War widow's pension together with any small additional income as could then be mustered. They must have felt the financial pinch considerably. Mama referred to having one Sunday dress and one school dress, which often had to be washed and ironed overnight. Yet there was family pride and she greatly prized her relatives.

Pictures of our mother as a young woman show her as attractive in every way. She had sharp features, chestnut brown hair, and a good figure. She was gifted as a musician, well trained in piano, and possessed of a lovely alto voice. She studied music at Ohio Northern University and attained about the equivalent of a junior college education. She had many beaux. One later became a very prominent American churchman. She might have had an easier life if she had gone in that direction. But, in that event, there would not be this story to tell!

Mama was a strong, stable person, in many respects a truly remarkable woman. Endowed with an affectionate nature, she showered love upon her considerable brood. She did not need to be reminded to "hug her children," as seems necessary nowadays; for her, that came naturally. She was a peacemaker on occasion and always a good manager. How she could make ends meet on a small income we shall never know. She could cook, sew, bake, make do, and do without. She made her own dresses and those of her daughters, too, as well as her boys' clothing when we were young. She cut the hair of her sons and husband. Indeed, she filled all the domestic roles to perfection. She was not a gourmet cook, but her noodles, dumplings, and creamed veal, as well as her cherry pie, spice cake, and bread, had to be tasted to be believed.

Sometimes Mama fell ill. Her children concluded that she had to – to get some rest! Her contributions to her children were great in every way. So far as I am aware, she played no favorites with her children but gave them all about equal attention according to their particular need.

Mama had a good sense of humor and loved a good story – for hearing or telling. If there were an amusing side to a happening she was sure to find it. She was reared that way, for her sisters and brothers showed this characteristic and were each possessed of a hearty laugh. They laughed until the tears came!

She also liked to read and did a great deal of it, mostly fiction, magazine articles, or biography. She read aloud to her children, which was something we could never get enough of. She was an excellent conversationalist and raconteur; things were lively when she was around. She never lacked for friends and seemed to culti-vate them easily. Other neighborhood children liked us to share her with them. This she did not seem to find onerous.

Her husband's humor was more reserved and subtle. He was a master of timing and delighted in straight-faced overstatement or understatement for effect. He liked what in quiet fashion he called a pleasantry, but this did not extend to so-called practical jokes. Mentioning this dimension of living is not to suggest that success in marriage depends upon good humor, but it helps. It also depends on shared interests, similar cultural traditions, mutual understand-ing, respect, and a full measure of God's goodness.

Every member of Joe's family had a rich endowment of humor and their life together has been marked by considerable merriment. That continues among our descendants where gatherings have of-ten been hilarious occasions. There is much to be said for the lighter side of life.

3
GROWING UP

If it seems that this record has been painfully preoccupied with Joe's background, there is good reason. He himself was interested in his origins and he enjoyed being a part of a sizeable family. It helped to shape him.

The book of Psalms reminds us that God places "the solitary in families" (Ps. 68:6). This is evidently true and advantageous in most every way. A dreadful toll is often exacted when this is not the case. On this score Joe was exceedingly fortunate, for his was a good family. This is not to suggest it was a perfect one. At times it was indeed dysfunctional (a word not used in earlier days). One recalls the word of a wise pastor who said that he had never seen a family that was not dysfunctional.

Joe had seven siblings. Daisy, the first born, died a few days after her birth. Of the seven who reached adulthood, Margaret – Mary Margaret, to be exact – was the oldest and took her role as eldest almost too seriously, as a sort of surrogate mother to the rest of us children. She had strong convictions, which she readily expressed, a real human touch, and a unique sense of humor. The next sister was Elizabeth. She had a wonderful disposition as a child and became a really splendid woman. Making close friends seemed easy for her, and her girlfriends became like sisters to her younger brothers. She was a good student and was graduated from Ohio Northern University. Before marriage she taught English in high school. In our day she could have excelled in management. At a far too early age she died of cancer.

The firstborn son was Donald, actually Hugh Donaldson, whom the family called Don. Don had real gifts of tenderness. Physical fitness seemed to come naturally to him, but life itself was not easy. He was bright enough, but he did not like school nor did he excel in academic matters. He did have one year of college training, after which he married and went into business: real estate, insurance, filling stations, and the management of a small hotel. Blessed with a good wife, he had a fine family and lived comfortably. Yet he could not handle alcohol well, and in his mid-fifties Don died of cirrhosis of the liver.

Joe was next and was born about two years after Don and about eighteen months before me, James Kenneth, known by our immediate family as "Ken" or "Kenny" (later, friends called me "Jim"). Joe and I were particularly close throughout Joe's whole life, save some seven years when I was a missionary to India and during the years of World War II. I was quieter and more reserved than either of my brothers. For years I planned a medical career and indeed undertook premedical studies. Then, like Joe and largely influenced by Joe, I was called to the ministry. The careers of both of us were for years intermingled and our stories intertwined. I was largely consumed in church administration and as a bishop. I married Eunice, the only child of Dr. and Mrs. E. Stanley Jones.

The three brothers were separated in age overall by only three and a half years, so we were close. Don, Joe, and Ken Mathews attracted attention wherever they went. We played together, worked together, studied together. In World War II, all three of us served in the military: Don in the navy; Joe and I in the army.

Seven years after me, in 1920, Alice Louise was born. Alice was a beautiful child. She was a quite serious girl, good sport, and playmate. Her brothers delighted in "furthering" her education, a role for which they thought they were superbly fitted because of more advanced years and experience. She did not always accept this kindly. She showed particular aptitude in speech and theater. She could have become a fine actress. She earned a master's degree and became a teacher of high school English, in which she highly excelled.

It cannot always be an easy experience to be the last child of a large family. That lot fell to Virginia Alleene (called Alleene). She was a pretty child with blondish hair. In many ways she was the most sensitive of all the siblings. No wonder she became an artist and poet. Her paintings delve into the depths of the human experience.

Joe at birth weighed in at seven pounds. He was always shorter in stature – five feet nine inches – than either of his brothers. What he may have lacked in size he surely more than made up for in energy, of which he was endowed with a plentiful supply. He was breast-fed and usually quite healthy. As a small child he did undergo a precarious illness diagnosed as typhoid fever that caused Mama and Papa much anxiety.

He was an appealing child and was not one to be unnoticed. He had especially attractive eyes and long eyelashes to go with them. He could at will turn on a kind of pitiful expression. This characteristic he put to good use as long as he lived.

He had a more venturesome side to him than did either of his brothers. He could be the daredevil and often appeared to be fearless. His willingness to take risks sometimes resulted in painful injuries. He played hard and frequently emerged as a leader in childhood games. He liked baseball, particularly the role of catcher. Somehow a large catcher's mitt came into his possession and he was immensely proud of it, and with it he could lay claim to his favorite position. In track he was a miler and cross-country runner. In football he liked the role of halfback or running back. In swimming he achieved some proficiency. He was pretty much an all-around boy.

There are recollections of what Joe's earliest years were like. The family moved frequently – from Breezewood before he was two years old. Then it was on to Hammondsville, Ohio; then to nearby Wellsville, then to Upper Sandusky and finally to Ada. Why these moves? First of all, Papa was an itinerant preacher, subject to frequent moves, after the Methodist Episcopal manner. Then his health deteriorated and doctors recommended outside work. For a time father worked as a salesman. Finally, during World War I, since he was too old to serve in the armed forces, he was employed by the Pennsylvania Railroad, where he worked, interrupted by periodic illness, until his retirement.

Vital religious practice was encouraged and cultivated in the family, especially during earlier years. We children were brought up in the fear of the Lord, yet it was *not* a home of stifling spirituality. Some of the earliest memories are about family prayer, to which we devoted ourselves consistently.

Joe was always glad that he could remember his baptism, for it did not occur in infancy, but when he was about five years old – together with his older brother, Don, and me, eighteen months younger. It was at an evening prayer service in the First Methodist Episcopal Church in Wellsville, Ohio, on September 3, 1916. There the three of us received the sacrament of holy baptism and formally entered the family of God. This was to be confirmed experientially and liturgically later on. (Wellsville, by the way, was in pre-Civil War days on the Underground Railway, a part of the avenue to freedom for hundreds of slaves.)

The family would often gather around Mama and sing as she played the piano. She liked old-fashioned songs, which were of late 19th and early 20th century vintage. The family also liked Civil War songs and some of the more lighthearted music of the First World War and following. The same was true of hymns. Charles Wesley's were favorites. Papa enjoyed Cowper's "God Moves in a Mysterious Way," while others insisted on "The Little Brown Church" or "O, For a Thousand Tongues to Sing." Sometimes, as we sang, Papa would get "happy." Papa "could not carry a tune in a basket." Neither could Joe. The rest of the family had rather better voices, but regardless of quality we all sang lustily and enjoyed ourselves immensely.

Family mealtimes frequently were celebrations. When Papa was present he would often deliberately direct the conversation in a useful direction. Both parents enforced strict manners. We were never allowed to sing at the table, nor were we ever to speak disparagingly of anyone. No racial or ethnic slur was acceptable, so almost never were derogatory terms voiced even indirectly. Profanity was, of course, proscribed – even the mildest expletives. Nor was slang tolerated. Moreover, mispronounced words or mistakes in grammar were immediately corrected. When on rare occasions one of the siblings happened to be in homes of friends where these practices were not followed, they were deeply shocked and were glad to be home again. We did not regard ourselves to have been at all hampered by family restrictions. Quite the contrary! Be assured that the paternal admonitions on proper speech affected Joe.

Of course, the Sabbath was carefully observed. Until rather late in our family experience, we were not allowed to read a Sunday newspaper. Playing cards were never allowed in the house, but "Flinch" and "Rook" were acceptable. We were allowed on Sundays to play Bible cards, involving biblical questions and answers, seeming to concentrate on the various kings of Israel and Judah. So far as is known, no harm ever resulted from this modest pastime.

People managed to enjoy life in those simpler days. It is remarkable how little one missed what had not yet been invented. This meant that we often devised our own games and needed little or no equipment. Then, of course, in a large family one never lacks playmates. A big family can be fun and allows free social development in a more or less controlled environment. It is a school that prepares the young for effective living and working with others.

Papa always encouraged solidarity among his children. Very often he would tell the morality tale from McGuffey's reader – about a large family in which dissension ran rampant. A father asked each of his sons to give him a stick. He demonstrated how individually the sticks could easily be broken; but when bound together they were unbreakable! Mama too had cautionary advice. Typically, she would say, "Look the devil in the eye, and he will disappear!"

Christmas among us was celebrated modestly. While honoring its religious significance, presents were not frivolous but emphasized the practical and the necessary – for economy's sake. Mama had a very special Christmas morning song that she would invariably sing to launch the happy day.

A great deal is made nowadays of sibling rivalry. Intense competition for parental approval does not linger in my mind as a serious problem among our family. Mama was skilled in equitably sharing her affection. She seemed to engender in each one of her brood a sense of being "special" to her without appearing to be partial.

One is astonished at the individual differences that are manifested among siblings, all of whom share the same heredity and are shaped by the same environment. A part of this must be in the mystery of individual response to these givens. Some would say that brothers and sisters do not grow up in the same family; it constantly changes. This could be understood as significantly true in Joe's family, where sixteen years separated the eldest from the youngest. The mood or style of a family can change with this passage of time. Or perhaps the difference lies in varying perceptions at separate stages. In any event, siblings share an immense store of common experience, possibly more than accrues even between spouses. The fact is that sibling rivalry in Joe's experience was not notably destructive. The family managed a full measure of mutual sharing and help.

Though carefree childhood in a small town, where everybody knew everybody – from the mayor on down – could be fun, it was not all fun. There was work to be done, too, and the Mathews boys and their sisters could always find small-time jobs, making pocket money available and also contributing to the slender family coffers. There were lawns to be mowed and leaves to be raked. There were paper routes. Every summer there were the nearby onion marshes that needed regular weeding. Joe's two older sisters also engaged in this work. Straddling one row and crawling on your knees all day, you were paid one dollar. If you could manage two rows it was two dollars and three dollars for three rows. It was hard, hot work. However, it put us in close touch with a sometimes rough life!

The Mathews were, one supposes, poor; yet, as Dwight Eisenhower said of his own family, "We didn't know it." When this is so, families do not become captives of poverty. In fact, they often experience themselves as rich. They might well possess good breeding, a cohesive family life, pride, self-respect, adequate housing, clothes and food, dreams, hopes for the future, cultural advantages, and community respect. Are not all these a form of riches? Moreover, most neighbors were also rather poor.

Joe always displayed a great regard for family. He had a particular affection for his mother. There was an heroic side to him. For example, when he was about eight years old he exclaimed one day about his mother: "I'd die for that woman!" While young, he stood more in awe of his father but later in life regarded him in almost a fraternal way. Among grandparents he knew only one, his maternal grandmother. She was the very picture of what a grandmother should be. Her grandchildren always regarded her with warm love. During her last months she lived with us and died in our house – Joe's first brush with death.

There were aunts and uncles too. They play a most positive role in human development. They love their nieces and nephews but exercise less restraint over a child than parents do. So Joe and his brothers and sisters rejoiced to be in their company. They seemed to be involved in exciting things and were always an endless source of stories. Aunts and uncles also meant cousins, and cousins meant kids, and kids meant family reunions and fun. All this meant that life was for living.

Family life is not, however, isolated from the world. While Joe was very young, World War I broke out and the United States entered it. Older cousins were in the Army. Troop trains passed through Ada. Patriotism was stirred. The kids were a part of it. They played soldiers, totally unaware that someday many of them would be a part of other conflicts.

Joe always thought of himself as a small-town person. He lived the first twelve years of his life in villages. Then he lived for two years in a large city, Houston, Texas, and after that in a small city, Mansfield, Ohio. Then it was on to New York City, New Haven, Hamilton, N.Y., Austin, Dallas, Chicago, and short stays in many global centers.

There is a kind of symbiosis between our dwelling places and us. Philosopher Jose Ortega y Gasset stated that if one told him the landscape of habitat, he would be able to tell who that person really is. The truth of this insight has often been noted with respect to mountain people. For example, there is a striking difference in every way between Himalayan people and their counterparts on the plains of India. The same might be observed of those who dwell in Appalachia. This is even more pronounced among island dwellers, whether in Nantucket or the South Pacific. It is observable with those who inhabit peninsulas such as the Delmarva. It is marked among plains dwellers, and in the tension between inhabitants of town versus country. Where we live makes an indelible stamp on us.

For Joe this is especially true of his childhood years in Ada, Ohio, whence came his formation as a person, from his seventh through his fourteenth year. Ada was for Joe everybody's hometown. It was for him a little like Tom Sawyer's Mississippi River hamlet.

We Americans almost always subscribe to the virtue of small towns. In them and on the rural scene generally one's outer space is immense, no matter how confined the inner space may be. There the experience of time is, or was, more leisurely – one experience at a time in contrast to the frantic pace of urban living. In a town, life is not piled up on life. There is more space between bodies, but there is room also for deeper acquaintances and mutuality. In small towns one's experience is rooted more deeply in the past; in cities it is likely to be more future-oriented. In towns, one's close relatives are likely to be there. Linkage with a more remote past is afforded by a visit to the nearby cemetery or by listening to the tales of elders. There, in little communities, foundations are laid, ideals and values shaped.

Ada, Ohio, is the home of Ohio Northern University. One can sing the praises of a college town. A certain cultural atmosphere permeates a college community. Kids there grew up knowing the college students, some of whom were from remote corners of the world. They knew the college president, the professors and their families, for they went to school with their children. They had access to sporting events, to cultural events, to musicals, to lectures, to religious programs, and to great moments when dignitaries on occasion visited the community. To grow up in a college town is to experience the early desire to go to college oneself – to take this for granted. It was almost as if one were already enrolled in college when very young.

During Joe's early childhood the most common vehicles on the streets were buggies pulled by horses. It was an exciting event when a car drove by. Our parents never had a car but owned a succession of four horses. Nellie is recalled with particular affection. Joe saw the evolution from that point to supersonic jets and rockets. As a kid he would run outside to glimpse the sight of an occasional airplane flying over.

The main line of the Pennsylvania Railroad passed through Ada. Two trains a day stopped, one each way. Gathering at the station to see the train come in was an event. More important were the trains that did not stop, for in imagination, a child could easily escape Ada by passing "flyers," such as the *Broadway Limited*, that would arrive in Chicago or New York City a few hours later.

Radio emerged also during the first decade of his life. One can still see him and his friends hovering around a crystal set listening to station KDKA, Pittsburgh. How they thrilled to hear pianist Harry Snodgrass, "King of the Ivories!" He was an inmate at a Pennsylvania penitentiary, but became so popular that the governor of Pennsylvania, in response to thousands of pleas, pardoned him.

Joe often joked about Ada but it was for him an exciting place. There he went to Sunday school, joined the Boy Scouts, marched in Memorial Day parades, celebrated the Fourth of July, attended the annual Farmers and Merchants picnic, and swam in Grass Run, Hog Creek, and abandoned stone quarries. He played childhood games, learned to sing lustily the high school and college songs even before he could read their texts, fought with friends and quickly made up, got into mischief, and in general learned life by living it. He did not experience being deprived of anything.

Kids often made their own toys and made up their own games. Joe and his brothers imagined themselves cowboys. Our steeds were small wheels or hoops that we pushed along on the crossbar of a T-stick. It was great fun and we rode our "horses" everywhere. We would stage drama on the haymows of barns that were a part of almost every residential property. Some plays were impromptu. At other times we would attempt bits from Shakespeare's plays.

Every summer, roving theatrical groups would come to Ada. In those days there were still "Tom Shows," which put on *Uncle Tom's Cabin*. The Shannon Shows would present melodramas, and on the lighter side was the Kinsey Komedy Kompany. More serious was the annual Chautauqua, which brought to town variety music, famous lecturers, and drama. These were tent shows, and the kids would help put up and dismantle the tents in exchange for free admission. All these experiences contributed to Joe's flair for the dramatic.

4
SCHOOL DAYS

John Calvin is often cited as observing that the Christians all their lives "go to school to Jesus Christ." To Joseph Wesley Mathews those were words of truth. More than that, the whole world is a school that is lifelong in its duration. Thus, one must be seen as a learner all his days and very often a teacher, too. This was evident to Joe's dying breath.

We have already seen that his home was a school. So was the church. His parents and siblings were his teachers, always on a reciprocal basis. His neighbors and friends were his teachers. So were the doctors who tended him, and so on. This matter is emphasized here because through the years Joe himself emphasized it.

Joe and his siblings walked to school. This happy practice continued through high school. There were no school buses in those days and no student had a car. Often this meant four miles a day on foot. It was good exercise. Students carried lunch boxes, or when times were tough we all went without.

Years ago there was a bumper sticker that read: "If you can read this, thank a teacher." Immediately on seeing it Joe tested himself. He could name all of his elementary and high school teachers. He loved them all; indeed, he was secretly "in love" with some of the younger and prettier ones. They were all women in grammar school. The school superintendents and principals were kindly in his experience. It was a delight for him later in life to be asked to send greetings to one teacher and one principal when they celebrated their one-hundredth birthdays.

Joe did well in his school work. He related well with other pupils. He was conscientious and earnest about his homework. He recited frequently and prided himself in bold, legible, and rather unique handwriting. His grades were mostly A's and B's, and he was disappointed if ever given a C.

As we have seen, not all education was in school; it continued at home with parents and brothers and sisters. Joe's parents insisted on excellence. His father particularly stressed this. He was a born teacher and was concerned about his children. At one stage he secured a roll-up blackboard on which we were drilled on the multiplication tables, spelling, grammar, and geography. He often repeated the adage, "The roots of an education are bitter but the fruits are sweet."

Papa would take us three boys afield. We went with him on long jaunts in the country. He taught us to swim the breast- or dog-stroke. He showed us how to collect edible mushrooms and puff-balls. He gathered watercress and hunted snapping turtles, for he loved turtle soup. He taught us to identify trees, flowers, and rocks. He knew of such things and imparted much knowledge to us. However, he did not take to hunting because he detested the use of firearms. And he did not neglect imparting appropriate sex education.

Our parents believed also in corporal punishment and practiced the same. They advised their children that if we were ever punished in school, we would be punished again at home. Actually, neither ever happened. When warranted, our mother would use a stick – a "switch" she called it. She would insist that offenders choose the instrument of reproof. We would at first return with a mere twig. Sent out again, we would bring back a club. By this time she would be so amused that when the proper-sized implement was finally found, her ire had subsided and the outcome did not amount to much. If shortcomings were judged of sufficient magnitude, Papa would administer reproof to his sons with a belt or razor strop that would sometimes leave small welts. Yet we would never have dreamed of thinking we were suffering from child abuse. Reciprocal love would soon assert itself and all was set right again.

Sunday school attendance was insisted upon. Joe admired these teachers. Among them was a Mrs. McDowell, who was the Sunday school superintendent. She continued to be for Joe the very image of a saint. Another teacher was named Ben Smith, son of the president of Ohio Northern University, and later himself a preacher.

Others were a Mr. Henderson and a Mr. Kramer. These and many others were held in honored memory.

We all went to Sunday school and church every Sunday. We had no car, so we walked. Alice and Alleene, the youngest two, would lead the procession, followed by me, Kenny, usually walking alone; then came Don and Joe, Margaret and Elizabeth, and finally our parents. It did not create any remarkable sensation because most other families did the same.

Already mentioned, in a college town there is much entertainment, and much free of charge. Liberal arts colleges in those days had what were called literary societies. They were like nonresidential sororities or fraternities without the Greek letters. Every Friday evening they would meet to put on an entertainment, such as a recitation, monologue, or musical recital. Sometimes they held intercollegiate debates. One learned the rules of debate so that years later in college it was relatively easy to undertake this form of public speaking.

Ada had one small movie theater and we kids often attended the Saturday afternoon matinees. One could get a lot of entertainment for a dime in those days. In addition to the feature film, there was a newsreel, a comedy, coming attractions, and above all, the serial. These were about one-half hour episodes of some very exciting continuing dramas. Real cliff-hangers, the serials ended abruptly at the most exciting and perilous moment, which wooed the viewer back the following Saturday. The leading ladies were beautiful. Tom Mix was in those days every boy's hero, a real cowboy. Like all boys, the Mathews boys enjoyed westerns, then called "cowboy movies." They were regarded as necessary training for their intended lifetime vocations as cowboys – they were certain that at age twenty-one or thereabouts they would transport themselves to Colorado and enter this exciting and dangerous field of endeavor.

As it happened, Joe's father also enjoyed westerns, but none so much as one of Zane Grey's features, *The Last of the Duanes,* to which he took his sons. It had all the necessary ingredients: the hero – "Buck" Duane – a good guy, a beautiful heroine, a community at peril, saloons, and people "dying with their boots on."

Everything was right. For years afterwards, Joe and his brothers vied for the honor of being called "Buck." At that time none of us, possibly including Papa, grasped the theological significance of a cowboy movie, so well portrayed much later by Gary Cooper in *High Noon*, but the story of redemptive deliverance was somehow present in *The Last of the Duanes*. Thus it was that from this unlikely source came help not only for our fantasy career as cowboys but for Joe's and my actual careers as shepherds.

Kids somehow got into college football, basketball, and baseball games free. We attended track and field events and witnessed college and high school dramatic presentations. Our older sisters were in operettas. As they learned the songs so did their brothers. The music swirled in our minds for years afterwards.

In the early fall of 1925, Joe and his siblings were broken-hearted for a while. The family was moving from Ada and they all realized how deeply they were rooted there. Joe used to speak of the painful lump in his throat as he experienced the breaking of ties with friends and teachers.

The destination was Houston, Texas, where Papa's brother lived. The basic reason for the move was that they wanted to live closer together. The brother was a physician, Finley Mathews, whom we called Uncle Doc, a pleasant and affectionate man. His wife had the unusual name of Keturah. We called her Aunt Kit. She was a bit stern on the surface but had a caring nature underneath.

Houston in the mid-1920s was beginning to be a burgeoning metropolis. It was exciting to live there in those days. A ship canal had been dug from the Gulf of Mexico to Houston so that the city was becoming a seaport. Its leaders were very aggressive in business and trade. The city had a large radio station designated as KPRC (an acronym for Kotton Port-Rail Center) that used to proclaim that Houston was "where twenty-one railways meet the sea and ships of all nations find a friendly port." Cotton was king and oil followed close behind. Jesse Jones and Will Clayton were prominent citizens. "Ma" Ferguson and Dan Moody were governors of Texas.

The city boasted three major newspapers: the *Houston Post-Dispatch*, the *Houston Chronicle*, and the *Houston Press*. Experienced newsboy that Joe was, very soon he found a paper route for the *Press*. Meanwhile, brother Don dropped out of school for two years and got a job as office boy in the Kirby Lumber Company. The next year, Joe dropped out also and worked for the same firm for one year. Once again we all worked to help support the family. Joe's eldest sister, Margaret, entered nurses' training and the second, Elizabeth, enrolled in senior high school.

We all learned the special songs that relate to that great state: "The Eyes of Texas Are Upon You," "Texas, Texas, Pride of the South," "The Yellow Rose of Texas," and others. These songs Joe long continued to sing with appropriate gusto. Texas did elicit large-mindedness, and the family doubtless benefited in this sense.

The family had a considerable financial struggle during the two Houston years, and those years were not notable for the family religiously speaking. Possibly economic restriction and poor clothes had something to do with it, because during those years we scarcely darkened the door of a church. Maybe it was religious rebellion of short duration and mild intensity. It was not rooted in any great intellectual perplexity. Why it should have occurred Joe never really analyzed in depth. It must have been more family-related than inner-related. Joe's spiritual rootage was, however, of sufficient depth that he readily sprang back to his rightful heritage. This brief wilderness wandering did not appear to have damaged him much. Maybe there was some value in not being a practicing Christian for a while.

The Texas venture never really worked out. In the late summer of 1927, the family moved back to Ohio, this time to Mansfield, which is located almost exactly in the north central part of the state. The surrounding territory of Richland County is shaped by rolling glacial hills, marked by good farmland and prosperous agriculture. Many of our ancestors had been pioneers in the region. The city itself had a population of about 40,000 and extensive industry: a steel mill, the Ohio Brass Company, a large Westinghouse plant, a tire factory, and various foundries. It was a major commercial nexus for a large area. At one time in the 1940s,

Mansfield was ranked as the "number one" small urban center in the country.

Generally the community spirit was good. It also had a considerable presence of racial and ethnic minorities. All in all, it was a good place to live. The feel of Mansfield was a mixture of the progressiveness that characterized Houston, with a bit of the small town atmosphere of Ada. It was not difficult to adjust to living there. The schools of the city were excellent. Joe's two younger sisters, Alice and Alleene, enrolled at the primary level. Don was in junior high. His siblings always admired Don, who, although he had dropped out of school for two years, was prepared to return at a class lower than his two younger brothers. Joe had worked for one year, so he was now in the same class of high school as I was. We studied together and that began a collaborative relationship that was to continue for the rest of his life.

Joe and I were privileged to be a part of the first classes in a brand-new school building. The facility was located in the western part of the city, about two miles from our home. The brothers, as before, walked back and forth daily. Earlier comments refer to the physical benefits of this practice. It had social values as well. One often walked with friends – a splendid way of bonding with one's fellows. We all had great pride in this new school, and we engaged together to carve out appropriate traditions and to develop a genuine *esprit de corps.* M.H.S. was blessed with an outstanding principal, Jesse L. Beers, and a number of stellar and memorable teachers.

Joe and I already began to be leaders. We both did well and had records of nearly all A's. In those days we did not have SAT tests or scores, but there was a statewide test of high school juniors. The two of us came out well toward the top. Joe won a statewide oratorical contest. That sort of thing boosts one's morale and self-esteem.

We might well have been friendly rivals, but were actually colleagues. Frequently we were in the same classes. This facilitated homework. We could quiz each other and talk over reading and writing assignments. We shared a love for geometry and were surprised to find that solid geometry was easier than plane. The teachers were exciting and knew how to inspire interest in their pupils. We delighted in French, in history, in current events, but even more in the sciences. We worked together in preparing for chemistry class with a large chart of derivatives of coal tar. We collected our samples in small bottles and mounted them on a plywood frame. We were delighted to discover that our work was still on display after several years. In a word, Joe took his studies with utmost seriousness and was determined to excel.

In athletics, M.H.S. had a superior football team. Coach Russell Murphy was outstanding. Decades later he was still the talk and toast of Mansfield. He was of small stature, wiry, and entirely dedicated to the sport. He had an unusual ability to inspire his charges to give their best to football. In those years the great Notre Dame Coach, Knute Rockne, conducted summer football seminars for high school and college coaches. Murphy always attended these and his teams in turn benefited from the very latest in techniques. They were thoroughly drilled and encouraged to master solidly the rudiments of football, and they did. Joe enjoyed the game and showed reasonable prowess in it.

Joe's special interests and activities, however, included public speaking and debate. On occasion Joe was allowed to preside at school assemblies. He always excelled in dramatics. He had a real gift for histrionics and could get into character and really sway an audience. People long recalled he played the leading role of Captain Jack Absolute in William Brinsley Sheridan's *The Rivals*. He was a stunning figure clothed in the scarlet and white regimentals of a British army officer. He also played the lead in our senior class play, Rollo's *Wild Oats*, a contemporary comedy that on Broadway had starred Roland Young.

Joe's last year in high school (1929-30) coincided with the beginning of the Great Depression, and by the end of the school year financial stringency was becoming increasingly evident. The strain became visible among fellow students, and even teachers. Joe was elected president of the senior class. It fell to his lot to assemble a planning committee for the senior prom. It was a resounding success in spite of the depression.

Joe and his brothers always worked in Mansfield – sometimes trying to fill three jobs at a time – as bellhops, as handymen in local stores, in part-time chores in foundries, ushers in a movie theater, and as door-to-door salesmen. It is surprising what young people will do when they must.

Joe also did well in his relations with the opposite gender. He always seemed to be able to find the best looking girl in town. Maybe it was his soulful eyes that did it. He also had a special knack in being able to criticize the taste of his two brothers in this regard. He apparently wanted to be sure that we did not make serious mistakes of judgment. Needless to say, neither brother ever warmed to this proffered aid and effectively declared their independence from "helpful" fraternal assistance.

Joe was graduated from Mansfield High School in June 1930. Neither he nor his brothers went on immediately to college. For nearly another decade Mansfield was their home, though with the passing years they returned there with less and less frequency. A number of times they returned for class reunions. (Sometimes loyal spouses attended as well; surely they should have some special reward for this devotion.) Mansfield is one of the places Joe looked back on with real nostalgia.

5
AN AWAKENING

The autumn of 1930 should have seen Joe departing for his first year of college. This did not happen. But it was only a question of when and where.

During his last two years of high school he pursued an appointment to West Point. After all, his father had achieved this through a statewide competition initiated by a member of Congress. His father had attained the highest marks and thus the prize. In 1930, no such contest was open for Joe. Presidential appointments to the academy were jealously guarded. Appointments through Senators and Representatives from Ohio were obtained through political influence. Joe tried but did not succeed. One could say this was a pity, for he had great potential as a leader, military or otherwise.

Besides, the Great Depression was just beginning and the family's resources were not sufficient to support even one son in college, let alone two. As Joe's younger brother, I was in the same situation, for I too sought collegiate training. Consequently, according to the language of a later day, college was "put on hold," one year for me and two years for Joe.

As high school juniors Joe and I found summer jobs in a wholesale grocery firm, the Bissman Company of Mansfield, which distributed products through a large section of north central Ohio. It was hard physical labor: off-loading railway freight cars and stowing their contents in a large warehouse. Later, the goods were reloaded into trucks and distributed to retail grocers.

A carload of sugar, for example, typically consisted of 400 or 500 one-hundred-pound bags – burlap sacks. For years the employees there had taken a day and a half to unload a freight car and warehouse the product. Young, strong, and innocent, Joe and I did this easily in half a day. This made us popular with management but unpopular with fellow workers. In time the tension diminished. Two persons unloading sugar develop a kind of rhythmic, swinging motion, each grasping either end of a bag and tossing it onto a trolley and then again stacking it in the warehouse. Salt bags weighted 150 pounds and green coffee bags even more. It was burdensome toil. For this work we received $21.80 a week, which seemed a lot at the time. Things are relative: we could get a full lunch for a quarter in those days – soup, main course, and dessert.

There were unanticipated advantages in such work. For instance, it was good physical exercise. Along the way, we learned a great deal about the business. We could have engaged in any part of it, including roasting and blending coffee. We learned also how to drive large trucks – semitrailers. Backing them up into a narrow space is an art that is not easily mastered. When we drove these vehicles and delivered the goods, we came to know the countryside thoroughly and gained the acquaintance of retail merchants as well. Also, we profited by serving side by side with men who were a part of the labor movement.

In many ways Joe saw 1930-32 as lost years, at least at the beginning. His best friends had gone to college and he felt left behind and left out. Social life was at a minimum. He participated at times in a church youth group. He would spend spare time in the library reading in a wide variety of subjects.

His real interest, however, was in theater. This seemed to provide motivation like nothing else. His participation in high school dramatics had thoroughly piqued his interest. He took part in a church drama group which was of better than average quality. In a local Little Theater group he was deeply involved. This included some Shakespeare and a leading role in *Witness for the Prosecution*. This led to a tryout at the Cleveland Playhouse. One of the judges on that occasion was the well-known feminine character-actress, Marie Dressler. She recommended that Joe go to Hollywood and try out for the movies!

Perhaps it should be mentioned at this point that Joe took up the habit of cigarette smoking. One drama part called for this and he was determined to master the stage business related to the practice. He succeeded, but he never succeeded in breaking the tobacco habit, though at times he tried. He tolerated my complaining to him about smoking, although he thought the admonitions arose out of some sort of moralism. In my view, his addiction hastened his death, but the Creator at no time entrusted me with control in such matters. One thing was always sure, Joe would let no other person be the keeper of his conscience.

Joe took the suggestion of Hollywood seriously. He decided to head for California and toward some of the most transforming events of his life, which may well be termed a "first awakening." He had formed a close friendship during high school days with Edwin (Ed) Norris. Ed too became restless in the tough early days of the Great Depression. So it was, on a cold February morning, the two of them began their westward venture. It was tough going as recalled in notes Joe recorded a few years later. He likened their journey to Columbus setting out on his voyage and even attempted a parody of Joaquin Miller's poem about "Sail On!" In their case they did not sail, but often walked, for rides were few and far between.

The pair first of all headed for Florida, sometimes staying with friends and relatives. Their time in these warmer climes was short; their real goal was to heed Horace Greeley's advice, "Go west, young man, go west." So they followed roads through the southern tier of states toward California.

As spring approached, Joe and Ed found themselves at nightfall stranded in west Texas at the "end of nowhere." Motor cars were proving sparse in those wide expanses, let alone those who might be willing to pick up two hitchhikers. Therefore, they camped out one night on what proved to be the dry bed of a stream. All went well until near midnight when a sudden thunderstorm broke out in the distant mountains that marked the horizon to the north. A flash flood quickly descended on them and the stream took on a life of its own. Scarcely were they able to reach higher ground with their few sodden possessions. Miserable, soaked to the skin, they made their way into Langtree, the nearest hamlet, where they found refuge in an empty freight car on a siding. They bedded down for the rest of a night in complete misery.

Years later my family and I visited Langtree, Texas, and it became a part of our story. Langtree was known in a radio drama at the time about "Judge" Roy Bean, who was dubbed "the law west of the Pecos." It was named for Lillie Langtree, a famous English singer and actress, whose beauty attracted many admirers, from George Bernard Shaw to Roy Bean. It was there that Joe and Ed awoke to greet another day. It proved to be unpromising.

To their dismay they discovered that cement had been unloaded from that freight car in which they slept. Their wet clothing had become impregnated with cement dust. As they dried out, the cement began to set and their clothes, they said, resembled suits of armor!

The weather became milder at noonday, and they washed their clothes in the Rio Grande and contemplated their next prospect. Ed proposed they hop a freight train to California. Joe reported that it was as if a voice within him cried out, "Don't go, Joe. If you do you will be a bum." Hitchhikers can keep their self-respect. After all, no one has to give them a ride. To accept a motorist's hospitality does the host no harm. When they resumed "thumbing a ride" the following day, the very first driver who came along took them all the way to Los Angeles! In frequent references to this striking episode, Joe concluded that "God struck a blow at his heart."

They had reached their destination, or was it only a way-station? To them it was a major scene in the drama of life. Los Angeles in 1931 was home to more than a million people. It resembled the rest of the country in the sense that thousands were out of work. Joe and Ed, between them, had sixty cents. Talk of starting at the bottom!

They found that even the most marginal housing was beyond their reach. Finally, a distant cousin of Joe's took them in. Gradually Ed Norris dropped out of the story and went his own way. But Joe's desire to become an actor remained undiminished and he pursued his dream for months. In a word, his effort was fruitless. He did not get into the movies. That was possibly Hollywood's loss, for he was a good actor.

Apparently God had other plans for Joe. His cousin and benefactor was an earnest Christian and tried to open up the way. He saw to it that Joe obtained enough work to be sustained, but more, he put Joe in contact with missionaries. For a time Joe assisted an evangelist in erecting and maintaining a tent for his meetings. His name was Dr. R. E. Neighbour, who might have been described as an enlightened conservative Calvinist. He was also a musician of considerable accomplishment. He was billed as the "Greatest Interpreter, Arranger and Technical Master of Christian Hymns on the viol and viola d'amore in the World" (a viol has numerous sympathetic strings, resembling strings of the sitar). He was also gifted as a Bible expositor. His influence on Joe was deep and in some respects lasting. During ensuing years, Joe's friends, in jest, used to remark that "he started out with Neighbour and ended up with Niebuhr."

During this period the young seeker was thrown into association with many a person of great piety and deep Christian commitment. Among them was the saintly Mrs. Charles Cowman, whose daily devotional classic *Streams in the Desert* had enjoyed a wide readership. Increasingly Joe was influenced by such earnest believers. More and more, observing the vibrant Christians surrounding him, he knew he was lacking in something essential. These people appeared to live on a higher plane. His search intensified as he attended camp meetings at Pacific Palisades and Fenwick, near Los Angeles.

The climax came with the Olympic Games that were held in Los Angeles in the summer of 1932. At the same time the churches of the region organized what was called "The Olympiad of Religion," with the nation's outstanding preachers and evangelists taking part. Among them was Bishop Arthur J. Moore of the Methodist Episcopal Church, South. Somehow the Christian message, as Moore could so effectively convey it, penetrated the very depths of Joe's being. He responded to its appeal. Joe's was a classic conversion experience of the Pauline and Augustine and Wesleyan model. His life was renewed and entirely redirected. This was followed by a clear call to Christian ministry to which he responded with equal ardor and enthusiasm!

What had started in a boxcar in Langtree, Texas (where, as he later recounted, he first really prayed), had reached a climax in Los

Angeles. This whole episode constituted what may be termed his "first awakening." Others were to follow – each building on the other – and helped to shape him into the authentic apostle he was to become. He constantly reiterated and reinterpreted this event, just as St. Paul is recorded as doing in the Book of Acts. The fact of his changed life remained.

Joe used to testify to this in an oft repeated sermon he first preached in 1932, titled, "Presume Not That I Am What I Was." This title he borrowed from one of Shakespeare's plays (the Second part of *King Henry IV*, Act V, Scene 5, line 56) and dealt with his spiritual awakening and reversal of life direction. He referred to his excessive ambition, conceit, desire for success, and other short-comings, which were replaced by a sense of forgiveness, an awareness of God's presence in his life, a desire to live a life of divine approval, and of caring for the down-and-out – indeed for all. He had found a new center, a new goal, and a new incentive to live for others.

After these startling developments, he did not linger long in California but made his way rather quickly back to Ohio. Once there he shared his newfound zeal. At first his excessive enthusi-asm and quite dogmatic beliefs put others off. But gradually his zealous approach awakened me as well. I, too, drastically changed vocational direction from medicine to Christian ministry, which we both were to pursue – often in unison – through ensuing years.

College Years

Hardly had he arrived at home when it was time to go on to col-lege. He enrolled in Lincoln Memorial University at Harrogate, Tennessee, near Cumberland Gap. I had already completed one year there. A boyhood friend of Papa was chancellor of Lincoln Memorial University. This college was founded by Civil War Gen-eral Otis Oliver Howard, who had also been a founder of Howard University in Washington, D.C. Just as the latter school afforded opportunity to African-American students, the former gave a chance to southern mountaineers and others. Legend has it that President Lincoln himself had suggested to Howard that following the war the general should establish such a school. He did so and named it for Lincoln.

One could attend Lincoln Memorial University tuition-free and work to cover all expenses, a little after the manner of Berea College in Kentucky. It was an opportunity to snatch, but the going was hard. The average student was obliged to work three or four hours a day. Joe dug ditches, toiled in a limestone quarry, and engaged in farm work. Then he was fortunate enough to work as an electrician, less arduous but more dangerous. This was particularly true following a small tornado that wrought chaos on the community electrical system. Neither of us brothers engaged in intercollegiate sports; fatigue from overwork was a factor.

Hard work is supposed to be useful in the development of strong character. One manages, but at a cost. Both Joe's and my academic records were good. Prizes for speech, debate, and pre-medical studies in my case, and in speech and dramatics for Joe, came at the price of not attaining the thorough mastery of subject matter that would have been desirable. Lincoln Memorial University was no top drawer institution, no Ivy League. Nevertheless, the fact of the Depression brought the Ivy League to less exalted colleges and universities. Some of the professors were of that caliber, offering excellent teaching in English, chemistry, physics, mathematics, social science, and philosophy.

This must be said about the college: it was set in countryside of unsurpassed beauty, considerable historical significance was attached to the region, and the mountain people proved to be solid and unpretentious.

Joe became actively and immediately involved in the religious life it offered. He continued to exercise his dramatic talent and performed in both religious and secular plays. He certainly tried to be an effective Christian witness and was in demand in nearby churches. He gave leadership in organizing a new congregation among rather isolated mountaineers in Tipperell, Tennessee. One could walk there, about three miles across the mountains. The growing congregation met in a one-room school house. Joe and other students did the preaching and singing. If their hearers were not edified, they were at least patient and polite. Some lives were changed.

If these people encouraged the brothers, our pastor back home did not. When we solemnly announced our vocational intention to him, this somewhat severe and scholarly cleric responded with discouraging words. We were not to be deterred; we could only conclude that he must have been discouraged in his own ministry and had no incentive to encourage others in this path.

Others helped us on the way. The pastor and his wife of a Methodist Episcopal Church in Lafollette, Tennessee, opened up their hearts, their home, and their pulpit to us.

We began to take the first faltering steps toward the Methodist ministry. This was to secure a license to preach. It meant that we were recognized local preachers, or lay preachers. After examination, written and oral, a successful candidate is issued the appropriate certificate or license. Joe recalled the district superintendent in that area as counseling him especially to guard his relationship with women. He reminded him that Genesis records that Joseph had to flee from a woman, leaving his robe behind! The district superintendent knew the perils of improper sexual relationships. Countless pastors have stumbled at this point. Both brothers appreciated his advice and caution.

We brothers were urged along the way by the university minister, a kindly and scholarly Presbyterian, Dr. W. B. Guierrant, whose wife was also supportive. It was this same pastor who later made it possible for both of us to attend seminary. He was a fine Bible teacher and led many students into eventful journeying through the Book of Books.

After three years at Lincoln Memorial University, Joe transferred to Asbury College in Wilmore, Kentucky, an evangelical college with Wesleyan connections and in the holiness tradition, under which he had been converted in Los Angeles. He was quite at home at Asbury and became quickly known on the campus for his prowess in speech and dramatics. Like many other students in the school, he preached and evangelized in nearby communities. Joe received his bachelor's degree there in 1936.

During the summer that followed, once again we two preacher brothers joined forces. We engaged in evangelistic preaching in the southern mountains, in three different coal-mining communities in Lee County in the extreme southwestern corner of Virginia, wedged between Tennessee and Kentucky, not far from LMU, by this time familiar terrain to us both. In many ways we were ill prepared intellectually, but we made up for it in energy and zeal. We were a team and would preach in turn every other night. This fact in itself was helpful, because we had precious little material in the form of revival sermons. But that was not all. Joe was made of sterner stuff than I, and his manner tended to emphasize the wrath and judgment of God. My inclination was to stress the love of God. Between these two poles a fruitful ministry seemed to develop. It was a kind of "divine pincer movement," which had the effect of embracing everyone. One of the church bulletins listed an "alter call" (rather than an "altar call"), which we thought quite apt.

Nor did we leave attendance to chance on mere posters that announced our meetings. Instead, we made personal calls on every home in the community and did the same in the surrounding area. Sometimes we would walk because we had no car, or would borrow horses and ride from door to door. As we recorded at the time, "We walked until we could not stand up and rode until we could not sit down!" Having been directly and earnestly invited, the people responded in large numbers. The churches were crowded to the doors with people of all ages and of all denominational backgrounds. The first series of meetings was held at St. Charles, Virginia, a small mining town. Finally, everyone in town confessed conversion and we young preachers moved on to the next place, but not before we had baptized those who newly confessed their faith. This was partly a "precautionary measure," for the Baptist notion of adult believers' baptism was highly prized in that vicinity. We took the further step of baptizing by immersion in a nearby river. Thus there was no more a possibility of another evangelist following, insisting that baptism by sprinkling was invalid. They had already been as thoroughly baptized as they could possibly be!

This evangelistic effort was further enhanced by holding vacation Bible schools for the children in the mornings and Bible classes for adults at night. The local pastors of all the churches were supportive and cooperative, and the laity worked together harmoniously. After finishing the work in St. Charles, we repeated the whole exercise in a rural community surrounding Robbins Chapel, a few miles away. The results were the same. We then proceeded to a third church in a rural setting at the foot of the Cumberland Mountains. This was a more sedate center. Although the response was encouraging, it was by no means as sweeping and enthusiastic as the former two. But, all in all, we were being shaped into effective evangelists, Methodist style. We learned that summer to declare the Gospel in clear, convincing, and winsome terms.

After the summer of evangelism, Joe and I turned home to Mansfield. Our older brother, Don, and his wife were visiting our parents at the time. Since they were driving back to Texas, we decided to accompany them.

When it came time to return to the East Coast, we had to arrange some mode of transportation, probably hitchhiking. Since Don lived in a port city, Corpus Christi, we found an alternative. We discovered a freighter that was to sail for Wilmington, Delaware, where our sister Elizabeth McCleary lived. To our astonishment, the captain was willing to let us serve as deckhands on the voyage in exchange for passage.

This was our first venture upon the briny deep. The passage took us across the Gulf of Mexico, around the Florida Keys, and up the East Coast. We experienced a heavy storm at sea, complete with seasickness. We saw flying fish and waterspouts for the first time, observed sporting dolphins, and marveled at the fluorescent foam around the ship's prow at night – all very new and thrilling. The food was good and abundant, available at any hour of the day or night. The older sea-hands tolerated us to a point that almost resembled friendliness. The work was hard and long. We earned our keep by swabbing and "holy stoning" the deck, by endless painting, and by being gofers. At night we were sometimes assigned to lookout duty on the prow of the freighter. We were to alert the bridge about any oncoming vessels, with a special ring of the bell for ships on the starboard or port side or dead ahead. One time we rang the bell for a star that was just appearing above the horizon! After about ten days we landed at Wilmington, Delaware, and were picked up by sister Elizabeth. We really did not take to the life of sailors. When war came, both of us chose the Army instead of the Navy!

Seminary Education

We proceeded immediately to New York City where Joe was to embark on his first year of theology at Biblical Seminary, now known as New York Theological Seminary. I had already completed two years there. We were directed there by Dr. W. B. Guierrant, our university minister, a Presbyterian. He secured for us tuition-free scholarships with an opportunity to work to cover other expenses. Biblical Seminary was nondenominational but had a Presbyterian bias. It was neither conservative nor liberal. Its middle-of-the-road theological position was well suited to both brothers' thought and dispositions at that time.

As the school's name implies, there was strong emphasis on English Bible, which was studied systematically book by book. It was proud of its tradition of studying the Bible itself. Secondary sources were studied, also, and students were trained in critical scholarship. Methods of study and teaching were particularly emphasized. One did learn how to study systematically and to teach effectively. We were taught an inductive method of Bible study and we employed a method of extensive charting of texts.

To be effective in a professional field, one must come into touch somewhere along the line with highly proficient persons in that field. Specifically, one must sit under great teachers, the more the better. Joe and I had that privilege at Biblical Seminary. One of these was Wilbert Webster White, founder of the school. He had come under the spell of William Rainey Harper, founder of the University of Chicago and a master teacher, particularly of Hebrew. White was also a product of Yale with a sound foundation in theological disciplines. He became profoundly convinced that the greatest failing of preachers was that they did not really know the

Bible. It became his mission in life to try to correct this, and he went far toward this goal.

There were other fine teachers and visiting professors, such as Edwin Lewis and Karl Heim. Much appreciated were the lectures of Dr. Julius T. Richter, one of the great lights in the history of missions, a German who had been at one time a pastor to Kaiser Wilhelm in Berlin.

There could scarcely have been better training in Bible, especially the New Testament. Joe became a kind of walking concordance, for if someone cited a verse of scripture, he could have called out its chapter and book in the New Testament. As to the Old Testament, he could certainly have named the book. It was assumed that with such "raw exposure" to Scripture one would at the same time gain a working biblical theology. To a certain degree this was true, and also liberating, for sooner or later one must do one's own theologizing. The weak spot in this approach was that the student suffered from not being adequately grounded in systematic theology.

Biblical Seminary was located at 235 East 49th Street in the heart of Manhattan. The Waldorf-Astoria was two blocks away and the theater district was within walking distance. Years later the United Nations was built nearby. Across the street lived Katharine Hepburn, on whom students delighted in spying from time to time, as well as such visitors as Anne Harding and Spencer Tracy. The violinist Efren Zimbalist lived next door. The subways were near at hand and travel anywhere in the city was a nickel. All of us students took full advantage of this opportunity to learn in the city.

Students also systematically went on escorted tours to significant places all over New York City, including the New York Public Library and the offices of the *New York Times*. Other excursions led to the Cloisters, to the Metropolitan Art Museum, and to the Metropolitan Opera. We also visited Sailors' Snug Harbor, a heavily endowed retirement home for merchant mariners located on Staten Island. One of its notable buildings was the chapel built on the model of St. Paul's in London, but on half-scale. We also went to settlement houses, mental institutions and hospitals, as well as to the great churches – Riverside, St. Patrick's Cathedral and St. John the Divine, Christ Church (Methodist), and Fifth Avenue Presbyterian. We also had the rare privilege to hear all the great preachers of the day. We occasionally attended theater, the symphony, and the opera. The city afforded unparalleled opportunity for outstanding cultural fare.

Joe brought his particular brand of zeal to Biblical Seminary and soon made a place for himself. We were delighted to be fellow students and colleagues once again. Joe also took it upon himself to be in charge of my social life, as in times past, freely passing judgment on choices in the realm of female companionship.

Joe was fortunate in securing a job which afforded him pocket money and expenses not covered by his partial scholarship. He was made student assistant in Broadway Temple Methodist Church in New York City. The senior pastor was the Rev. Dr. Christian F. Reisner, an imaginative and fearless prophet. This appointment lasted for nearly five years as Joe pursued his theological studies. Reisner and Joe were a real pair, each encouraging the other. Joe's youth program was outstanding and remembered for years. Many truly came alive in Christian discipleship under his tutelage.

During the summer of 1937, Joe and I engaged in a rather interesting enterprise in northern Ohio. We established about thirty Bible classes. These were scheduled in five or six counties in north central Ohio. We had an itinerary which we followed every week the whole summer. We would move into a community, see a pastor, usually a Methodist, and ask if we could teach a Bible class. We were received with amazing receptivity. We did a good job of teaching Bible by books, by methods we had learned at Biblical Seminary, which really did know how to teach Bible and how to teach teachers to teach Bible. Altogether about seven hundred people enrolled in our classes. We were especially proud of a class of children to whom we taught the Gospel of Mark; they proved particularly responsive. We were astonished to find that some of these classes continued some twenty years later!

It was this lack of adequate systematic theology that prompted Joe to transfer to Drew University after two years at Biblical Seminary. In this new setting he learned theology under Dr. Edwin Lewis, Dean Lyn Harold Hough, and others. He was awarded his

Bachelor of Divinity *cum laude* in 1939. One of his classmates was Carl Michalson, with whom he developed close ties later at Yale and in academic colleagueship.

Immediately afterwards, Joe enrolled part-time in Union Theological Seminary, to which he commuted from a pastoral appointment in Sharon, Connecticut. He had become a member of the New York Conference of the Methodist Church and was ordained in turn as Deacon and Elder. At Union he was further exposed to the theological training of Professors Reinhold Niebuhr and Paul Tillich.

Joe had come a long, long way, having had his "first awakening" and was pointed toward larger ministries in the future.

Photo Memories

Early Years

Legend:
Top Left:
Back Row: Parents
James Davenport and
Laura Mae Mathews
Front Row: Joe, Margaret,
Elizabeth, Ken (in front),
Don

Top Right:
Joe's Mother: Laura Mae
Wilson Mathews

Bottom Left:
Back: Elizabeth, Margaret,
Don
Front: Joe, Ken

Marriage to Lyn

Legend:

Top Left:
Evelyn (Lyn) Johnston

Top Right:
Lyn

Bottom Left:
Wedding, Jan 3, 1941

The War Years

Legend:
Top Left:
Joe and Lyn
Top Right:
John Vayhinger with Joe
Bottom Left:
Joe in Okinawa
Bottom Right:
Chaplain Joe Mathews

Raising a Family

Legend:
Top Left:
Joe and Lyn with Joseph, Jr.

Top Right:
Joseph, Jr., Joe and James

Bottom:
James, John, and Joseph, Jr.

My Brother Joe

Legend:
Top: Bishop Jim with his son, Stanley, and Joe
Bottom Left: Joe in the Guild Hall in ICA Kemper Building, Chicago
Bottom Right: Bishop Jim with Joe at ICA gathering in Chicago

Joe in Chicago

Legend:
Top Left: Joe presents Iron Man to Mayor Richard J. Daley in Fifth City;
Top Right: Joe with William Glover and George Walters at Fifth City
Festival – David Reese in background

Bottom Left: Joe with guest speaker in Room A on Fifth City Campus
Bottom Right Joe with David P. Wood, Chairman of the Board for
Ecumenical Institute and Institute of Cultural Affairs

Joe around the World

Legend:
Top: Maliwada Human Development Training School, India, 1975, Joe in group
Middle Left: Joe bows to India leaders, New Delhi, 1975
Middle Right: Joe with village youth
Bottom Left: Joe with Asia leaders, Chicago
Bottom Right: Joe with women leaders from India

6
OF LOVE AND WAR

Life Partner

As the 1930s turned into the 1940s, Joe must have experienced rather vividly that "time was marching on." His thirtieth milestone was rapidly approaching. He had already made two of the three basic life decisions. He had determined that his life philosophy and commitment would be profoundly Christian. His life vocation would follow from this as he began training for Christian ministry: he was called to preach. A third decision – a life partner, if indeed he was to have one – had not yet been made.

His two brothers outpaced him in this respect, which one would not have guessed. The elder brother, Don, had already been married for several years and had with his wife, Jane Phelps, started a family in Texas. Then came word from India that I had also married in 1940 to Eunice Jones. It would never do for Joe to fall behind in this way. This is not to suggest that anyone should really have worried about the matter, least of all Joe himself.

Along about 1937, his family began to notice that Joe was paying some attention to a lovely young lady in Wilmington, Delaware. Her name was Evelyn Johnston. Joe's sister Elizabeth and her husband Ray McCleary lived in that city. Joe managed to visit Elizabeth and Ray with increasing frequency. Elizabeth soon discovered that these visits were not directed as much to her as toward Evelyn, or Lyn, as she came increasingly to be known.

Lyn, born in Wilmington, June 19, 1917, was more than simply a pretty face. She also had a ready mind, which she sought to cultivate. She was a hard worker and possessed management skills, which she put to work in various settings throughout her life. Hers was a family of modest means, but highly respected in the community. She had adoring parents who shared pride in Lyn and her sister, Eleanore, who was six years her junior. In high school Lyn was a straight-A student, immensely popular, and graduated at age sixteen. She then studied at Beacon Business College in Wilmington, equipping herself as a secretary. She always longed for more advanced education. For some years she was secretary to the Rev. Dr. Benjamin Johns, beloved pastor of Grace Methodist Episcopal Church in Wilmington. She often recalled him as the finest man with whom she ever worked. The skills she cultivated there were put to thorough use in later years.

Though Joe and Lyn's relationship may not have been love at first sight, their bonds of mutuality strengthened through several years. It soon became clear that their eventual wedding was only a matter of time.

Delay was due to circumstance. Joe needed to complete his seminary training. He also had the weight of family responsibilities, which he took with great seriousness. His father had recently retired with only a modest pension. Consider, too, three sisters who were at least partially dependent upon Joe – not just financially, but also emotionally. His job was at first that of a student assistant pastor in a large New York City church. When he finally received his own pastoral appointment in northwest Connecticut, it offered little financial security.

According to Methodist practice, a pastor was supplied with a furnished parsonage. In Sharon, Connecticut, the not unattractive house was just across from the church and near the village green. But who was to take care of it? Joe's own considerable accomplishments did not include that of homemaker. So it was that for a period of months his older sister Margaret filled this role, until she herself married a local man. Joe performed the ceremony. She was succeeded by one of his younger sisters, Alice, who had completed one year of college and needed a residence and a job in order to continue her studies. For some extended period his other younger sister, Alleene, made her abode there. Thus, for many months, it could have been said that there was no room for Lyn. She, as it were, had to wait in the wings.

This rather extended episode in Joe's saga shows him in a role in which he excelled all his life, caring for others. His two brothers, it should be noted, were far removed from the scene: Don was in Texas and I was in India. Thus it fell to Joe, aided by his sister Elizabeth, to assume some of the heavy burden of their extended family. This involved helping various siblings to find jobs and entrance to college, partial support for their school expenses and transportation to and from colleges, and so on. These were burdens Joe assumed gladly and without complaint. His own needs and welfare had to wait.

It is moving to hear the stories from his sisters as they have told of his "life support" for them. One of his sisters wrote years later of this period:

> In recent years I wished that I had talked with Joe, about his asking me to go with him and all he did for me: teaching me how to drive; letting me drive his NEW car the first day he had it; teaching me how to critique a play, a book; how to deal with people; working with the young people's group; in a nice way advising me about how to dress; encouraging me to be more self-confident; and getting me back to college.... I sometimes wonder just what my life would have been had Joe NOT stepped in to guide me. There was no one else who saw what was going on. No wonder I loved him so much. He saved my life!

His other two sisters had different needs and separate agendas, but his devoted response and responsibility was the same. He demonstrated even then what was later clearly to become a *mantra* of his life, that we live for others; that when confronted by "the necessary deed," we must perform it! It was a good thing that Joe and Lyn were survivors. This period turned out to be a kind of training program for them.

Finally, the big day arrived: January 3, 1942. Joe and Lyn were married in the beautiful Grace Methodist Episcopal Church in Wilmington, with Dr. Johns officiating. They were said to have been well and truly wed. Pictures taken at the occasion show Lyn to have been a radiant bride. For his part, Joe was clothed in striped trousers and swallowtail coat, together with all the accessories – rented for the occasion. Among the attendants were the bride's sister, Eleanore, and Joe's sisters Alice and Alleene.

The entrance of the United States into World War II had only been declared, so the happy couple could still drive on a rather lengthy wedding trip. Their destination was Mexico where they stayed for a few days in a mountain retreat near Saltillo. They were much taken by this spot of beauty and their oft cherished hope was to visit it again.

Two happenings occurred during their honeymoon that they often mentioned later. They stayed for a night in a fine hotel somewhere in the southeastern states. They had just sat down for a dinner when another young couple was seated at an adjoining table. The woman turned out to be a beauty that Joe had dated in high school. They too were on their honeymoon. The groom had also been Joe's high school acquaintance. It was not exactly the kind of encounter either couple would have chosen!

The other event was often recounted by Lyn, much to Joe's distaste. It was the occasion of their first quarrel. Joe had been driving while his bride had fallen asleep. They had just completed the causeway which crossed the famous Lake Pontchartrain, near New Orleans. This was a sight Lyn very much wanted to see. She worked her new husband over pretty thoroughly about this episode, giving him a much needed lesson.

Sooner than they might have wished, they were back in Sharon, Connecticut, ready to undertake the responsibilities and challenges presented them in this attractive New England community. Its population was a combination of rich and poor, retired and active, those whose work was local and those who journeyed by train each day to New York City. The newlyweds devoted themselves wholeheartedly to caring for the needs of people there. If Joe Mathews was around, people were bound to be aware of it. The new and attractive couple residing at the Methodist parsonage added greatly to community interest. The stunning pair made a difference in Sharon. Joe was an exceptional pastor and Lyn a perfect partner.

Joe always drew a response from people. They either loved him (and a great majority did) or were turned away from him. Wherever he showed up, Joe tended to awaken the community. His sermons were unusual – striking – wonderful, some said. The listeners could not be indifferent to what they heard. They invariably were confronted with a challenge, an invitation to change. Young people flocked to the little Methodist church and the membership grew. As the pastor seemed to be tireless, so the people were energized. They became participants and not mere observers in the church and community. He sought out people in his incessant calling on them at their homes. He showed the people that he cared deeply for their total welfare.

Since the church building was small, and the land on which it was constructed miniscule, they sought ways of expanding the facilities. Joe's startling solution was to propose digging out a basement under the sanctuary. In this excavation process, Joe himself took a leading part, often working alone late at night. In the process he injured his back and was troubled by this ailment until the end of his life. He spoke in schools – as a pastor could still do in those days – especially in the Housatonic Regional High School. There, too, the students responded in a most positive way. For a period he taught religious education there. He fought also to gain the time for the study required to undergird his ministry. To be an effective pastor was a demanding task. Through it all, though, he felt sustained by a rich fellowship with God and the unfailing support of an adoring wife. She made their parsonage a shrine of welcome and hospitality.

Compared with many other periods of his life, the Sharon experience must have seemed at times idyllic. However, it did not last long. The specter of war had become a reality in the sudden and unexpected attack on Pearl Harbor. A man like Joe Mathews was not one to remain a silent observer. Within a period of months he volunteered for service in the Army of the United States. The notion of trying to avoid such service or seeking exception would never have occurred to him. If his community, his country, the welfare of humanity itself was at stake, he had to be part of it. This conviction, of course, he shared with millions of his fellow citizens.

I have tried to point out that Joe confronted a number of crises in his life. One was his sudden spiritual awakening. Later we will see how he was awakened also to the global demand placed upon him. Still, his war experience was perhaps the most crucial awakening of all. To that we now turn.

The War Years

It should not be concluded that Joe was swept into the conflict solely by a tidal wave of patriotic fervor. Rather, he left abundant evidence of having wrestled long and hard with this issue. In an address he gave in Sharon, Connecticut, shortly after Pearl Harbor, we find him stating very clearly the position he had finally come to:

> In recent weeks, we have heard frequently the question put: which side is God on? Napoleon is reported to have stated that God is on the side with the largest battalions. To say that this is an impossible remark is decidedly an understatement. The nature and dealings of God were outside the little emperor's realm of knowledge. Napoleon was admittedly a great general, but he was not a great man in his heart. Only the great in heart can speak authoritatively about God. Which side is God on? I do not know that you can say that God is on one side or the other. A Catholic Archbishop of New York recently stated that God was on no side but the side of his own righteousness. The Archbishop is right.
>
> The question is not whether God is on our side but whether we are on God's side. If any man, if any nation is on the side of God's righteousness, then indeed he is on God's side and then and only then God might be looked upon as being upon his side. Such is the question a thinking Christian person must face today: Is he on the side of God? He or she cannot permit oneself for any reason to be swept headlong into any situation, but rather enter into it guided only by his understanding of God's will in the confronting problem. What is God's righteousness for men in this hour?
>
> The world is at war. Our nation has again taken up the sword. This has placed the world, the nation, and you and me at a crossroads. Choosing a course to tread in this crisis is our common problem. It is our problem as members of the human race, as citizens of the United States of America, and as disciples of Christ in the Kingdom of God. Before this present conflict I did not sign the pacifist pledge. I certainly was not allied with

the war parties. My sympathies were definitely on the side of the former. My policy was to dedicate my energy and resources to the preservation of peace. But now, despite the efforts of all who labored that it might not be, war has come. This is a new situation. A new view must be taken, and a new course of action must be mapped out.

It has been my belief that it is impossible for a Christian to make hard and fast decisions about what he will or will not do before he faces a particular situation. Christian ethics consist of great life principles which are to be converted into definite action. Before the war I could not be absolutely certain of what I would do in case of war. I had never been faced with war. I knew that if and when a war came I must love God with all my heart and my fellowman as myself, which I feel are the basic principles of the Christian ethic, but I could not know exactly into what form of expression these principles might be poured. Now, however, whether we wanted it or not, our nation is at war. And my ethical principles must be turned into specific forms of Christian conduct to meet the issue of the hour.

I wish to share with you the four resolves that I have laid down by which I am to be governed today. They have come slowly, with no little fear and trembling. . . . But you must understand that what I have to say is not *the* Christian point of view but *a* Christian point of view. Or should I say a Christian's point of view. It is my own. And I in nowise ask anyone to accept it as his own.

1. I resolve not to forget that the Christian ideal is absolutely and eternally opposed to war.
2. I resolve to give myself fully to this cause though it demand my life and though I must take up arms against my brother.
3. I resolve, in the midst of war, to hate war the more earnestly while I refuse to hate those individuals who are temporarily termed my enemies.
4. I resolve to dedicate my energies and resources now to the building of a just, durable, and Christian peace.

So it was that in the spring of 1942 Joe volunteered for service in the Army of the United States. He desired to serve as a chaplain. Accordingly, he had to obtain approval of the Chaplains' Commis-

sion of the Methodist Episcopal Church, for any chaplain was required to be certified by the appropriate agency of the religious
body of which he was a part. (There were no female chaplains at
that time.) On May 5, 1942, he was commissioned as 1st Lieutenant. While awaiting permanent orders he attended classes for a few
days at the Chaplain School in Fort Harmon, Indiana. He was assigned to the 27th Division Artillery and attached at first to the
125th Infantry, 3rd Battalion. This unit was based at Camp Rucker,
Alabama, and then at a camp in Gilroy, California. He weighed in
at 150 pounds, 5 feet, 8 inches in height. At age 31 he enjoyed excellent health. (Without Joe's knowledge, I was also commissioned
a 1st Lieutenant in the A.U.S. in India – at almost exactly the same
time.)

Since for some time Joe's unit did not depart for overseas, Lyn
was able to join him for a period in California. Sooner than they
had expected, Joe's outfit was moved forward to Hawaii for duty
and further training. He and Lyn were not to see each other for
three years. This was the lot, of course, for millions of couples during World War II! For a time, Lyn roomed with and worked with
her two sisters-in-law, Alice and Alleene, in Sharon, Connecticut.

The 27th Division had been a National Guard unit in New York
State but was federalized in the autumn of 1940. The division
moved to Hawaii during the summer and fall of 1942. For more
than a year it was responsible for the defense of various parts of
the Hawaiian Islands and went under intense combat training for
more than a year. It was a very concentrated experience of learning
to be soldier, and for Joe, learning how to be a chaplain. We know
that he took this responsibility seriously, for there is abundant tes-
timony to the fact. He gave himself with utmost intensity to
whatever assignment he had. This was true in the past and would
mark him also in the future.

Originally attached to an infantry regiment, in the spring of
1943 he was assigned to a headquarters' unit, the 249th Field Artillery Battalion, where he served seventeen batteries using 105mm
cannons. One can readily imagine what this entailed, especially
under heavy combat.

Before proceeding, a broad sketch of World War II should be drawn. At the time these words are being written, the war has been over for nearly sixty years. When one considers what has transpired in the intervening years, including several other wars in which the United States has been involved, the Great War has become a kind of blur. It involved unpleasant aggressors such as Adolph Hitler, Benito Mussolini, General Tojo (not to mention Emperor Hirohito). It occasioned unbelievable suffering and cruelty, the loss of life by the millions, the destruction of many cities, and the threat of ending human history itself. Though its devastation is very real to the veterans who still remain, World War II has moved into the field of interest of historians and military specialists. It remains the most violent and wide-ranging conflict in human history. It called forth an unparalleled united effort of nations who were determined to overcome the aggressors.

Our immediate interest in the Pacific portion of the conflict had to await the focusing of the war effort in the Atlantic and Europe. The war was fought on land, sea, and air, and on a scale never before seen in world history. At first, Americans remained mainly observers of the struggle mostly waged in Europe. The events at Pearl Harbor on December 7, 1941 – a date recalled in infamy – changed all that. Americans were then united as never before and engaged fully in the effort. At first the Pacific war was waged at sea and then in the air. The U.S. Army, too, had its full share of involvement on the ground. First, there was the thrust of General Douglas MacArthur up the Western Pacific, through or around island chains, past New Guinea and to the Philippines – pointed always at Japan. Other Army operations or combined Army-Navy operations were directed toward scattered islands of the Central Pacific, the Ryukyu Islands (especially Okinawa), again headed toward Japan.

To outline the broad sweep of the campaign is more than a mere geography lesson or a list of faraway places with strange sounding names. A similar exercise could be undertaken with respect to other parts of the world – to equally distant locations and no less strange sounding names, for World War II was virtually *world*-wide. For those troops who were about to enter armed conflict for the first time, romanticism was swept aside. It was for them more like a descent into the maelstrom, or more likely, descent into hell!

Years later, newsman Tom Brokaw was to write what proved to be a best seller concerning the American men and women who served in the 1941-1945 conflict. He titled it *The Greatest Generation*. Those actually involved would never for even a moment have thought of themselves as the "greatest generation." They were simply doing their duty, fulfilling their responsibility as citizens in a ghastly struggle for which they either volunteered or were drafted. Joe would have laughed at the very thought of being regarded "the greatest."

The units to which Chaplain Joseph W. Mathews was attached saw action in three bloody battles in the Pacific. As a schoolboy, Joe was an avid and informed student of geography. At that time he did not realize that he was destined to be involved intimately in a lot of geography – applied geography, if you will. He was to spend much time in miniscule islands or atolls in the Central Pacific. So small were many of them that they could only be found on a large-scale map. Though Joe never liked to speak about the horrifying experiences of battle, he reveled in rolling off his tongue the names of obscure island groups at the end of nowhere.

Just to give a glimpse of the area in which he battled, think first of all about the junction of the Equator and the International Dateline. Just west and a little north of that point are the Gilbert group of atolls. Then well to the west and slightly north lie the islet chain of the Marshall Islands. Directly to the west of them is the Caroline group of more than five hundred islands. Off to the north lie the Marianas, sweeping for nearly five hundred miles south to north. Far to the northwest of them is Okinawa, much larger and relatively close to the Japanese main islands. The whole was a vast region that the American Army, Navy, and Marine units island-hopped as they battled across the Pacific Ocean. This region was to become very familiar to Joe.

Although Chaplain Mathews threw himself thoroughly into his military service, it was his being in actual combat changed him profoundly. After this sustained combat experience he was never again the same. It toughened the sinews of his being, even though from boyhood he had manifested unusual hardiness. He engaged in three bloody battles, namely, Eniwetok, Saipan, and Okinawa. A chaplain was not to bear arms, but could if under sustained fire or "in harms way"

The 27th Division had from the spring of 1942 been in Hawaii engaged in extensive combat training. It was charged with the defense of all or part of the Hawaiian Islands. The war in the Pacific during ensuing months was carried on largely by air and by sea. Then in November, 1943, a task force of Joe's division, jointly with Marine units, invaded Makin Atoll and successfully took it in three days' time. This achievement was reported tersely with the message, "Makin taken." Joe did not take part in this assault. The force then returned to its Hawaiian base.

It was quite different shortly thereafter. Joe was very much a part of the landing in Majuro of the Marshall Islands (January – February, 1944). Years later, toward the end of his life, Joe frequently visited Majuro where he and his colleagues established a Human Development Project. What memories these later visits must have stirred in him! More specifically, his unit went ashore at the lagoon of Eniwetok Island, the site in 1952 of the test of the first nuclear bomb. Here a furious battle raged – Joe's first experience under fire. He did not remain at a safe position in the rear but was in the thick of the fighting, serving in ways that were then open to chaplains.

He acquitted himself well, for here it was that he was awarded the first of several citations for courage. Orders from Headquarters of the 27th Infantry Division read:

Award of the Bronze Star Medal to Chaplain (Captain) Joseph W. Mathews, 0468664, Chaplain Corps, U.S. Army. For heroic service in connection with military operations against the enemy at Eniwetok Atoll, Marshall Islands, during the period 19-23 February 1944. Chaplain Mathews displayed marked disregard for safety by engaging himself throughout the attack on Eniwetok Atoll in forward areas, constantly exposing himself to enemy fire. His continued labors with casualties resulted in a great saving of lives and his shining example of fortitude was in-

spirational and had a highly favorably effect on the morale of all
elements ashore. The appropriate burial place and memorial service provided for those who gave their lives in this operation are
testimonial to Chaplain Mathews' achievement following the assault phase.

After this engagement his outfit remained for garrison duty on
Eniwetok for three months. Imagine the surprise of his family
members when fifty years later in a national periodical they observed a full-page picture of officers and men on the beach of that
island. The battle over, there stood a greatly relieved Chaplain Joe
Mathews, youthful and trim in Army uniform!

Back in Hawaii the full division began intensive training for a
far larger engagement, beginning two months later (June 1944) on
Saipan in the Marianas. This island was considerably larger than
Eniwotok, measuring about fifteen miles long, north and south, and
an average width of seven miles. After intense naval and air bom-
bardment, the Division began landing June 16, 1944, and joined
the fight with the 4th and 2nd Marine Divisions. The island was
strongly fortified by the Japanese and stoutly defended. The advance of the three divisions across the island was slower than
expected, and the two Marine divisions outpaced the 27th Army
Division. This led to interservice rivalry, for here was an Army
unit under the command successively of Naval and Marine officers. Thus Army Major General Ralph C. Smith was subordinate to
Marine Lieutenant General Holland M. "Howlin' Mad" Smith. In
spite of the rivalry, the U.S. forces prevailed and secured the island
by July 7, 1944.

Once again, we find Joe performing well under heavy fire. He
was among those awarded an Oak Leaf Cluster. He must have been
aware of the rivalry between the two Generals Smith, but, if so, he
does not mention it. This conflict was widely reported at the time
with two leading publishing interests taking sides: the Hearst
newspapers supporting the Army's side while the Henry Luce organization backing the Navy and Marines. Lt. General "Howlin'
Mad" Smith" removed his counterpart in the midst of the battle
and replaced him with Major General George W. Grier, Jr. The
Marine general apparently lost his temper and was convinced that

his adversary did not lead the Army unit aggressively enough. This, in turn, reflected upon the record of the 27th Division, which can hardly be supported. The Army unit was confronted by exceedingly strong enemy resistance from caves, which had to be flushed out by flame-throwers and severe hand-to-hand struggle. In fact, the Army supplied about a third of the U.S. fighting men and accounted for a third of those killed in action (1053 out of 3119 U.S. troops), while accounting for a third of Japanese losses that totaled nearly 18,000.

At battle's end, Joe had the numbing experience of burying hundreds of young men, who were the vibrant youth to whom he had offered spiritual comfort only days before. This experience, which he went through three times, left deep scars on him, as his family and friends can testify. Typical of those who went through such devastation, he seldom referred to it. He had immense respect for the soldiers he served and they invariably reciprocated. He admired the heroism and sacrifice he so often witnessed. Once he spoke of a young colonel, a West Point graduate, who had remarked to him one day, "If I ever die in battle, let no one say that my life was taken. Rather, let it be said that I *gave* it." Shortly afterwards, the officer was the victim of a sniper's bullet.

Yet, Joe spoke of these matters rarely and wrote of them not at all. Sometimes for weeks and even months he scarcely penned a line to his wife or family. He was just too consumed with the burdens he had to bear. (Perhaps his war letters were lost, or they were consumed in one of the two fires which destroyed family possessions after the war.)

Most of his family members wrote to him very regularly, save, perhaps his two brothers, who were also in uniform. Lyn wrote almost daily – high marks for her! He wanted to know in detail what life was like at home: health, finances, family stress, and so on. This information was supplied to him in abundance. Far more important, Lyn literally poured out rivers of affection for him. If love was what sustained him, it was endlessly supplied. Lyn would speak of the family cares and expenses. She would share with pride her fine record in Maryville College near Knoxville, Tennessee. While at Maryville she made almost all A's. Her roommate was

Carol Titus, fresh from a missionary family in India, and a cousin of Eunice Jones Mathews, Lyn's sister-in-law, whom she had not yet seen. Lyn transferred to Stanford University to be closer to Joe and continued her daily letters, but it was mostly affective adulation, almost adoration for her absent spouse. This was, of course, multiplied million of times by millions of families supporting their loved ones. One can say this was a "plus" of war!

It is a moving experience to read the letters they interchanged six decades ago. Precious little humor accompanied Joe's enforced separation. One exception might be recorded: Joe once wrote Lyn telling her that "there was room for two" in his foxhole! Enough of that! Such a word, however, must have lifted her sagging morale.

Lyn received scholarship aid at Stanford and opportunity to work at jobs which served to cover her other expenses. She spared him the word that she almost collapsed from overwork, but her grades were excellent. During the course of her work in California, she had occasion for putting on a party for nine-year-old girls. One of them asked if she was studying to be a teacher. She replied, "Maybe." The child then advised, "You shouldn't because all the boys will whistle at you!" When she reported that to her long-absent husband, it must have lifted *his* morale!

Her affectionate name for Joe was "Josef" (another was "Josephus," when she wished to chide him). She often expressed her approval of his chaplain's activities, even though she was at times depressed, despondent, and blue, but endeavored to shield him from this. She did report the death of her father on June 4, 1944, and she relayed to him word of the frequent illness of *his* father. Papa was confined to the Methodist Hospital in Brooklyn, N.Y. She confided at times her inmost thoughts, her intellectual struggles, her wakening mind and thirst for knowledge, and the subjects that forced her to reflect deeply.

Her interest in religion increased immensely. She attended Palo Alto Methodist Church, whose pastor, Marvin Stuart, later became a bishop and a close friend of Joe's. She found this preacher "young, enthusiastic, and, above all, has something to say!" She also became acquainted with a visiting professor, the Quaker theologian Dr. D. Elton Trueblood, whom she greatly admired.

Her thoughts often turned to love. She read somewhere with approval, "Love is constantly finding something new in those we love." Mostly she thought of the future. When mail didn't come, she reflected, "Maybe tomorrow." She wrote, "I could not live without tomorrow" (hope) or "I could not live without yesterday" (memory). Whether original with her or a quotation, this was pure poetry! Above all she repeatedly referred to "That Day" – their re-union. Both of them lived for that! Again, this was the almost universal experience of couples separated by war.

It is now time to say a little about what chaplains do in war-time. Far more than might be supposed. In large part, fulfilling this significant role is not something that is specifically taught in theo-logical seminaries. It is rather more caught than taught. Joe did have an ancestor who served as a chaplain in the Revolutionary War. (A more remote forebear was said to be an Archbishop of York, some of whose descendants settled in the American colo-nies; so some disposition to war was in Joe's blood.)

For those who survived, there was a respite after each conflict. This was true after the return of units to the base in Hawaii from Eniwetok, for a period of about two months. After the Saipan bat-tle, bloody engagement that it was, the 27th Division was moved to the south for an extended stay on the Island of Espiritu Santo (Holy Spirit Island), located in the New Hebrides group, northeast of New Guinea. This was a much needed rest. The men were physi-cally and spiritually exhausted. Besides, their morale had been sorely tried due to the acute episode of interservice rivalry in which their fortitude had unfairly been called into question. They also had to engage in highly specialized training for the Ryukyu engagement to follow. Their stay in the New Hebrides lasted for more than seven months.

These several intervals did not relieve the chaplains of duty. Rather, in some respects their work intensified. There was plenty to reflect on regarding the past; there was foreboding about the fu-ture. Joe and other chaplains made good use of these periods.

The work of a military chaplain was far from being a copy of the service of a minister in a conventional pastorate. Clearly it was more intensive. Those called to be priests, pastors, rabbis deal with the boundary or focal dimensions of life: birth, baptism, marriage, life pressures, illness, injury, and death. Such matters punctuate the life of mortals, but in wartime they are more immediate and urgent. Some military personnel are baptized or otherwise inducted into a religious body. Sometimes there are marriages. Chaplains had a role in the approval of weddings while in service as well as conducting the ceremony. It is the threat of impending death and serious injury that is more immediate and pressing. Questions of the meaning of life come to the fore: fear, courage, and inner resources become matters both urgent and compelling.

The U.S. Armed forces provide a place for spiritual care and advice. This has been true since the very beginning of our country. It really has no relationship to abstract notions of separation of religion and the state. It favors or denies no particular religious affiliation. It provides help to men and women who suddenly find themselves up against the meaning of life itself.

It is no surprise, then, to find that chaplains have a great deal to do with morale. An examination of Joe Mathews's files reveals a wide-ranging field of concern: sermons, funerals conducted, morale, fear, Thanksgiving, "My Country," "Why We are at War," "The Christian Soldier in Action," "New Year's Talk," "Japanese Religion and Culture," prayer, death and care for the dead, war and peace, religious holy days, lectures on Washington and Lincoln, "After the War," lessons from the war, and so on.

In some sense, his work was not very different from the role of a typical pastor, but it was more urgent. He preached regularly and his notes show that he planned his messages with care. In those days, lectionary preaching (that is, following a stated scriptural cycle) was not in vogue, but he covered the whole range of spiritual needs. He taught Bible lessons regularly and with considerable effectiveness. He displayed pastoral care both to individuals and groups. He often traveled a lengthy circuit, for the various units were often scattered. Great attention was given also to prayer, a particular need of fighting men.

Of course, Chaplain Mathews dealt with *morale* topics. He was certainly his own man, no automaton giving voice to prescribed propaganda positions. This latter approach he regarded a misuse and corruption. Actually, morale in his view was a high and noble goal, essential to effective living in both civil and military contexts. As his notes suggest, he saw morale as inner spirit, the emotional and mental attitude which undergirds the fulfillment of objectives in any life situation. It enables courage, motivating and activating the will; it concentrates the ability to decide a course of action and carry it through. It involves one's whole philosophy of life; one's understanding of the external situation with which we are confronted; the action required by others in a mutually demanding situation. Then he turned from trying to define the concept to a list of those who were upheld by morale. Here his list ranged from John Bunyan to Joan of Arc, from Jesus to Disraeli. He typically concluded with making clear that morale makes better men and women, better soldiers, while at the same time equipping them to face death and to approach life with a sense of worth, of acceptance, and the power to see it through. He admitted later that he never grasped morale's meaning to the degree the situation demanded.

Again and again, out of sheer necessity, Joe turned to a discussion of *fear*. He did not hesitate to emphasize that everyone is subject to fear, especially in the time of impending battle. Those who would deny this are either fools or liars. He noted that fear begets fear; that fear has useful roles in alerting to danger and awakening all senses. Therefore, fear can either harm or help. It can immobilize or stimulate. It can arouse courage. It can stimulate faith in one's self, in the cause, in one's comrades, in God. Fear presses a person to the very edge of existence: to life's purpose, to loneliness and isolation, to self-esteem, to overcoming cowardice, to the courage which is found in facing the threat to life and well-being.

Sometimes, when most overwhelmed by terror, peace and power breaks into our consciousness. Tillich's *Courage to Be* was not available to him then, but he would have embraced it immediately. For many, this will come as the awareness that even in "the valley of death" God is present as the sustaining force. But whatever Joe said about such matters, he readily admitted how feeble and ineffective he was in addressing the deep realities of the situation. Nevertheless, he and his fellow chaplains tried.

Even grimmer was the necessity of chaplains to deal with *death* itself, the dying, and with the dead. The Army charges the Grave Registration Section of the Quartermaster Corps with the actual burial of those killed in battle and the attendant record keeping. The chaplains were responsible for the collection of bodies. Their careful and respectful handling was essential for morale of all concerned. Thus, the dead must be cared for as soon as possible. For example, their bodies might be covered by blankets or even palm leaves. Then they were to be moved to collecting stations. Chaplains, too, had to choose sites for cemeteries.

Chaplains had to train parties to search the field. They had to care, as much as possible, for the enemy dead as well. These parties were advised to wear "dog tags" and helmets, not to walk alone, to watch out for snipers and "booby traps," "keep moving"; "don't collect souvenirs"; remove NOTHING from bodies; moving bodies to aid stations. One can readily understand how difficult it was to speak of such matters and even more how demanding it was to fulfill this sort of mission. Of course, the chaplain's role was crucial in the burial of the dead. Survivors were deeply concerned that their comrades were cared for with great dignity in the end.

Joe had to go through these services hundreds of times. He found this always to be a devastating experience, and he invariably felt the inadequacy of his ministrations. At times there had to be mass burials, but an effort was made to make the services as individual as possible. Typically, the service would involve scripture, prayer, a meditation, sometimes a hymn, and committal with benediction. Joe would speak of a God who cares, of a Creator who suffers, too, of the "indestructibility of life," of the "Eternal Qualities of the Good."

And there were the *letters* that had to be sent to families. These could often be quite personal because strong bonds were created between a chaplain and his men. When one is privileged to read such letters and some of the grateful replies, the sanctity of life comes through.

Care for the soldiers did not end there. The folks back home needed to be reassured concerning those who were still alive but so far away. A letter sent at Christmas 1943 will convey the mood:

My dear Friend:

Some months ago I became the chaplain of the unit in which a member of your family is serving his country. Because of this relationship, I feel a very personal interest in your home and wish to extend my sincere greetings at this Christmas season.

You can well understand that Christmas this year for our soldiers will be even more difficult than last year. As days pass we yearn the more fervently to be home with those we love. Nonetheless, we will not be deflected from our course by home-sickness or any other hardship. I do not think I am wrong when I say the foremost desire of the men is to finish the task that lies before us out here. Only when it is done will we turn toward home. I'm sure that is the way you want us to feel. In the mean-time, the most important thing that you can do and are doing for us is to write. Mail is of supreme importance! Write frequently, cheerfully, and encouragingly. It is a mistake, in my opinion, to put anything in a letter that may be disquieting news, unless it is absolutely necessary.

To me, the grandest men in the world are those in my unit. I'm undoubtedly a bit prejudiced, but they are splendid fellows. I thoroughly like them. I visit with them regularly and try to make myself available for consultations and friendly talks at all times. Religious services are held regularly and opportunities are pro-vided for every man to attend those of his own faith. I want, more than I can express, that our solders not only conduct them-selves honorably on the field of battle, but that they return to those who love them even finer men than when they left.

As to Christmas here in the Pacific, you may be assured we are endeavoring to bring to all a happy Holiday Season. Every-one is putting forth his utmost effort to make this the best Christmas possible. I pray that the true spirit of Christ will abide with us here and with you at home. And I join with you in pray-ing that "Peace on earth, goodwill to men" may be more of a reality across the world before another Christmas time comes.

If I can ever be of any assistance to you, or if you know of any way I can help your loved one here, please do not hesitate for a moment to write.

Very faithfully yours,
Chaplain Joseph W. Mathews

Such letters often elicited deeply grateful responses, as in the following example:

Dear Friend: Ohio, August 28, 1944

As we received a letter from Verum the other day stating he had been to church that morning and you had delivered a good sermon but he also stated he would like to be in his church here again which I know he would and he would sure like to see again. When a person looks at the pictures taken at Saipan it is a miracle that there are still some amongst the living that were there we sure feel thankful again. I came upon your letter the other day of April 3 and felt I should write a few lines and am glad that you feel you are rewarded and thanks for the few lines you wrote underneath your letter that we have a fine a son and we are proud of him and may God speed him home to us again and we will appreciate it if you will write again sometime and good Luck to you.

(Mrs. E.C.F.)

Repeatedly Joe turned to *prayer* and *devotional practices*. He insisted that prayer holds a central place in the life of the Christian, who is one called to fellowship with God. This linkage is established through prayer and maintained through prayer, the very way in which humankind communes with God. Therefore, he would reemphasize the importance – the necessity – of habits of devotion. Devotion and doctrine are linked together. He speaks of "time for prayer," "a place for prayer," especially in a foxhole. He outlines the types of prayer, insists that God answers prayer. So insistent was he that one has to conclude that the message must have gotten through.

The lengthy respite that the 27th Division had on the Island of Espiritu Santo gave occasion for different types of *addresses* from the chaplains. So it was that Joe turned attention to heroes of American history, lectures on Washington and Lincoln, always his personal heroes. He often shared reviews of significant books he had read: *War and Peace*, for example. Or he would give occasional addresses related to the various holiday seasons. Then he engaged in preaching missions to other units or served as "guest preacher" for other chaplains, thus exposing other troops to his unique style.

It was while Joe was on this large island that he came for the first time to be familiar with *missionary work* close up. These particular missionaries were Presbyterians from Australia and New Zealand. In whatever spare time he could muster, he visited some of their stations; he preached in their churches through interpreters and observed their medical and educational work. As was the case in other parts of the world, the troops were generous in their support for the work of these missionaries. I recall the letter of one pilot who wrote home to his mother these words, just prior to a flight in which he lost his life: "These missionaries are doing a great job, in an out-of-the-way place, without an audience to cheer them. See that you folk keep them supplied!"

Joe came to have great respect for the Polynesian people and developed an immense interest in their *culture*. He used to recount a particular journey to the interior, for the island was a large one and quite mountainous. He was led up a steep incline on a hot day. His guides brought him refreshing spring water in bamboo cups. Finally they reached a high plateau. There he was welcomed by a tribal chief and his people and treated to a sumptuous feast of roast pig and all that went with it. They worshipped together and Joe preached. So it was in Christian fellowship he was made to feel at home while far from home. Letters from missionaries to the chaplains and G.I.'s expressed the great gratitude that they felt for their help. Such insights into mission work were not easily forgotten. Joe's interest increased.

During their rather lengthy stay on Holy Spirit Island, the 27th Division was not really experiencing rest and rehabilitation, but was going through intensive training exercises for the heavy combat which lay ahead of them. They knew to a man that they were soon once again to be under heavy fire, for the land forces were inching ever nearer the Japanese home islands.

Saipan had taught those engaged in the struggle how fanatically the Japanese military tried to cling to the territory they occupied. They had shown the intensity with which they would try to defend their turf. It was precisely Joe's division which had developed the tactics of driving the enemy out of caves by flamethrowers, by Bangalore torpedoes, and Molotov cocktails. There would be more of the same – much more.

It was as well for American troops to understand their *enemy* and to grasp as well as possible what motivated them to behave as they did. As I write, I have before me Joe's notes on a highly concentrated lecture he often gave on this topic nearly sixty years ago. He had concluded from his study that two factors were present in Japanese psychology. One was the universal urge for self-preservation. The other was supplied by Japanese culture and history: the glory that was associated with dying for the Emperor. These two promptings were in conflict. We all are largely what we are due to our habits and culture. Their traits were not inborn, as it were, but acquired by cultural indoctrination.

Among Japanese culture's contributing factors are its geographic insularity and prolonged isolation. Religious elements were derived from ancient times and subsequent new religious trends from Buddhism, Taoism, and Confucianism. There were likewise influences from China and from the West. There was a long-standing element of militarism and the glory associated with it. There were also genuine fears of exploitation from other nations.

A more modern philosophy emerged which was seen as controlling human conduct.

    a.   Shinto – the way of the gods – religion
    b.   Kodo – the way of the emperor – politics
    c.   Bushido – the way of the soldier – militarism

In summary, there had emerged intense racial pride, a belief in their divine origin, deep-seated loyalty to Emperor and native land, a fear of and contempt of foreigners, the glorification of war, and a willingness to be regimented. The twentieth century abounds in evidence of such trends in other cultures as well. Regardless of the accuracy or inaccuracy of this analysis, the "bottom line" was: Watch out! Be careful! Don't underestimate the adversary. They were out to destroy, so expect no favors.

This is harsh realism indeed. Use of this understanding was soon to be tested in the bloodiest land engagement of the Pacific war. The 27th Division left Espiritu Santo on March 25, 1945, for what was for most an unknown destination, Okinawa. The island was a sizeable one, stretching nearly sixty miles from north to south. Its irregular shape gave it a waist of from two to sixteen miles wide. It was highly mountainous. The irregular terrain favored defensive rather than offensive forces. Its population was about half a million, largely engaged in agriculture. Its hillsides are marked by striking womb-shaped tombs and are studded with numerous natural and man-made caves.

The 27th Division was a part of a much larger combined invasion force of services, total personnel numbering nearly 200,000. Joe's division, or parts of it, landed on April 9 and later in many smaller operations. They secured the important Kadena airfield. They flushed out cave and tunnel positions and worked their way up the western side of the island until the battle ended on August 8, 1945. It was intense fighting all the way.

The division was then posted for garrison duty for several months at Onna, on the west coast of Okinawa. When they settled in, Joe led his men to build a respectable church, which was bequeathed to the Church of Okinawa, a part of Kyodan, the United Church of Japan, organized during the war. Joe befriended local pastors and Christian people. The church was built of ammunition cases and other war-wrecked material found near the site. When I visited Okinawa in 1956, the attractive church was still in use. By the time of a later visit in 1995, it had been replaced by a solid and beautiful modern structure.

No attempt is made here to give details of a very complicated and bloody battle. The losses were heavy on both sides. About 12,500 Americans were killed – about 5,000 from the Army alone. The Japanese lost many more. Joe and other chaplains buried hundreds of men. It was an overwhelming experience.

Although Okinawa was subsequently returned to Japanese sovereignty, a large presence of American military forces is there today. Toward the southern tip of the island there is now a large Peace Park. Nearby are cliffs and caves where Japanese combatants were slain and hundreds of civilians committed suicide, preferring death to capture. Thousands of square, black marble pillars, or obelisks, cover the area. Engraved in English, Korean, or Japanese on the stones are the names of those who fought and died there.

There is an exception, however, for a number of pillars have no names inscribed, save one, where five names are to be found, all in Korean characters. These were in memory of some of the Korean "comfort women" who were forced into prostitution for Japanese soldiers. Most of the families would not consent to their names to be written; so they remained blank. This prompted the following Haiku:

> *Cold black obelisks,*
> *Nameless amidst thousands named,*
> *Pronounced chaste at last.*

Joe's division was then sent to Japan for garrison duty for a period. He often spoke of the devastation there, mostly from the firebombing of Tokyo and other cities. He observed the Japanese at close range, admiring the rich aspects of their culture. He never ceased to be interested in these matters. He sought out Japanese church leaders, including the renowned Christian, Toyohiko Kagawa of the Kyodan. He found him brokenhearted, for he himself was a convinced pacifist.

The 27th Division left Japan, arriving in Seattle on December 24, 1945. The division was deactivated at Fort Lawton, Washington, December 31, 1945.

Then it was home again and joyful reunion. For Joe and Lyn THAT DAY had arrived! They could now get on with their lives, raise a family, and make a major contribution to church and society.

Of this Joseph Wesley Mathews was sure: having seen thousands of strapping young men cut off before life had really begun for them, he was not really prepared to deal adequately with such realities. He was thirty-four years old. Half of his life was behind him. Difficult as that part had been, how was he to know that the last half would be even more demanding! And deep down he had been awakened to his need for a far deeper grounding in theology.

7
RETURN TO ACADEME

We have seen that Joe's experience in World War II was the second of three great turning points in his life. He had spent much of the decade of the 1930s in preparation for the role of Christian minister. This period saw him involved in the life of five different institutions. Their very variety is a testimonial to the fact that for him the pursuit of professional preparation was a very rough road indeed. Nevertheless, the war showed him how unprepared he really was to meet the demands of ministry. He determined to change that. Hence, for him the next step was a return to academe. This designation covers a highly dramatic decade of his life as a graduate student at Yale University and as a teacher at Colgate University and Southern Methodist University (Perkins School of Theology).

To repeat, Joe learned at the hard school of combat that he was far from adequately equipped to fulfill the demands of his vocation. Of this he was thoroughly – almost viscerally – convinced. He was not alone. War changed the outlook of many of his contemporaries. Joe felt this experience with great depth and intensity. He became aware that in many ways the whole church seemed unprepared to fulfill the demands a new day placed upon it. In order adequately to serve the present age, he was convinced that he, his contemporaries in ministry, and the whole church needed to be re-educated and retooled for the unfinished task at hand. All this bore in upon him with compelling force and he felt obliged to respond to this demand.

There can be no doubt that Joe's experience in the war greatly shocked him, for firsthand he was reminded repeatedly of the brevity of life and its profound finality. He saw hundreds of the soldiers he served literally obliterated in a second's flash. Thereafter he never ceased to explore the depths and limits of human existence.

This note was sounded again and again in his rather sparse correspondence from the battlefield. It is echoed repeatedly in the far more extensive responses from his wife to him somewhere in the Pacific. She shared his eagerness for reeducation: thus, her letter to him on September 13, 1944:

> Your two letters about future plans have just reached me, leaving me thrilled about your proposed plan for our life together after the war. I am so excited that I fairly tingle all over and I know I am glowing as only you, my darling, can make me glow. Your second letter was far more logical than the first. It is workable and even sensible. To a conservative, it would sound a bit venturesome, but the world has progressed because of men who have dared to go forward, unmindful of future security, inasmuch as they were giving themselves to some cause that was worth their efforts.
>
> I have so much to learn. I can't seem to get enough. I sometimes wish I had a little system of education all my own. I'd like to do concentrated study with you until I had partially quenched my insatiable desire for science. Then go to English, history, psychology, sociology, economics, and lastly philosophy, theology and religion.
>
> We can easily work the school angle from a financial viewpoint. I would like to have it so that you could devote all your time to schoolwork while I worked to keep things going. I place not too much importance on your degree, but years [of study] would bring you so close that it would seem a shame not to go on and get it.

In one of Joe's letters to me (April 1945), he becomes specific about his concern for the church:

> I have found the chaplaincy a laboratory. It has driven me to stand for certain reforms in the church. I'll name the main ones without taking time to enlarge:
>
> 1. There must be a unity in Protestantism.
> 2. The Christian faith must be restated in 20th century thought forms which people can understand and apply to life today.

3. The Christian faith must be reinterpreted to envelop the whole of life – the whole of the individual's personality and relationships, the whole of the orders of society. Christianity must be judged on its contribution to life.
4. The Church must reorganize her educational system and program. Christians today haven't the slightest intelligent idea about their faith.
5. Modern versions of the Bible in language folk can understand must be put in the hands of the people by the Church. King James may be beautiful, but what if it can't be understood and as a result isn't read? The Church has made a fetish out of the Bible during this war.
6. There must be a stronger and intelligent emphasis on the unique Christian experience that created the Christian church of the New Testament.
7. There must be a further reinterpretation of missions. We have sent too many souls to heaven and their bodies to hell – taken away their culture and have offered them nothing in its place but the white man's stinking superior attitudes. The Christian natives I've seen are lost souls.
8. The Church must have a united, clear voice to raise against the glaring social evils of the day and not be afraid to raise it.

These things are not new, I know, but they have been firmly impressed upon me after working for three years with a cross section of American youth at war. My basic creed has been simplified. What do you think of this?

1. I believe in God
2. I believe in a Christ-like God.
3. I believe that man can know God.
4. I believe that in knowledge of God man as an individual and as society, in this life and the next, comes to the fullness of life.

Is this enough for bare essentials? Many of my men who have been overseas three and a half years will be going home before long. I want to sternly and passionately review with them the Christian faith before they go. Maybe later I'll send you the ten topics I cover.

It is clear that Joe was earnest in his search for a more solid grounding in his search for religious truth. At times he seemed to be almost obsessed, trying his hand repeatedly at stating his concern. Two more examples reinforce his focus:

1. I stand for an interpretation of Christianity for our age.
2. I stand for an emphasis of the "Christian experience" of power.
3. I stand for an application of the faith to the whole of life.
4. I stand for a reconstruction of our religious education programs.
5. I stand for an ecumenical church.
6. I stand for a united Christian voice on glaring social problems.
7. I stand for a reinterpretation of missions for other people.
8. I stand for a modern version of the Bible in the hands of people.

Second example, from notes:

Reforms for the church:
*   statement of the Christian faith for our age
*   emphasis upon Christian work (individual and group) with ways and means pointed out and provided (specifically)
*   means for bringing individuals to definite decision for Christ
*   clarification of the Christian experience with special steps to that experience made clear
*   further striving toward union of the Christian church
*   more definite criticisms of all orders of life that depart from first principles
*   more thoroughgoing education of Christians in Christian faith and application
*   study and reemphasis upon the experience of prayer
*   further rethinking of missions – more action (Christian) than talking
*   youth and lay participation in Christian work

Such goals, aims, and perspectives Joe continued to keep in focus during the years that remained for him. They were his North Star throughout his life.

It is worth noting that there exists an almost silent fraternity among those who have undergone combat. Almost universally they prefer not to talk about it. There remains deep within the psyche of combat veterans a hurt that can neither be erased nor fully expressed. A part of one's self was lost and can never be retrieved; a kind of paralysis sets in. Veterans of other wars felt the same things. There is a wound there which must be treated, but how? This deep-seated emotion drenched Joe, and his soul cried out for release and relief for himself and others. This drove him for decades.

The earnestness of his pursuit is seen in the fact that within weeks of his discharge from the Army he was already enrolled as a graduate student in the Divinity School of Yale University. He had also considered applying to the University of Chicago or returning to Union Theological Seminary in New York, where he had already tasted of its offerings. In both of these institutions he interviewed professors. It was not, however, until he had met with Professor H. Richard Niebuhr at Yale that he came to a decision. Happily he was admitted as a graduate student in contemporary theology and theological ethics. Yale became his intellectual center for three years.

For the first time in his life he was freed to give himself to concentrated and relentless study. This was possible for two reasons. First of all, Lyn worked full time in a variety of jobs to help support the family. The other factor was the G.I. Bill of Rights (Public Law 346), which Congress – exercising unusual vision and wisdom – enacted in June 1944. It became law with the prompt and ready signature of President Franklin D. Roosevelt.

This legislation has sometimes been described as the "best deal Uncle Sam ever made." Millions of military service personnel availed themselves of the higher education opportunity. It covered tuition costs (at the time this averaged $15 for an hour of credit, even at major universities), plus $20 a week in unemployment benefits for a year, dubbed the "52-20 Club." Tuition, books, and fees of up to $500 were paid directly to the institution for a maximum of forty-eight months. The legislation also guaranteed to the veterans a year of education for each ninety days of service. In addition, it underwrote one month of study for each month of active duty, up to a maximum of forty-eight months. Plus, married students could receive $75 a month for subsistence.

All veterans were grateful. Seasoned and made serious by their wartime experience, the recipients of this aid excelled in their studies, oft times putting to shame regular students. Most of all, our country benefited immensely, since the result was a more highly trained citizenry than any other nation could boast. This is another reason that such veterans can truly be called "the greatest generation."

Yale Divinity School

Joe and Lyn were on their way, soon ensconced in a Quonset hut at 24 Armoryville, New Haven, Connecticut (near the Yale Bowl).

Yale Divinity School at the time was the scene of a number of stellar players in the theological field. Among them was Robert Calhoun, H. Richard Niebuhr, Roland Bainton, Albert Outler, Kenneth Scott Latourette, Liston Pope, Halford Luccock – to name only a few. Joe's mind was stretched by many professors. He both learned and debated with Albert Outler and finally admitted an intellectual debt to him. Very often he spoke with appreciation of Professor Bainton for leading him into the wondrous world of Martin Luther. A little later we shall turn to H. Richard Niebuhr, his principal mentor. To him he owned an enormous debt of gratitude.

One of Joe's earliest courses in Contemporary Theology was under Professor Albert Outler, with whom he was later a faculty colleague at Perkins School of Theology at Southern Methodist University. A requirement of this course was the submission of an extended essay to be titled, "How My Mind Has Changed Theologically in the Last Decade." It is highly revealing and in part touches on factors which have already been mentioned. The paper is a good link between his past and his future.

Joe writes of his immature thinking, naiveté, and confusion. He observes that he was not alone in a confused state, for it seemed also to describe the condition of other young (and even older) preachers and chaplains. In his case, during the decade just behind him he had moved strangely enough from a strong conservative influence, through an emphasis on critique of liberalism, then to liberalism itself, then to a phase where liberalism and conservatism were side by side in his thinking.

> At the very beginning of theological awakenings, I was attempting to ride two horses – Conservatism on the right and Liberalism on the left. My home was not very religious, I suppose one would say, but what religion was present was, in nature, definitely conservative. I recall attending, as a boy, Holiness Camp Meetings of the Methodist Episcopal Church, and much of this reactionary theology found its way into my mind. On the other hand, while growing up, for the most part I attended churches which were out-and-out liberal. So, although I did not understand it all, I was early exposed to these conflicting and opposed stresses.

He probes further by reference to one year in a theologically-slanted college and three theological schools in which he was, in turn, influenced by the positions he had just expressed:

> The first emphasized fundamentalism with a Wesleyan cast. There is no doubt in my mind but what this Holiness movement served well a particular need in a particular past day. It may well be that they are keeping alive today something vital for the future streams of the Christian faith. I absorbed from them a certain temper for which I am grateful. But on the other hand, there is no denying that these Holiness people are almost hopelessly out of touch with modern culture. They are ever too prone to forget that the Christian faith is a living principle to be re-clothed again and again as history unrolls. They have so solidified their forms of Christian thought and experience that I fear the forms are oft times mistaken for the thought and experiences themselves. At the time, I reacted mildly against some of their positions, but the theology I learned there was the only theology I knew. It left a deep mark on me. . . .
>
> At the next school (a seminary) I did not meet much in the way of any systematic training in theology. I did receive some-

thing invaluable which carried me through six years of preaching when my theology was on feeble legs and which will play no small role in any future system I may be able to construct. I refer to a thorough training in the content of the Bible placed in its historical setting. The theology I managed to gather was Calvinistic in tone over against what I had met previously and it was certainly somewhat more liberal. . . .

In changing schools after two years I met head-on, through Professor Edwin Lewis, the dialectical theologians and their great reaction to the Liberal Movement. It was difficult for me to appreciate thoroughly the oppositional nature of Neo-Protestantism, for I had not really gone through liberalism. Perhaps I missed most of the point of the whole movement. Barth and Brunner were a welcome advance to me, incredible as that may sound to some. They seemed to resolve the tension between my conservative foundation and my undefined liberal leanings. Here was a theology that was respectable to the modern mind (in some quarters) and still had a note of urgency and a point of decision. Modern Biblical scholarship was taken into consideration and yet The Book remained a Living Word. The individual situation was realistically viewed and, at the same time, the social side was not entirely dismissed, by Brunner at least. Moreover, Christ was given a central and vital place and yet not garbed in penal theories of salvation, which were growing more meaningless to me. I could go on, but this will suffice to show the effect these Continental theologians had on my thinking. In brief, because I felt that this was a theology more in tune with the age than my ultra-conservative views, I proceeded to restate my ideas of God, Man, Sin, Christ, Salvation and the like more and more in the terminology of the Barthians. But, even while I was succumbing to the wiles of the dialectical school, I was being introduced at Drew to a more thoroughgoing liberalism than I had elsewhere known. This prepared me for the final chapter of my school career in the pre-war period.

At Union in 1939 I was set down into the midst of liberalism under men such as Lyman and Van Dusen. Regardless of how certain minds in that institution were changing at the time, regardless of the fact that I also sat under men such as Paul Tillich and Reinhold Niebuhr, I was here formally indoctrinated in liberalism. I do not mean that liberal views were all new to me. I had met most of them before even though rather indirectly and unsystematically. It is rather that I now was laid hold upon by them. The idea of God immanent in man; history and the world coming into His own; the theological importance of social evils; the scientific method with its liberal and tolerant spirit; the notion that man was a better creature than we had thought; and maybe he could bring in the Kingdom – all these and more were views I largely accepted, and they found a place in my preaching. The odd part of this is that I did not surrender my conservative and Barthian views when I accepted the more liberal ones. This is where my real confusion set in, although it was potentially present before. I attempted for the next four or five years to hold on to both poles. I do not like to admit that I saw no difficulty in the holding of all these views at the same time. Perhaps I saw the contradiction and would not admit it to myself. Maybe I imagined I had some sort of a synthesis. I finally attempted to conceal from myself and others my jumbled thinking behind some catch statement as: I am conservative in my theology and liberal in my social outlook. Such methods have been employed by those far more worthy than I.

This was the theological equipment I took to the New England church, which I was to serve for two years. It should have been a time of thinking through what five years of studying theology had given me. It was not. The work of rescuing a rundown parish and setting it on feet strong enough to carry it into the future did not leave sufficient time for the kind of thinking I needed to do. There was study enough but it was of a practical nature, which did not directly touch my problem. What work I did do in theology and what other theological influences that reach men in the parish ministry was of a liberal turn. I think that if there was a shift in my thought it was more to the left. Yet all the while I took pride in considering myself a more than moderate conservative. When the war came, I was trying to hold together, single-handed, liberalism, Barthianism, and an almost fundamentalist view.

In the early months of 1942, I entered the Army as a chaplain. Before I was done with this phase of my life, some decided alterations had occurred. That there were changes is not surprising. Four years of the stark business of war must leave its imprint. To such a position as mine, something was almost certain to happen. And it did. In short, the war did five things which radically affected my thinking. These I shall list and then discuss briefly:

1. The war brought me inescapably face to face with the turmoil of my mind and with the impossibility of an 'on-the-fence' position.
2. The war revealed to me the insufficiency of both an extreme conservative and a radical liberal view.
3. The war showed me the absolute necessity for a view of life which was realistic, honest, and unmistakably my own.
4. The war gave to me certain insights about men and methods which must serve as guideposts in any reconstruction of my thought in the postwar period.
5. The war so clarified my mind at some definite points as to give me a basis upon which to begin that construction.

The war, to summarize, had uncovered my confusion, criticized the schools of theology which were involved in that confusion, and had led to an intense investigation of personal beliefs which resulted in an interim creed in which I could function with sincerity. I turn now to the fourth influence of the war. This had to do chiefly with certain techniques and viewpoints. . . . One in my situation could not help having impressions along these lines which would alter his outlook. I think I can sum them up in four compound statements:

I was impressed with the need of further efforts toward the reinterpretation of Christianity for our age and the further application of the Christian faith to the whole of life.

I was impressed with the need of a thorough revamping of the religious education program and a rethinking of missions.

I was impressed with the need for an all-out endeavor toward a unity in Protestantism and for a clean, strong, united Christian voice against the tragic social evils of our day.

I was impressed with the need of the further elimination of superstitions attached to our faith and with the psychological necessity of clarifying our methods of calling men to a decision concerning the Gospel.

Looking back over what has been said, it seems very like a network of disorder. Nonetheless, it is my story as I understand it.

Nine months after his release from the Army, Joe could report progress:

> First of all, I have become clearly persuaded that a true recovery of theology for me must come through an understanding of the development of Christian thought through the centuries, with particular reference to the New Testament.
>
> Secondly, there are several schools and theologians who have been particularly enlightening to me in this period of study. The Neo-Thomists, especially A. E. Taylor, have given me greater appreciation of the importance and place of the Christian community. My problem of self-interest in relation to the Christian ethic, which was raised during the war, has had some light from Bishop Butler and Sidgwick. Dostoyevsky, Berdaeyev, Kierkegaard, and Brunner have had much influence on my further thinking on man and the human situation. In the matter of "natural" religious experiences and the relation of natural and revealed theology, I have been deeply affected by both William Temple and A. E. Taylor. Karl Barth and William Temple have aided me in my search for a better understanding of God. I have also been impressed anew with the way in which the dialectical theologians approach and read the Scriptures. This is to mention but a few of the more recent men to whom I am becoming indebted. Many others, among them several classical theologians and philosophers, aroused my interest and will make their contributions as I have further opportunity to become acquainted with their minds.

He concluded:

> Although I cannot know what lies ahead, doors are open which once were locked, and I am persuaded that the way will be found.

If apology is required for quoting at length from this essay, it is to let Joe tell his own story, even as the story itself was being radically changed by his Yale experience. He never ceased to talk about how much this intensive study meant to him. He would from time to time refer to particular courses and professors he especially admired.

At the same time he was experiencing family life with his lovely wife – so long deferred by the war years. On September 17, 1947, their first son, Joseph Wesley Mathews, Jr., was born in New Haven.

Association with other G.I. Bill students was for him exhilarating; there was a strong sense of community among them. The cultural offerings of a great educational center offered them an intellectual feast after a long famine. Regular and usually inspired worship nourished their spirits, just as great teaching was constantly a stimulus to their minds. New Haven was within the bounds of the New York Area of the Methodist Church, so Joe could also be involved once again in some Conference affairs. Not infrequently he would preach in nearby churches and was thus afforded opportunity to convey his newly acquired theological insights with his gifts of vigorous preaching style. He was readily recognized as the same Joe Mathews who had long ago acquired the skill of awakening the dormant spirits of his listeners.

H. Richard Niebuhr's Influence

Far and away the most potent influence for Joe's theological awakening was the teaching and writings of Professor H. Richard Niebuhr, brother of Reinhold Niebuhr. Joe had studied under Reinhold at Union Seminary before the war and had appreciated his thinking. It has often been observed about the Niebuhr brothers that Reinhold was most interested in the reform of society; Richard was most interested in the reform of the church.

Given the search that Joe was pursuing, it is not surprising that he was more attracted to the latter. That is not to infer that he was not interested in the former goal. Rather, Joe's passion was to be involved in the renewal of the church as instrumental in changing the world. So it was that he sat at the feet of his new mentor as much as possible. Richard Niebuhr had many intellectual skills in church history, sociology of religion, theology, and others. Primarily, he was an ethicist. In his work he resisted excessive systematization, and in his role of professor he resisted being made a kind of a cult figure. He was of modest tone and preferred to point beyond himself. This was prompted by both his nature and on principle.

He was a popular teacher and lecturer. His classes often filled the Divinity School's largest lecture halls. Earnest students learned to get to his classes early, for not infrequently there was standing room only. He always spoke from the cutting edge of his subject matter. His style was sometimes described as "theological poetry," affording solid theological truth for his hearers. A transcendent note was often sounded, but this did not come across as mere piety, because he did not address the emotions but the intellect, and that at a very penetrating level.

Viewed from four decades later, the solid core of his emphases endures (though critics can complain of the mostly masculine terminology which, of course, prevailed at the time in most everyone's speech and writings.) The tenor of his thinking was unique, provocative, and constantly opened up new vistas for his students. Many could hardly wait to return to their rooms in order to put down in fuller form the insights they had just heard. As I write, I have before me fifty pages of careful classroom notes written in my brother's bold, highly legible hand from one course taught by Richard Niebuhr. Be assured that Joseph Wesley Mathews drank deeply at this well and was refreshed.

Then, too, he often buried himself in the library and read Niebuhr's complete works and basic theological tomes for the first time. Nor was this all. During the academic year of 1947-48, Joe and a future colleague at Perkins School of Theology, Herndon Wagers, were afforded an exceptional privilege. Through the whole school year they had lunch daily with Richard Niebuhr. Whether or not the professor did this with others at other times is not known, but one contemporary remarked that it was "just like him." Niebuhr sensed the earnestness of their theological longing or resonated to their common pain, for Wagers also was a perplexed Navy chaplain who had served in the Pacific. One colleague has referred to this gesture of their mentor as "warm and genial humanity." One can almost listen in on such occasions. There they were in some quiet eating establishment or with sandwiches in the professor's office. (If in the latter, the lights were turned down low to protect the teacher's eyes, so sensitive was he to light.) Both students frequently referred to this dialogue experience during the years that followed. Sometimes as Joe would lecture, it was as if the curtain opened and he was in dramatic dialogue with his mentor. It was awesome to observe.

Surely the interchanges turned on occasions to Niebuhr's writings from his earlier years. This included his own unpublished doctoral dissertation, "The Religious Philosophy of Ernst Troelsch" (1924), the towering German historical theologian and sociologist whose lengthened shadow covered Niebuhr's own career. Conversation must have arisen repeatedly about Niebuhr's own first published work, *The Social Sources of Denominationalism* (1929). This was a basic critique of American churches, revealing the essential flimsiness, not to say, sinfulness, of their many divisions. Through his scholarly and informed analysis, he made clear the bondage and blindness of the religious establishment to their own captivity to secular ideologies. These notes were essential for those who would labor for church renewal in a post-World War II period. Into the discussion must have come the continuing critical appraisal of the ecclesiastical order, as set forth in Niebuhr's *The Kingdom of God in America* (1937). Essentially it unmasked the idolatry of the bondage of the churches to the lesser but compelling gods of racism, economic forces, and nationalism. It was more likely that their discussion turned to what was then Niebuhr's most recent publication, *The Meaning of Revelation* (1941), in which the hinge swung from what ails the church to what its rightful role might be in history.

I have found myself wondering whether or not it was during the discussion of these themes that Joe's attention was called to Wesley or Calvin. At any rate, more than once Joe would cite with enthusiasm the first two sentences of Calvin's *Institutes of the Christian Religion:* namely, "True and substantial wisdom consists principally of two parts: the knowledge of God and the knowledge of ourselves. Although these branches of knowledge are intimately related, which of them precedes and produces the other it is not easy to discover." Here the issues are joined. God's absolute sov-

ereignty must be upheld: the sovereignty of a God who was both
Great and Good. Before God all humanity must repent. There is no
other proper stance before the Divine. Life is to be lived in relation
to God, the source of all being, and in response to what God is doing. Whether we know it or not we are constantly responding to the
will and action of God. This became crystal clear in Richard Niebuhr's *Radical Monotheism* (1966). While others were concentrating in the analysis of more immediate social issues, Richard
Niebuhr was concerned about what to him were deeper matters:
how and from what basis is the church to address the specific problems of the social order. So we find him writing *Christ and Culture*
(1952). The two young seekers were afforded life-changing dialogue with their teacher.

Joe became acquainted quickly with H. Richard Niebuhr's sur-
vey of theological education, *The Purpose of the Church and Its
Ministry* (1956). At the time he paraphrased for me that the purpose was "to increase in society the love of both God and
neighbor" – basically Biblical but basically forgotten. Too often
the churches seemed to imply an either/or rather than a both/and. A
short citation from that book (p. 35) displays both Niebuhr's poetic
theology and his analogy of love for both God and neighbor:

> Love is rejoicing over the existence of the beloved one: it is
> the desire that he be rather than not be; it is longing for his pres-
> ence when he is absent; it is happiness in the thought of him; it is
> profound satisfaction over everything that makes him great and
> glorious. Love is gratitude; it is thankfulness for the existence of
> the beloved. . . . Love is reverence; it keeps its distance even as it
> draws near; it does not seek to absorb the other in the self or
> want to be absorbed by it. . . . Love is loyalty; it is the willing-
> ness to let the self be destroyed rather than that the other cease to
> be.

Joe and Herndon must have rejoiced at Richard Niebuhr's last
and posthumously published book, *The Responsible Self* (1963).
They had surely been nurtured already by its insights into Niebuhr's ethics. In this respect Joe was by no means alone, because
Richard Niebuhr was, during this period, having a similar influ-

ence on scores of other students. It has been rightfully observed of him that in his generation he contributed to the preparation and development of more persons who became teachers and leaders in the field "than any other theologian of the twentieth century." And it is reported that Richard Niebuhr had the very highest praise for Joe's gifts as a teacher.

On October 30, 1947, Brother Joe passed his qualifying exams and was accepted as a Ph.D. candidate. A bit later he qualified in French and German as well. He chose as the topic for his dissertation, "A Study of Love and Faith in the Thought of John Wesley." This was not surprising, for he was a thoroughly committed Methodist and "Wesley" was his middle name!

The fact is, Joe never completed this thesis. It became a major burden to him as he was caught up in the demands of academia at Colgate and Southern Methodist University. Multitudes of aspiring doctoral candidates have experienced this particular form of anxiety and will empathize with what Joe was going through. As his brother, I was passing through the same experience at Columbia University while engaged in a full-time appointment in church administration. After much agony I finally completed the process. Naturally, and with great sympathetic understanding, I encouraged Joe to do the same. Finally, for personal and family reasons, but mostly for reasons of Christian conscience, he did *not* complete this demand. To him a Ph.D. as a goal in itself seemed a kind of idolatry. Incidentally, I personally met Richard Niebuhr only once. I spoke to him of Joe's dissertation and in response he seemed to imply that Joe's "idolatrous" conclusion was valid.

The fact is that Joe did complete a document of some four hundred pages, and to my mind it reads rather well. Some United Methodist seminaries have a copy of it, although it is entirely devoid of the usual footnotes and other stylistic features one associates with such documents. A few Wesley scholars who have examined the draft have said in a kindly way that the effort tends to be more of a reflection of Joe Mathews' mind than of Wesley's. That may well be, but at the same time this might be seen in a positive way, that a doctoral student's probe into the thought of another, by the very nature of the undertaking, results in a large measure of subjective involvement.

The time soon came when Joe and Lyn left New Haven. Many associations begun there continued through the years. Their family had grown further with the addition of their second son, James Johnston Mathews, who was born in Oneida, N.Y., on July 11, 1949. This happy couple had themselves grown immensely, both intellectually and spiritually. It was time for Joe to try his wings in another field of academic venture. This time it would be in the role of teacher.

He proceeded to this stage of his life far better equipped for the fray. He had in large measure found what he sought, a reorientation of his Christian thinking. He was delivered from much of the confusion which prevailed in his mind when he came out of the Army. Nor would he be alone, for he had found not one mentor, but four. Their pictures were to be found hanging in his study or classrooms for the rest of his days. They were Rudolf Bultmann, Paul Tillich, Dietrich Bonhoeffer, and H. Richard Niebuhr. All were pioneers of church renewal. Bultmann had opened the Scripture to modern minds. Tillich laid out a systematic theology for a new day. For instance, he often said that existentialism was the "good luck" of modern theologians. Joe was not exactly an existentialist but he learned much from them. Bonhoeffer led the way to a fresh understanding of and commitment to Christian discipleship and community. Niebuhr seemed to put it all together in ways that appealed (and did not affront) modern men and women. Joe never ceased to enjoy intellectual companionship with these four along the difficult road ahead.

Colgate University

As his days at Yale were drawing toward a close, Joe was naturally concerned about "What next?" Avenues opened in several places. One was to a pastorate in Stamford, Connecticut. Another was to teach at Centenary College in Louisiana. There was an opening for him as professor of philosophy at Hanover College in Indiana. Then he was invited to teach in the Department of Religion at Vassar College in Poughkeepsie, N.Y. It was nice to be wanted and even sought after. Finally, though, he decided to accept an invitation as instructor in Philosophy and Religion at Colgate University, Hamilton, N.Y. The salary was $3500 a year, an almost unbelievable figure when viewed from more than fifty years later.

If Joe had accepted any of the alternative opportunities, the course of his career would have been vastly changed. Nevertheless, it is fair to observe that wherever he might have gone a shaking and religious awakening was sure to follow. And it did.

The family arrived at Colgate in September 1949. The setting was beautiful; a small town set among the rolling hills of central New York State. Only a few miles away in Norwich lived Joe's younger sister Alice and her husband. The budding professor again moved into a Quonset hut, by this time a very familiar experience. Fortunately Joe had a knack with tools. He built some of the furniture himself, including a desk. A corner of a room became his study, and they were snugly installed in what was to be their home for four years. Lyn, of course, added her special touch to the scene. She was skilled in all the domestic arts and fulfilled her promise of working at least part-time to add to family support, even with two young boys.

The files during the three years he was at Colgate show Professor Joseph Mathews trying to fit himself into a quite new and challenging situation. From the beginning, his classes were found to be interesting and the enrollment was large. Clearly he worked very hard on a wide variety of subjects. There are notes on his reading. He devised a number of core courses in the fields of philosophy and religion. He taught Bible. Besides New Testament he led classes in prophetic religion, especially Amos, Hosea, and Micah. Courses were also taught with particular reference to Roman Catholic students. Of course, he taught ethics, with a Niebuhrian slant, we may be sure. His files show that he assumed responsibility in faculty affairs and was involved in campus activities as well. He found time to write some articles on contemporary issues: basic modern beliefs, conditions of working men, and so on.

Not infrequently he preached in neighboring churches and usually created excitement when he did. From time to time I have met students who studied with him. He was well remembered. Quite often also he would speak in chapel. Once he preached there on Mark, chapter 2. It was the well-known story of the paralytic carried on a litter by four friends to Jesus for healing. The place where Jesus was speaking was so crowded that they had to lower the sick man by ropes from the roof. Jesus noted that his need was as much spiritual as physical and said to the paralytic, "Your sins are forgiven." Then he told the man to get up out of his litter and walk. Joe repeated with emphasis: "Get up! Get up!' Two young men in the balcony, thinking they were being addressed, arose to their feet, much to the consternation of others present. Joe expected reaction and response, and usually got it.

Joe's sister Alice promised to recount her recollections of the Hamilton years. Her e-mail, just received, is inserted here verbatim:

Colgate University, 1951

Alex and I had just moved to Norwich, a half-hour away from Hamilton, NY. After we had settled in, Joe had invited me to come up to Colgate to attend his classes. Really to follow him about for a day. Afterward we could discuss my experience, commenting on what I had observed, make suggestions, etc. I really was pleased to be able to do this. He was an instructor in the Department of Religion and Philosophy.

From the first class through the third, it was very obvious that the students wanted to be there and were very attentive. I do not recall the classes in any detail, but I was impressed by the students' responses to Joe. Between classes, some of the students wanted to talk with me, telling me how much they liked the classes, how surprised they were to be finding religion so intriguing. One young man told about how Professor Mathews one day had suddenly jumped up on the radiator and began peering up into the sky, and then asked a student nearby to join him. Joe began asking him, "Do you see Him? Do you see the figure of a man in a white robe with a long white beard?" Finally, the whole class joined them, peering through the windows! Well, as you can imagine, the students were entranced. The young man telling the story mentioned how mesmerized he and other students were by Joe and so pleased that they could be in his classes. Joe's classes were frequently the topic of discussions on the campus.

I also remember that Joe, with some other professors, developed a core course for freshmen that gave them a deeper perspective about life: suggesting ways they could really benefit from being in college, helping them raise questions about their lives, their futures. This program proved to be successful and was used for a long time at Colgate.

Joe's years at Colgate did have impact on students, some of whom wrote in later years saying that Joe had changed their lives. This I learned from others.

Lyn and Joe enjoyed their time at Colgate, forming friendships of some significance for the rest of their lives.

On January 19, 1952, there was another addition to their family, for John Donaldson Mathews arrived on the scene as an Epiphany gift. He was the first baby to be born in the new Hamilton hospital. He was a fine, attractive lad and grew into a splendid young man. He was blessed with a gracious spirit. His untimely death in an automobile accident in Wyoming during the summer of 1976 deprived the world of a fine example of humanity. How greatly he was missed by all who knew him. How crushed were his grief-stricken parents!

Joe and Lyn Mathews were at home in Hamilton, New York. They liked the atmosphere of a community of learning. They enjoyed their many friends and colleagues. Joe was drawn by the beauty of the countryside in mid-New York State. Moreover, he became interested in matters concerning the original inhabitants of the region. He reveled in walks in the hills, in learning about feeder channels providing water for the historic Erie Canal. Most of all he liked teaching as a profession – as a vocation – and the access this gave him to the eager minds of his students.

And yet he longed for something more. After all, he was a child of the Church; he was an ordained minister of the Methodist Episcopal Church. He wanted to teach in one of its halls of learning. Just as there came to him offers of teaching posts in various institutions during his latter days at Yale, so they continued to come. One invitation was to teach in the religious field at Martin

College, Pulaski, Tennessee. Then another one arrived from Perkins School of Theology at Southern Methodist University. To this
he found he could not say no.

Southern Methodist University – Perkins School of Theology

Since he said yes, the Mathews family of five moved to Dallas,
bought a home there, and in September 1952, Joe began his stint in
teaching sociology of religion. He was not really a specialist in that
particular field, but at the same time his tutelage under Richard
Niebuhr gave him excellent qualification. Besides, that was the
only post available. It has been observed that, qualified or not, he
undertook the responsibility and quickly turned it into "Theology
According to Joe." Under his guidance and that of some other professors of similar perspective, students very soon had their eyes
opened to a completely new world of theological learning.

It was indeed a time of awakening at Perkins. Only the year before, a new dean, Merrimon Cuninggim, had arrived on the scene,
fresh out of Yale, together with Albert Outler, one of Joe's professors there. It was the dean's task to recruit an entirely new faculty,
for all the older members were to retire within seven years. Along
with Joe there were two other new arrivals: Edward C. Hobbs, a
New Testament scholar, just out of the University of Chicago, and
Marvin Judy, a pastor from Texas, who was to instruct students in
practical theology. Here was an opportunity for a new beginning at
Perkins. Actually, there emerged a not always friendly rivalry
among the faculty. Edward Hobbs together with Joe formed the
more liberal pole of the faculty. It was no real surprise when it became evident that there was considerable interest in this side of the
divide. The trend was resisted from the other pole, particularly
from Dr. Outler.

At the same time, the seminary community experienced a renewal of authentic worship in the campus chapel. It was stimulated
by the use of John Wesley's morning service. Later, Edward
Hobbs published a small volume titled *The Wesley Orders of
Common Prayer*, earlier published in *Motive* magazine. This was
Wesley's revision of *The Book of Common Prayer,* which came to
be widely used in the Methodist Student Movement. It was not

merely a reprint but a carefully reconstructed, reedited, and rein-terpreted work. Hobbs' introduction to this book was one of the clearest and finest essays on the meaning of Christian worship that had appeared to that date. Its effect was wide and profound. These same professors were instrumental in another initiative, the intro-duction into the curriculum of a seminar on "Christianity and Contemporary Art Forms." This effort also stimulated wide inter-est on the part of students and faculty alike and contributed significantly to the shaping of the life of the community.

Joe had a knack for devising programs in the life of the church and demonstrated this even from his first years in the faith. He therefore played an important role in the reshaping of the curricu-lum at Perkins. Essentially, it consisted of two didactic years of a basic Core Curriculum of Bible, Systematic and Philosophical Theology, Christianity and Culture, and Practical Theology. The third year was devoted to seminars according to the particular ma-jors of students. The revision was, on the whole, well received and regarded as successful. Joe certainly felt it to be so, and, in an ef-fort to stimulate recruitment, assured all concerned that Perkins was able to give students a theological education of the first rank. In this enterprise of revising the curriculum, Joe was seen as a chief force in reenergizing the school. His efforts had a profound effect and were still being felt years later.

This is only a sample of his activities. A kind of log-book shows that he was with increasing frequency called upon to speak to university student groups and church gatherings all over the country. He created something of a sensation wherever he went. He was fully engaged in faculty responsibilities of all kinds, and he seemed always to be involved with students as well.

Through the years, I have met or have had letters from many of brother Joe's former students at Perkins. They give evidence that his teaching manner was unique and impressive. He simply could not be forgotten or ignored. One lengthy communication was from Dr. James T. Clemons, who became a professor of New Testament at Wesley Theological Seminary in Washington, D.C. He relates his experiences as a student in Joe's classes. At first he was baffled and confused; then intrigued by his style and the content of lectures; then profoundly influenced. He speaks especially of Joe's relations with other faculty members: congenial yet candid, always ready to debate in an atmosphere of mutual respect.

This chapter closes with students' accounts of reactions to Joe, in their own words. The first comes from a Mexican-American student, Roberto Escamilla, who reached back over fifty years to recall that Joe's impact upon him was great. Then he added:

> How I remember Professor Joe Mathews: He was prophetic in the best sense of the word.
>
> - He had the capacity to shake the students out of complacency and lethargy.
> - He was an evangelist in the classroom with a liberating Word that went beyond personal piety into social action.
> - He could deal with Niebuhr and Wesley, Tillich and Bultmann, Ritschl and Barth with powerful eloquence.
> - The seeds he planted for the renewal of the church are rendering abundant harvest even fifty years later.
> - He had the capacity to dramatize his lectures and to make the Word come alive. No one ever went to sleep in his classes.
> - He took the claims of the Christian faith with great seriousness and became indignant with some "mickey-mouse" (as he called them) ways.
> - In the Ecumenical Institute he developed a theological curriculum designed to engage in serious reflection/dialogue and to engage in the discipline of participatory, creative worship.
>
> From Professor Mathews, I learned
>
> - not to be afraid to ask hard and difficult questions about God and about life and the world
> - to understand the gospel in wholistic terms – personal and social, individual and collective – the sacred and the secular – the past and the future – and what it means to be "eternally loved and accepted by God"
> - to read the Word as if for the first time and to hear it with new ears

Another student from Texas, Gene W. Marshall, wrote the following:

> My first experience with Joe was in 1953 at Perkins School of Theology in an ethics course on H. Richard Niebuhr's book, *Christ and Culture*. This happening transformed my vision of myself, of the human self, of God, sin, faith, good action, Church history, human history, virtually everything. It began a personal relationship of mentor and friend with Joe Mathews that endured from that time onward. It is almost impossible to exaggerate the force with which he confronted me and my fellow students with life-changing decisions for us to ponder. A picture that remains in my mind is the time a student protested, "If I believed what you just said, I would leave the ministry." Joe walked over the entrance of the classroom and said, "Well, here's the door."
>
> A second major healing event with Joe Mathews was a course on the works of Søren Kierkegaard. Our small class of eight or ten read several works together and then divided up Kierkegaard's remaining works, wrote reports and read them to one another in the living room of Joe's home. Perhaps that is when I realized that I had entered into radical Christian community on a permanent basis. . . .

Another commentary by a student, William Holmes:

> I recall he had a terribly wonderful and wonderfully terrible reputation. His lectures were unpredictable, provocative and inescapably existential. They were so existential that a few students took great offense and registered their opposition to his teaching. However, most of us were so existentially addressed by studying with Joe that we found ourselves moved to a whole new level of understanding the Gospel, and our lives were changed at the very core. . . .
>
> I do recall my first day in his class. At the very beginning he said: "I knew more about each one of you, when you came through the door, than you would want your mother to know!" Of course, he had little, if any, superficial information about us. But Joe knew himself, profoundly. He knew that the way he experienced life was not all that different from the way every

person in that room experienced life, and that all of us hungered for a word that only The Word would fill. To study with him, was to undertake a unique and radical journey, not only inwardly through personal introspection, but outwardly to Herculean ethical and social obligations. He grounded ethics in deep wellsprings, and never failed to remind us that the Christ-event was the primal source for everything we studied.

At a personal level . . . Joe was the major influence in the shaping of my understanding of the Christian faith and the meaning of the Church. When he went to be the Dean of the Faith and Life Community in Austin, I enrolled in all the clergy training offered there, and sent scores of lay people from my church to Dallas to study with Joe on the weekends. I eventually became one of the pedagogues for Religious Studies I, trained a number of lay pedagogues, and offered RS-I three or four times a year in Dallas. I continued this practice at all the churches that I served thereafter. . . . I have long ago mastered the five lectures, and am convinced that the RS-I curriculum on God, Christ, Holy Spirit, the Bible and the Church is timeless. I have personally seen several thousand peoples' lives changed by it – and my own.

Another personal story, by Harry C. Kiely:

I went to Perkins my first year of seminary, and during that year I had a very painful encounter with Charlie, a fellow student. He and I went out on a double date, and I was escorting a young woman I very much wanted to impress favorably. However, Charlie and I got into a conflict, the details of which are totally gone from my memory. All I recall is that he humiliated me in front of this young woman.

For all of the next week I was so distraught that I was unable to sleep at night. My stomach churned, and I rolled and tossed. I was filled with hatred for Charlie. At the same time I was ashamed of my negative feelings because here I was studying to be a minister, yet I was unable to get rid of these terrible feelings. My self diagnosis was that I was far from God. If I could find God, my feelings of hate would be overcome by feelings of love, and then I would be at peace.

I decided to call Joe and see if he could help me. I called him on a Saturday morning and he invited me to come to his home. He gave me a seat in the living room and sat opposite me. I told the story of what had happened on the double date, how it made me feel, and how I wished I could find God so that my negative feelings would be relieved.

I was totally unprepared for the response I got.

"What God are you talking about?" Joe asked.

What a question for a theology professor to be asking! "What do you mean?" I asked, frustrated by this kind of response.

"You said you wanted to find God. What God are you talking about?"

"Well, uh, uh," I stammered, feeling on the spot to come up with some kind of answer. Finally taking a stab at it, I said, "The God and Father of our Lord Jesus Christ."

"Oh, really?" he asked. "I suppose since you have given him a name that you think I know who you're talking about."

Silence.

"Tell me about this God," Joe said. "What's he like?"

Long pause. I was getting angry. I had come looking for some answers, and all I got were questions!

Finally, feeling I could not stand up and walk out (which is what I wanted to do at that point), I muttered an answer, one that did not convince even me. "Well, he's omnipotent, omnipresent, all-loving, all-knowing, infinitely compassionate."

"Are you sure?" Joe asked.

"Well . . . yes."

"You're absolutely sure about this God you are looking for?"

"Yes," I said, but not with much conviction. Where was all this leading? Boy, did I hate this guy by now!

Joe suddenly stood up. "Trade places with me," he said. I just sat there, bewildered. "Come on. Let's trade places."

So we swapped seats. Then Joe looked at me with great intensity and said, "I am so glad you showed up today because you are doing me a great service. All my life I have been looking for this God and at last I have met a man who has found him. . . . Tell me about this God. I want to know more. What is he like?"

I was completely floored. Of course I had no answer to his question and I am sure he knew it. I was bereft of any answer and all I could do was just sit there and stare at the floor. I felt I had been stripped naked. He waited patiently, as if he had all day, but he said nothing more.

I sat in silence for a very long time, wishing for a quick escape, but having too much pride to walk out.

I then began to ponder what might be the meaning of this encounter. Is there something to be learned here, something that, in a hidden way, may actually be the answer to my longing for God's deliverance? Is the answer to my search something that Joe could not give me, even if he wanted to, is it already present in me, in my life, but I have been denying it or trying to flee it?

Finally, after a painfully long time, I broke the silence. "I don't know what you are getting at, but I will tell you what all this stirs up in me. I think that the God I came here looking for may be the God I am running away from. Maybe all the torment I have been feeling was God doing something to my insides. Maybe what I want from you is for you to take this God away so I can be comfortable, and it probably wouldn't be a good idea for you to do that, even if you could, which you can't."

Joe was suddenly very excited. He ran upstairs to get his Bible and came back thumbing his way to Romans. Here is what he read: "If we live we live to the Lord. And if we die, we die to the Lord. So then whether we live or whether we die, we are the Lord's."

Joe said, "You see, you're right. You've been running away from the very thing you say you want. But this God cares too much to let you get away."

I have no memory of anything else he said, but what he did and what he said were enough. This was a life-changing experience for me. I was slowly awakening to the realization that the rhythm of life was not about my search for God, but about God's search for me. This experience opened for me the realization of grace – of being pursued by love.

Finally, one of my colleagues, Bishop Eugene Slater, once recorded his impressions of Joe:

In 1964 I was assigned to the San Antonio Area of the then Methodist Church. Within a relatively short time I had an experience in my continuing Christian journey that changed my conception of the Church from that of an institution to be supported, protected and defended to that of a company of Christian persons, called to lose their lives in service to Christian persons.

The agents effecting my changing conception of the Church were a half-dozen young pastors in the conference, all recent graduates of Perkins School of Theology. These young pastors claimed Dr. Joseph Mathews as the teacher whose influence shaped their theological understanding of the nature and character of the Church.

I continue to bless the memory of Joseph Mathews.

8
TWENTY-ONE YEARS TO GO – AND COUNTING

A difference between autobiography and biography is that with respect to the latter the writer knows how things turn out. Joe left Perkins and S.M.U. after the academic year 1955-56. His death occurred on October 16, 1977, so he had twenty-one years to go. Joe naturally did not know this, but during this period he lived the most productive period of his life. It was also the most public and controversial period, for he became increasingly involved in the religious enterprise and its renewal on a worldwide basis.

This chapter might have been titled, "Return to the Real World." He was certainly in the real world in a most concrete way during the years of World War II. It was this experience which drove him – and countless others of his vocation – to seek a firmer grounding in the faith as a basis for dealing with modern women and men. In Chapter VII, on "Return to Academe," we spoke of Joe at Yale, Colgate, and Southern Methodist Universities, where he served in turn as student and teacher for about a decade. It has seemed a little unfair to suggest that on these campuses the real world was *not* encountered.

By the end of the academic year of 1955-56, Joe seemed ready for a change of venue. This was occasioned by a number of factors. He had contemplated finishing his doctorate from Yale. There was naturally a concern at Perkins for him to complete this obligation. He had made some progress in spite of increasing demands upon his time at the seminary and as a speaker in an ever widening circle. He had a letter from H. Richard Niebuhr, dated May 3, 1955, in which his mentor stated that he was pleased with the progress of the dissertation. Nevertheless, by September 29, 1955, Joe wrote to Dr. Niebuhr that he had decided not to complete the dissertation.

During the ensuing academic year, he considered also a return to the pastoral ministry and had requested that his membership as a clergyman in the New York Conference of the Methodist Church be transferred to the Southwest Texas Conference. This was done, effective April 29, 1956, thus opening up the way for a pastoral appointment for him in that region of the country. In 1960, Lincoln Memorial University awarded him an honorary Doctor of Divinity degree.

Christian Faith and Life Community
Even earlier, however, on Christmas Day in 1955, Joe had accepted a post at the Christian Faith and Life Community in Austin, Texas. He was to be Director of the Men's Branch and Director of Curriculum beginning on July 1, 1956. Consequently he resigned his teaching post at Perkins at the end of May of the same year. He and Lyn and the boys sold their house in Dallas and moved into a very pleasant residence in Austin. As he often spoke of this change in later years, he emphasized that the new role offered him opportunity to teach laypersons as well as clergy. This wider scope of influence he trusted would quicken the renewal of the church for the renewal of society. His frequent speaking engagements across the country had only confirmed him in this conviction.

Without doubt, the most significant factor in the change of locus for Joe was the existence of the Faith and Life Community. It had its genesis at the time he was at Perkins. Great credit must be given to its founder and executive director, the Rev. W. Jack Lewis. Lewis was a prophetic figure, who pioneered in one of the first experiments in lay theological training in the 20th century. He was a Presbyterian minister and member of the Central Texas Presbytery. He had been a U.S. Navy and Marine Corps chaplain during the war, with service also in the South Pacific. Needless to say, he had gone through the same sort of traumatic experience as Joe and others. There can be no doubt that the war itself was an immense stimulus to general religious interest, for such devastation, death, and suffering has a clear effect of concentrating the mind. Jack Lewis had become aware of some of the efforts in postwar Europe toward church renewal as he visited some of the new European Academies, influenced by Bonhoeffer and others, studied in Scotland at St. Andrews University, and was stimulated by George McLeod and the Iona experiment, as well as by Taizé community in France. Jack was a man of some real theological learning and had organizational gifts as well.

During the academic year 1952-53, a men's branch of the Christian Faith and Life Community began, with about fifty men. This was followed by a women's branch of forty members, which was launched a year later. All students were enrolled at the University of Texas and were carefully selected from among those who had Christian commitment, intellectual gifts, and leadership potential. The new institution saw itself as a community of Christians, a fellowship of believers, a part of the Body of Christ serving the whole world. It was interdenominational in nature, not supported by churches, as such, but rather by highly motivated laypersons. Its governing Board of Directors was made up of thirty-five laypersons and seven clergy members from various denominations in Texas. It also had a national advisory body composed of prominent persons in various denominations. The residential students paid their own room and board. In addition to the residents of the two halls, a nearby university dormitory also took part in the program. A brochure is cited:

> In the beginning, the . . . [community] was a "corporate ministry" that began with the frustration of a Presbyterian minister, W. Jack Lewis, as a campus minister in 1952 at the University of Texas (Austin). He was having difficulty with the denominationally prescribed programs' relevancy for students. Being a good Presbyterian, he took a trip to where all good Presbyterians go when they are frustrated – Scotland. On the same trip, he went to Wales and England. This junket resulted in his meeting Lord George McLeod, a layman engaged in establishing the Iona community. The latter was intended as a prayer group among laymen, primarily in Britain, whose mission was daily prayer, and contributions to the fund McLeod was building for the refurbishing of the Abbey on the Scottish Isle of Iona (near the Isle of Skye).
>
> Lewis was impressed with the commitment of these people who willingly followed McLeod. Later in his visit to the British

Isles, he visited Cambridge and Oxford and was very fascinated by the manner in which religious education was conducted there, namely, on a residential basis, as the students went about their secular education.

Drawing all of this together, Lewis returned with a plan to establish what he came to call the Christian Faith and Life Community.

A further quote from their brochure states the nature of the curriculum:

> The curriculum of the Faith and Life Community covers a two-year period, with Bible study at the heart of the program. Members receive instruction in English Bible, biblical theology (roots of faith), and Christian ethics related to their field of study and life work, over the four-semester span. Lecture-discussion and seminar methods are used. Students may enter for two semesters minimum, but the full four-semester curriculum is strongly recommended.
>
> The curriculum deals with both Faith and Life, since these two are really one and inseparable. It attempts in content and perspective to provide students with a comprehensive, integrated, and relevant understanding and appreciation of the Christian faith.
>
> Within this one central theme of Faith and Life, the community studies its subject from two perspectives: 1) the Christian understanding of man, and 2) the Christian understanding of God.

All this was within the framework of a meaningful life of worship, enriched by visiting lecturers, and group discussion. The commitment involved weekly a total of five hours of disciplined study and five hours of worship, work, and fellowship. It was as demanding as it was rewarding for the participants. It was by no means "kid's stuff." In addition to Bible study, the leaders knew that laity were tired of being fed theological pabulum and were ready for real meat. They were confronted with the works of the Niebuhr brothers, Barth, Brunner, Bultmann, Herberg, Kierkegaard, Dostoyevsky, Luther, Calvin, Aquinas, and others. The students' influence began to permeate the University. Since they were serious in their pursuits, they were taken seriously by fellow students and professors alike. They were not regarded as religious fanatics or "Holy Joes." Above all, they were confronted by Jesus Christ in a contemporary way. For his part, Joe, as the new director of curriculum, "pronounced the lay students as good and in many cases better than those he had been teaching in the school of theology."

The whole enterprise was termed "the Austin Experiment" by some. It was indeed a laboratory of serious Christian living, given the generally complacent attitude toward authentic practice of the Christian faith in the churches. In one of their early efforts to define their conception of themselves it was stated:

> The Christian Faith and Life Community understands itself to be an experimental movement on behalf of culture and the Church. It seeks to pioneer relevant methods that will bring illumination into four pivotal areas: selfhood and common worship, selfhood and common study, selfhood and common life-together, and selfhood and common mission. These four focal areas embody the basic issues which claim modern man both inside and outside the Church and constitute the program of the College House.
>
> The earliest Christian community was composed of men and women from diverse cultures and occupations. They had nothing in common except their commitment to Jesus Christ as Lord. But this common commitment made possible a fellowship of *common worship, common study, common witness* and *common life together.*
>
> The Greeks called it *koinonia*, a community of faith and life in Christ. Laymen were dynamic participants. They had a living message, a vital ministry.
>
> The Christian Faith and Life Community seeks to recover this "ministry of the laity."

Those who pioneered the experiment realized that the post-World War II era created a radically scientific, historical world. They were perplexed by traditional other-worldly metaphysics; a complex world of technically psychologistic inwardness; and a bewildering world of space conquest and nuclear power, devoted to good or ill. The question was: How can human beings live authentic lives in such a new setting? It was clear that many reflective men and women were aware of a deep uneasiness and even emptiness. They could sense a breakdown in many human relationships and a growing entanglement among the multitude of the dimensions of life. Many felt caught by new pressures and growing anxiety. These forces were taken seriously by the Austin experiment. Thus they grasped their role as one of a new mission.

In one of their pamphlets they quoted with approval a statement of Canon Max Warren, General Secretary of the Church Missionary Society (of the Church of England):

> The Christian Mission in its primary sense implies a commission. Its true meaning derives from the purpose of the one who sends. For this reason the Christian Mission can never be identified with the individual, group or Church, for in each of these there is always to be found disobedience mixed with obedience. The mission always transcends the missioner. God's will is not affected or diverted by any failure in the carrying out of the mission. The will of God is constant. The Christian Mission, therefore, is that by reference to which, even while they are engaged upon it, the Christian individual, group and Church must always be reforming themselves, accepting the mission not only as their task but also as the judgment upon the way they are fulfilling it.
>
> The symbol of this obedience is the Cross, both because it is the place where the mission is defined in terms of obedience, and because it is the place where the Christian knows that he has reached the boundary of his own self-achievement, where man's impotence has been met by God's power. And just because he has been met at this boundary of his own impotence, he has a gospel with which to go into every human situation, to reveal that situation as itself a boundary, and thereto set forth the meaning of the Cross.

The Christian Faith and Life Community that began in 1952 with a lay training program for male university students was expanding rather rapidly. Within two years it expanded to include

women and married students. Then older laypersons were attracted
to what was offered. Finally the curriculum enlarged to include
parish ministers who were discovering that their conventional theological training did not equip them adequately for their work in a
new day. The offering for laity was called "Basic Theological
Studies," centered, appropriately enough, in Laos House in Austin.
For ordained ministers the designation was "The Parish Ministers
Colloquy."

There was also formed a "Campus Ministers Symposium" for
those assigned to student work at universities. The program was
expanding throughout Texas, then the southwest, and then the
whole nation. The budget was growing toward a quarter of a million dollars. The whole enterprise was termed generally the Austin
experiment.

All along the way the sense of mission was clarified and expanded. Always it was clear that the experiment saw itself as
involved in renewal and ecclesial reform, which has in one degree
or another characterized the church throughout its history. It therefore strived to help meet the challenges which faced the church
during the last half of the 20th century. Research and experimentation was undertaken in teaching, discipline, life-style, symbols, and
strategies required if Christians were effectively to penetrate contemporary culture. The mission of the Christian Faith and Life
Community was indeed becoming "renewal within the Church for
her mission in the world."

One could describe at length the liturgical life of the community. Its members often spoke of it as the essence or "inner being"
of their common life. The leaders knew the customary ritual had
become devoid of meaning, even for many Christians who were
regular participants in worship. They explored the reciprocal relations of private and public prayer, and the interrelation of the work
of worship in the sanctuary and the work of justice and mercy in
the world. The community gathered to worship and scattered again
to serve. This was its constant recurring rhythm.

As the Austin experiment pursued its meaning of contemporary
Christian worship, it acknowledged the debt it owed to renewal in
worship as manifested at Perkins School of Theology and particu-

larly to Professor Edward C. Hobbs. Public worship was understood as a drama in three acts, with a prologue of invitation and
invocation in which the participants are called from the world; and
an epilogue or benediction by which the worshippers are sent out
again into the world.

1. Act I was the *service of confession*, an expression of Chris-
    tian sorrow, of penitence, new intention, and pardon.

2. Act II was the *service of the word*, consisting of an Old
    Covenant reading, a Psalm, and then New Covenant read-
    ings from an Epistle and then a Gospel. In this act there
    was a witness or exposition of the Word, a brief sermon or
    homily. The emphasis was on Christian joy and praise.

3. Act III was a *service of dedication and offering of self and
    substance.* It emphasized Christian concern and responsi-
    bility.

Otherwise stated, Act I was about acceptance of self as sinner,
but forgiven sinner; it was about the mercy of God the Son and
Savior; about crucifixion and resurrection. Act II was the acknowl-
edgment with praise of God the Father. Act III was about life in
God the Spirit, the constant reminder of concern for others. With
such an understanding of worship (literally, "worth-ship"), liturgy
began to come alive with meaning and purpose; it was immensely
life-related. The form of worship was there all along; it remained
for the dynamic to be recovered. Dom Gregory Dix, for example,
made this clear in his great work *The Shape of the Liturgy.* Such an
understanding undergirded the activities of the Christian Faith and
Life Community and the Ecumenical Institute, which was to follow. This can scarcely be overemphasized.

In 1959, the community adopted, after Dr. Edward C. Hobbs,
"The Daily Office," which set forth the liturgy in a highly usable
form. A daily office had long been a vehicle of the historic church,
but largely lost to Protestantism. The "office" is in addition to private worship and public worship. It is prayer *with* the church; that
is, Christians in widely separated places were united in a common
discipline of prayer. It is not claimed that in recovery of this office
the Austin experiment was the sole initiator. Rather, it was a part

of renewal which was happening in many places, such as the Taizé community in France and other ventures in Europe, Asia, and the United States.

Mention must be made of the great skill and ingenuity which was developed in the area of criticism of art and literature. Many editions of "Letter to Laymen" were concerned with these topics. In March 1960, almost a whole issue was devoted to Stanley Kramer's great movie, "On the Beach," based on Nevil Shute's novel. It was really an imaginary account of Armageddon, of the last vestiges of life on earth following World War III, a nuclear conflict. It is still shown from time to time on television and it never fails to shake the viewer to the depths of being. Joe shared with others a great concern about the vanishing activity of serious conversation in our culture. This film was shown and then the conversation began, interspersed with various clips from the movie. The participants were drawn to an ever-deepening discussion. Each one present was addressed existentially with the meaning of life. This procedure, known as the "art form method" of conversation was extended to other movies, dramas, and books.

The work of this community in Austin was so multifarious that no effort is being made here to touch upon all of its activities. This must await some initiative to recount the entire history of this pioneering enterprise. It is a Ph.D. dissertation waiting to be written. Fortunately the community's periodical, "Letter to Laymen," gives a fairly complete account. Needless During the period 1956-1962, Joe Mathews together with Jack Lewis and their other colleagues were fully engaged in a multiplicity of programs.

No wonder that a stream of people from the ends of the earth made their way to Austin "to turn aside and see this great sight." They came from the World Council of Churches, the National Council of Churches, the World Christian Student Movement, from various denominational headquarters, representatives of other church renewal ventures, and from seminaries and universities. The list was long. Among the many notables was Dutch lay-theologian Dr. Hendrik Kraemer of Leiden University and director of the World Council's Ecumenical Institute at Bossey, Switzerland. He remarked after the visit that the Faith and Life

Community in Austin was "the most significant expression of the Church" that he had found in the U.S.A.

Bishop Stephen Neill, an Anglican of India and Britain and staff member of the World Council of Churches, in commending the Austin experiment's view of the role of the church, reminded them that "the Church is a place to get out of, not a place to stay in – in order to be in the world, to love the world, to be at home in it, to meet it, and to bear witness to it." In a similar vein, a Lutheran pastor from Germany, Manfred Linz, stated, "The Church appears to be trying to reach out to draw people into the Church. Theologically this is the wrong emphasis. The Church is the 'servant people' that goes into the world to remind the world of the Love of God." Dr. Roswell Barnes, American member of the World Council staff, observed that Joseph Mathews had a genius for expressing the elusive ideas of contemporary theologians in language that laity found understandable and attractive.

Other visitors may be named but they are only a small fraction of those who beat a path to the door. Hans Ruedi-Weber, George W. Webber, James I. McCord, Richard Schull, Fred Gealy, Schubert Ogden, Edward C. Hobbs, John Silber, Robert Spike, D. Elton Trueblood, Samuel H. Miller, Theodore Wedel, Roy Ross, as well as a long list of women who were just beginning to be allowed into the leadership ranks of the churches. The prominence of promising young women in the community would prove an important factor in changing this historic and wrongful disproportion.

As if to respond to the presence of so many visitors, Joe and Lyn, in the summer of 1957, visited similar experimental lay academies in Europe. Jack Lewis had made such a trip in 1950 and would do so again about ten years later. For Joe and Lyn, this would be their first visit to Europe. It was for both of them an enlightening and rigorous undertaking. One only wishes that they had kept a daily journal of their adventures. They sailed to Europe by ship. Once there they purchased a motor scooter with sidecar (not a motorcycle and side car). Onto and into this tiny vehicle they crammed their sparse baggage and themselves. It must have been a sight to behold to observe these two travelers wending their way through Europe – this for hundreds, yes, several thousands of miles. When one considers the speed which prevails on European roads, it seems almost miraculous that they were spared accident. What a surprise they must have been to their European hosts!

Their itinerary carried them through the Netherlands, Belgium, France, Italy, Switzerland, Germany, and then to England and Scotland. Their purpose was, of course, to touch as many places as possible where experiments similar to Austin were taking place. Among these were a number of lay academies in Germany, such as the Brethren Center in Kassel and Bad Boll, near Berlin, and the Evangelical Academy in Loccum. Work at Hanover also particularly interested them; CIMADE in Paris, under the direction of the renowned Madeleine Barot, was concerned especially with postwar refugees from Eastern Europe. They were greatly impressed with the AGAPE Community in Turin, Italy.

A kind of centerpiece to their tour was their participation in a conference at Chateau Bossey, the World Council's Ecumenical Institute, close to Geneva, Switzerland. The Institute was presided over by its director, Dr. Hendrik Kraemer, who had visited them in Austin. In this session, about one hundred representatives of lay training programs were gathered from many European countries, as well as from what later cane to be known as the Third World. Through contacts there, Joe and Lyn had the opportunity of expanding their tours to a number of centers not previously planned. When they moved over to the United Kingdom they were well received at various centers.

The learning experience of their tour was not just one-way. Joe and Lyn also had opportunity to speak about the Christian Faith and Life Community and other efforts at church renewal in the United States. At times, Joe recorded brief critical remarks about what they had seen. For example, he speaks of Switzerland's renewal efforts as a "bit romantic." Perhaps this stemmed from the general "aloof attitude" or "superior attitude" that the Swiss often seem to manifest, possibly related to their neutral status during the war. Of France he noted, "seems tied to Barthian theology and is afraid of Bultmann." On Germany: "Is tending to go back to rebuilding the old form of the prewar church and is losing the openness that was there just after the war." Of Holland: "sense of the church having a missionary task to the 'pagans' in the country, but not using the theological insights available to them, such as from Bultmann."

In one personal letter to me he stated his anticipation of this trip, and it became evident that his purpose was abundantly fulfilled.

> You asked about our trip to Europe. We will leave somewhere around the middle of May by freighter and perhaps return by plane around the end of August. Through the influence of Jack Lewis I am going to teach at the Ecumenical Institute this summer for a short period. I am interested in seeing the Institute (Bossey); the academics in Germany; the Church-in-world movement in Holland; some of the lay experiments in France; then in Scotland the Iona Community; and finally some of the universities in England. We will also stop off at the Agape Community in Italy, although this is not one of my particular interests at the moment. My concern will be to find out how these various lay movements understand themselves, where they came from, what they think they are doing, to try to get at the core of their activity. For if we start something on the order of an institute in this country, we feel that we ought to make use of the best creative insights of all lay endeavors on the Continent.

A year later Joe wrote about this journey, after he had had time for reflection upon its meaning. Here is a kind of précis of what he said:

> Last year I traveled in Europe from one lay center to another. In each I asked the question: Is there a lay movement in Europe? From their answers I began to see several different directions or emphases of the lay movement. The ones I will describe are types: none exactly fits any community that I visited. . . . Other lay groups are forging a whole new understanding of evangelism in its basic meaning, nature, and methodology. They have become aware that the pressures of our time force men to the very edge of life where the question is asked, Is it possible to live before this One who is un-synonymous with any human conception of Him? They understand that this question comes out of the concrete situations in which men find themselves. They know

that it is being asked in countless disguised ways. They are becoming aware that the Church, as an evangelistic community, must go out into the world and live beside the people to whom we would speak, a cup of water in one hand and a cup of wine, representing the blood of Jesus Christ, in the other. This is the evangelistic or "bridge" type.

Another is what I call the educational or college type. These are the people who perhaps realize that in the preceding century God brought into being a new concern for scientific knowledge, and that in this century he is bringing into being another emphasis – existential knowledge. Here, the questions raised are those of personal meaning, the question of the beginning points of values, or (to put it theologically) the question of faith.

The last type . . . is the cell or communal type. In terms of the sociological situation of our day, we do not need to ask how these groups came into being. Community has broken down. Many young people who come to college have never had what I would call a serious conversation with their parents. They have never experienced a time when the masks were taken off to become a family. It is frightening, but it happens. . . . We adults try to pretend it is not true, because it is such a horrifying reflection upon us. Our neighborhoods are gone. I know the names of the people on my street and their occupations, but seldom do I have a self-disclosing conversation with them. Friendship? What a rarity. Where is the person before whom we can dare to be who we are, and what is more important, the person whom we can permit to be who he is?

One of the things that has brought this last type of lay center into being is the lack of human community, that which I was born to have, and without which I cannot live. But there is a deeper question that they raise: What does community in Jesus Christ mean? God has shaken us until we at least are rid of our earlier naïve notions in this area. We are at least awakened to the fact that whatever else community in Jesus Christ may mean, it is not synonymous with that kind of community for which my soul cries out on the human level.

Out of this wrestling has come the awareness that the life of Christian faith cannot be lived alone.

Meanwhile, back in the Christian Faith and Life Community much work remained to be done. Joe and Lyn returned, though physically exhausted, to enter into the engagement with renewed intentionality. Yes, they did bring back the motor scooter and side-car! It was finally disposed of in Austin. Their many new insights were put immediately to work.

The Faith and Life Community's influence was being felt in widening circles in the United States and beyond. It awakened positive interest and was also the focus of not a little negative criticism. In contrast to the attitude of many others, who felt that the critics must be answered, Joe never did. This is not to suggest that he did not suffer from the blows he received throughout his active professional years. It goes without saying that the community's work created no little stir on the campus of the University of Texas.

In illustration of this, reference should be made to Joe's friend-ship with a colleague, Dr. John Silber, who arrived in Austin about the same time as Joe. He taught philosophy and became a dean at the University of Texas. Later he completed a very distinguished career as President and then Chancellor of Boston University. Silber had studied for a year at Yale Divinity School and had considerable theological knowledge. He and Joe became and continued to be good friends. Dr. Silber often appeared on panel discussions at the Faith and Life Community. On at least one occasion he and Joe engaged in a theological debate which aroused great interest on campus. They were in substantial agreement on religious perspectives and it was interesting that John Silber defended traditional Christian theology while Joe stood for an existential approach to the same.

At the very close of this biography an extended statement of Dr. Silber's view of Joe is included. For the present, this excerpt about Joe (April 4, 2003) summarizes Silber's impressions: "In 1955, [I] went to the University of Texas from Yale and there I met Joseph Mathews. . . . He and I became close friends and colleagues. He brought to that campus a spiritual depth and enthusiasm. . . . There he was at a largely secular campus of 25,000 . . . students, and he created something of a religious revival."

In bringing to a close this account of Joe Mathews and his work at Austin, it is important to emphasize an essential aspect of the whole enterprise: the common life of the community. When Joe and Lyn began their work at Perkins, they followed a typical middle class life style. Lyn in one letter expresses her great pride in their new home in Dallas, including also the family car with a possum tail attached to the radio aerial. When they first moved to Austin, they lived in a very attractive neighborhood not far from their work. Joe spent much of his spare time in looking after the appearance of their house and lawn. Suddenly, after three years, they sold this splendid residence and moved to a very modest house adjacent to the Christian Faith and Life Community. Other members of the faculty had begun to move in a similar direction. What Joe and others had observed in their visits to communities in Europe prompted them further to move in this direction.

So it was that the core members of the Christian Faith and Life Community (or most of them) headed toward establishing a new kind of religious order. It was a type of "third order," comprised of married couples as well as of devoted single women and men. To this end they drew up a "Moral Covenant and Corporate Discipline." This was the genesis of the later Order:Ecumenical. A kind of preamble read as follows:

> In the name of Jesus the Christ, our Lord, we take upon ourselves this corporate discipline:
>
> For the sake of our universal and particular mission as the Church of Jesus Christ:
>
> Being impelled by a sense of urgency born of certain events in the life of the church as she attempts to be the church in this present age:
>
> We, the Christian Faith and Life Community, by our free resolve, before the Creator of our personal and collective destinies and in the name of Jesus the Christ our Lord, take upon ourselves this moral covenant and rule of life, for the sake of a particular corporate mission within the total calling of the church, to which we have been commonly elected.

As the "Common Rule" was drawn up, however, not all members of the community were prepared for this drastic move. One can see that the stage was being set for the next step in the drama of Joe's pilgrimage, that would be anchored in deep communal experimentation.

During the six years that Joe was part of the Austin experiment, it grew immensely in program, in size, and as we have seen, in influence. As the years passed, criticism of the experiment increased. Basically the venture was successful, but with its fame so too its notoriety grew in some quarters of Texas. The focus of criticism was twofold: theological, for Joe's teachings were considered by some to be too unorthodox for their tastes; and, second, style of life: the move toward a more communal fashion of living was opposed by some. In spring 1962, a slim majority of the Board became fiscally conservative toward investing more in the lay education expansion that Joe was ceaselessly proposing.

Jack Lewis announced that he was accepting Joe's resignation, which had throughout the years rested upon his desk. To the Board's surprise, several other staff members resigned. Thus was precipitated what came to be called an "amoebic split." The Christian Faith and Life Community, as it had existed for more than a decade, ceased to be, though it did continue for a time, but with a far less vigorous program. (In 1965, Jack Lewis became the much respected and innovative director of Cornell University's United Religious Work until 1981.) The question arose as to the future of the staff members who had resigned. As Joe's brother, I invited them all to move to Boston, and this was considered.

The Chicago Invitation
In a rather short time an alternative arose. In 1954, when the World Council of Churches had held its Second Assembly in Evanston, Illinois, it authorized the establishment of an Ecumenical Institute for the United States. It was inspired by and modeled on the Ecumenical Institute in Bossey, Switzerland. The authorization was finally acted upon in 1957 when the institute was incorporated. Dr. Walter Leibrecht was asked to be the first director. He was a professor of historical theology at Garrett Biblical Institute in

Evanston. He had formerly been a professor of theology at Harvard Divinity School. A large building was acquired in Evanston for the headquarters. In initiating its planned program, the focus in Leibrecht's own words was on "what can be done to make the witness of Christians more effective in and for today's world. What we seek at this institute is a new type of Christian." This would appear to be entirely congruent with the aims that Joe and his colleagues had developed through the years. A difference lay in intensity, to say the least. Leibrecht had organized a strong group of church and business leaders in support of the new venture. Their letterhead lists some forty persons of great prominence. The National Advisory Board was composed of Bishop S. Uberto Barbieri, one of the Presidents of the World Council of Churches; Dr. Franklin Clark Fry, President of the Lutheran World Federation; Presiding Bishop Henry Knox Sherrill, of the Episcopal Church and also a President of the World Council of Churches; Dr. Paul Tillich, University Professor, Harvard; Dr. Elton Trueblood of Earlham College. The director's article in the periodical, "Religion in Life," winter of 1961-62, outlines the program in some detail.

By 1962, Professor Leibrecht wanted to be released from the directorship in order to become a Protestant observer to Vatican II. This left an opening for a director. In May 1962, the Ecumenical Institute was made a division of the Church Federation of Greater Chicago, where the Rev. Dr. Edgar H. S. Chandler was the Executive Vice-President. He was open and alert to the issues of church renewal. Happily his needs and those of the recently unemployed theological team from Austin matched reciprocally and an almost unbelievable agreement was reached. There was only one salaried position open, that of director. It was offered to Joe, who accepted immediately – provided his colleagues could come along. When Edgar Chandler pointed out that there was no budget for them, Joe offered their services at one dollar a year each! Surely church history affords few similar arrangements, although some of the disciples recruited by Jesus left their nets and followed him. The Austin families were certainly disciplined, and, accepting the plan, they might well have been dubbed the "Magnificent Seven."

The Great Trek to Chicago

The team moved from Austin to Evanston, where a house was available to them. Although metaphors have a way of breaking down if subjected to too much strain, when one reflects upon this episode, there comes to mind the Vortrekkers of the Africaners who journeyed from Cape Province to the Transvaal. There are also certain overtones of the Exodus from Egypt to the Promised Land. The reality was that the small company of refugees from Austin to Chicago hired a large semitrailer moving van and tractor. It was loaded not only with all the earthly possessions of the Joe and Lyn Mathews family but those of six other families as well. One of the company, Frank Hilliard, was licensed to drive such a vehicle and drove it all the way and later joined the staff. The truck was followed by a procession of the cars belonging to other members of the community. In addition to Joe and Lyn Mathews with children Joe, Jim, and John were Joe and Anne Slicker with Bill, Joann, and John; Joe and Joy Pierce with Cathy, Dale, and Mark; David and Donna McCleskey; Don and Beverly Warren; and Bill and Gretta Cozart. They were soon joined by Fred and Sarah Buss, after their marriage in Texas, where Joe officiated.

These folk settled into one house in sedate Evanston, Illinois. Walter Liebrecht facilitated the move in every way he could, and the same may be said of Edgar Chandler. The new families were all able to fit (snugly) into one house! As the most senior members, the Mathews and Slicker families each had one room in the basement. The others had somewhat more spacious quarters. All participants generously saved the master bedroom for the newly-weds, Fred and Sarah Buss, who joined them in August. Much time and energy was spent in working out details of living together: budgeting, division of labor, house rules. Their copious notes remain and reveal the attention they gave to every conceivable detail. Of vital importance was the matter of sufficient income for such a multi-family arrangement. To this end, several of the wives found employment in Greater Chicago and eased the situation. All means were pooled at the time in accordance with the principles of the emerging Order:Ecumenical. They were beginning to experience the pros and cons of life together.

As to program, it was mostly built upon the curricula worked out during the Austin years, as well as the experience at Perkins School of Theology. Now the playing field was much larger. They availed themselves of every opportunity and proceeded to relate to laity in the Chicago region, building relations over a broad denominational spectrum as they worked on a support base. Their interaction is revealed in a memorandum Joe wrote at the time:

> For the past several years our common history has been shaped under the external form of the Christian Faith and Life Community. Now at the beginning of our second decade, theological, cultural, organizational shifts in our thought and life call for a different manifestation before culture. In one sense, the first decade role created us as a historical mission group. The second requires building an adequate form in and through which we can effectively carry out the task placed upon us. The first years were a time of thinking through; now the emphasis is upon action. God called us to be and is calling us to be in a new set of circumstances To say this another way, our being as the Christian Faith and Life Community has brought us into history; that has been the role of the past. Now we must take up our historical destiny.

As time went on, the house they occupied in Evanston was bursting at the seams. A fire was accidentally set by one of the boys who was searching for some of his possessions stored in a large carriage house on the property. All of the families lost some of their belongings in the fire. It became more and more evident that they were in violation of ordinance: their part of Evanston was a one-family residential area. New accommodations had to be found, and soon!

Once again, as if Providence was acting on their behalf, a way opened up for them. One of the directors of the Ecumenical Institute (or Ecumenical Division, the Greater Chicago Church Federation) was also related to Bethany Biblical Seminary, founded by the Church of the Brethren, off Congress Parkway on the West Side of the city. The seminary was moving to the suburbs and their property was available for use. After lengthy discussion it was made available to the Ecumenical Institute on terms which were regarded as fair to both parties. Now much more space was available for a growing program; it was more central, located in a place where they could take the city more seriously and address the many pressing issues of modern America.

At this point the narrative will take a temporary break and will be resumed in Chapter 11, because an important event occurred in the spring of 1963, when Joe accompanied me and my young twelve-year-old son, Stanley, on a trip around the world. We were all altered by the experience.

Let me end this chapter by mentioning that Joe sketched a predictive chart, beginning in 1956:

> 4 years – Hearing from the College House
> 4 years – Forging the Church Dynamics
> 4 years – Probing the Cultural Mission
> 4 years – Launching the Prophetic Cadre
> 4 years – To be determined

As of 1963 Joe and his colleagues were on target.

9

ON BECOMING
A GLOBAL PERSON

In imagination, Joe had always lived in a large world. At heart he realized that the whole world belonged to him and that he had responsibility for all. This happened gradually and then dramatically as he, for the first time, circumnavigated the globe.

We have seen how once he worked his way on an ocean freighter from Corpus Christi, Texas, to Wilmington, Delaware. He concluded then and there that the life of a sailor was not for him.

World War II, as if in mockery, took him to the sea again, this time to land on the battle-strewn beaches of the Pacific. This was another of his transforming experiences, for life was never the same again for him. He saw in conflict what the South Pacific could be, hardly what the Broadway musical might suggest. There too he had witnessed firsthand for a time Polynesian and Micronesian cultures. In brief respites from battle he learned to admire these people and some of the missionaries who worked among them. This he never forgot. He returned there again and again in later years to be refreshed by the wisdom of that part of the world.

As a part of this experience, he first touched upon Japanese culture in Okinawa and then on the main island of Japan. He and his wife occasionally dipped into Mexico and made acquaintance with Hispanic and Pre-Columbian culture. Their world was growing.

In 1957 came their trip to Europe – their first. There they drank of many fountains and tested the roots of Western culture. Let others travel around by plane or train or bus or auto. That was not for these two. They did it by a tiny Vespa and its sidecar, entirely surrounded by their baggage.

But it was in 1963 that Joe entered into his full inheritance as a global man. Magellan and Drake, two characters he greatly admired, no longer had anything on him: he too traveled round the world. On the trip he had a notable introduction to the big continent: Africa. Its magic, its marvel, its mystery never left him. Then it was on to India, to Hong Kong, to Japan, to Honolulu, and home again. With me and my young son, Stanley, Joe left New York City on February 23, 1963, and returned there two months later. It was for us a voyage of discovery and at the same time an awakening, what I call Joe's third great awakening.

This passage may seem a little like the "we passages" of *Acts of the Apostles*, for the writer was along and indeed led the tour; hence the lapse into first person plural. The journey was a part of a mandate for Methodist bishops to visit every four years some part of the work of our church outside of the United States. Our family had determined also that just before each of our children reached age twelve we would see to it that they engaged in some overseas travel experience – while incidentally they could travel at half-fare. It was then concluded that my brother Joe should be invited, also, and I raised the money to include him. He was delighted and was assigned responsibility for observing the world of a budding college in the Congo, called Congo Polytechnic Institute. For the record, a trip around the world at that time was just over $1300, economy class. Young Stan's ticket was half as much.

Once aboard the plane and ready to settle down for the night, Stan would typically stretch out on the floor with pillow and blanket. This freed one extra economy seat for the adults to share. It was not exactly comfortable but it was acceptable.

An overnight flight brought us to Lisbon, Portugal, a first for all of us. Not only was this a significant visit in itself but a good port of departure from the "motherland" of Portuguese colonies in Africa. There we saw the usual sights: the Cathedral, St. George's Castle, a most intriguing "Coach Museum" (ancient horse-drawn carriages), a memorial to Prince Henry the Navigator, and the departure point of Magellan's journey. A visit to a fine restaurant with guitar music gave us a taste of the local culture, which whetted our appetites.

The next morning we departed for Liberia. A clear day offered a good glimpse of the Canary Islands. Then, looking out the left side of the plane, we observed for many weary hours the Spanish Sahara. A refueling stop at Dakar, Senegal, gave us an opportunity to set foot on Africa itself, which was to be our home for a whole month. A further short flight brought us to Roberts Field, which serves Monrovia, Liberia, but is actually far from the capital city.

At that very moment the whole continent of Africa was coming alive and making itself known in a new way to an emerging world. It was a continent in revolution, not so much in the Communist sense (though that view was by no means absent from the scene), but often described as a "revolution of rising expectations." It was a rejection of colonial rule and economic exploitation from the North and the West. It was a reaching toward nationhood, modernization, economic advancement, and the overthrow of economic domination by others.

The air was full of immediacy. The element of unity, continent-wide, seemed also present. Pan-Africanism was in vogue, a term which was at once poorly defined and deeply felt. "Black is Beautiful" and "Negritude" were meaningful ideas. Though doubtless a part of the movement in the post-World War II world to reject colonialism, it was a little delayed and with a peculiarly African slant. In Asia, for example, the struggle for freedom was the culmination of decades of struggle of both a violent and nonviolent nature. In Africa it came with surprise and suddenness. Once started, the movement took on a relentless quality. Sometimes it was swift, sometimes slow, but always present.

In many parts of the continent, war raged, sometimes in protest and struggle for freedom, sometimes civil strife, which followed independence. Such struggles were to persist recurrently even into the 21st century. Thus it was that Africa offered a vast laboratory for the study of massive issues, which were often global in nature and scope. To this Joe applied his powers of observation with complete abandon. His awakened conscience demanded that he be a participant in what he observed.

No better time could have been found for this tour of observation and discernment. The eyes of the whole world were fixed upon the Dark Continent, the hitherto Forgotten and Exploited Continent. It was now awakening; the people were finding themselves. They were no longer prepared to be ignored and neglected. They were no longer satisfied to be thought of as being infantile. As Sir Francis Ibiam, Governor of the Eastern Region of Nigeria, said at the time: "Some want Africa to remain the baby of the world – a good-humored, laughing baby!" But no more! Africa was coming of age.

Joe was acutely aware of this. How often as he reflected on this pilgrimage would he burst almost into song, for he spoke of

- "Moments of Agony" as he witnessed the sufferings of refugees from Baluba and Angola
- "Moments of Bitterness" at the plight of South African Blacks under the oppression of Apartheid
- "Moments of Ecstasy" as he danced on the brim of Victoria Falls
- "Moments of Revelation" as African peoples "took off their masks"
- "Moments of Perplexity" when he shared with the people "What then shall we do?"
- "Moments of Deep Seriousness" as some of their leaders confided in whispers their plans for freedom

At the 20th century midpoint there were only one or two really independent countries on the whole continent of Africa. By century's end all were independent, though, perhaps, not exactly free. During a 1954 visit to the Belgian Congo, an observer spoke to the Governor-General about independence. The quick and ready response was, "Independence? Come back in a hundred years and we'll talk about it!" That was, of course, Belgium's timetable, not Africa's, or history's, or, shall we say, God's? Ready or not, independence came to Belgian Congo in 1960! Others were to follow in rather quick succession.

Congo is about the size of India, or the United States east of the Mississippi. When independence came to Southern Asia in 1947, the whole region had a population of some 400,000,000. That was more than thirty times as great as Congo's estimated 13,000,000 at

the time. In 1960, when independence came to Congo, only thirteen Congolese had a college education, whereas Southern Asia
had several hundred thousand university graduates. Apparently
Britain had done something more or less right in preparing for the
end of colonialism, but not so in Africa's instance. The African
continent was afflicted by several colonial powers: Great Britain,
France, Portugal, Spain, Italy, and even South Africa – all moving
at a slow pace and attempting to hold on as long as possible.

Colonialism in Africa was not merely a political matter; it also
was very much a cultural matter (think "tribalism"); and it was also
very much an economic matter (think raw materials vs. internal
industrialization). Think also of linguistic and religious differences; climate and paucity of an infrastructure; and
commercialism. Easy solutions were not readily available. For example, agricultural production was often hampered by the very
fragility of the soil, easily damaged by sun and rain. For the most
part, the only agriculture that Africa knew was subsistence. Nevertheless, Africans wanted solutions, immediate solutions, for all
their problems, including the building of modern economies. This
was very often beyond their reach, so frustrations multiplied. So let
the song continue:

- "Moments of High Appreciation" of the spirit evidenced by
  young people, for half of Africa's population was below the
  age of fifteen. It was the same with women – so sensitive, so
  feminine, so quiet, yet determined.
- "Moments of Deep Gratitude" for the labor and devotion of
  missionaries, the concern the church had shown in its rooting
  in African soil, for African Christians who so often proved
  that they could stand tall, even without missionary help.

Back to Liberia, our thoughtful hosts had planned for us a kind
of bird's-eye view of the country. This included traveling through
100,000 acres of rubber trees planted forty years before by Fire-
stone Rubber Company. Then we had a stop at Gharnhga, in the
jungle, a fine example of African initiative. Our journey took us
next to nearby Cuddington College, a joint venture of Methodists,
Episcopalians, and Lutherans in theological education. More strik-

ing was Ganta, which offered a wide array of services in medicine, education, agricultural, industrial training, and work among women. What Africa most needed, here was provided. One could hardly praise enough the devoted labors evident here by Africans and missionaries alike. A tour of the capital, Monrovia, and a trip to Bossan on the coast, for a church conference session, completed our quick tour of the country.

Methodist Bishop Prince A. Taylor was our host. He and the others who entertained us could not have been more thoughtful or gracious. As already stated, much good work was being done by those who had come to help. Nevertheless, somehow Liberia was a disappointment. It seemed out of step with the dynamic and vibrant developments that were evident in many other places. A kind of decadence was manifest. That Liberia was forty-five minutes "off" what GMT indicated it should be spoke volumes. So did the fact that the local currency was U.S. dollars. We sensed that the people were exploited by their leaders. Decades later the land was still in deep trouble.

It was a great disappointment to our party that we were not able to visit Dr. Albert Schweitzer in Lambarene. He had graciously invited us, but a visit was simply not possible to schedule because of plane routes. What a shame! Instead, we spent a day "hedge-hopping" in West Africa: Accra, Ghana; Lagos, capital of Nigeria, and finally settled down for a night in Donali, capital of the Cameroons. This section afforded us only a touch of what British and French colonies were like.

Another flight brought us to Brazzaville where we experienced crossing the Equator. We found it interesting that two countries in Africa had the same name: one called Congo-Brazzaville (French) and the other Congo-Leopoldville (Belgian, until 1960). We were transported from the former city to the latter by a ferry across the vast, swirling Congo River, five miles wide at that point. We almost shuddered at the latent power of this river system, said to account for 25 percent of the whole water power of Africa.

Both these capitals were modern cities, by the way, and one was shocked by this fact. Nevertheless, Brazzaville was at the time far more prosperous than its neighbor, for upon the latter the cruel marks of war were clearly to be seen. Young Stan was delighted that his namesake, Henry M. Stanley, had marked the site of the city. His statue presided over a prominent square. In fact, this explorer's mark is left on many places, pleasing our young fellow traveler immensely.

At various meetings, in conversations with leaders, including the Deputy Prime Minister, Jason Sendwe, in taking in the city's sights and market we began to get the feel of this large, rich, and varied land. We visited a hospital at nearby Kimpese and the only university in the country, Louvanium, recently established by the Roman Catholics. This was of particular interest to us because Methodists were interested in initiating their first institution of high learning, the Congo Polytechnic Institute, at what was then called Stanleyville. Later it was taken over by the government, but at least the church tried.

Our intention is not to write a travelogue, but we did move around with some rapidity and with great difficulty. There seemed almost always to be a war just in the background, or impending, or recently interrupted. The presence of U.N. troops at various places maintained at times a kind of tenuous peace. In the midst of it all, restless, changing Africa was never really at peace.

My son was impressed that I could converse in simple Hindustani with some of the U.N. forces from India. It did lend a certain at-home feeling to the confusion. This confusion can hardly be overstated. Independence had come with lightening swiftness on June 30, 1960. The charismatic African figure Patrice Lamumba had emerged. He was a revolutionary person who could be rightfully likened to George Washington as a "father of his country." His star shone brightly for a season before he was assassinated. Rumor persisted that he was still alive. Civil strife followed as various groups sought opportunity to seize power. These in turn were prompted and supported by one or another foreign political or economic venture. There emerged three successive wars in the Congo: September 1961, December 1961, and December-January of 1962-63. Then came U.N. troops to render some sense of balance and stability. Nevertheless, strife continued almost constantly for the rest of the century and beyond.

The story of the church, caught in this cross fire, is one of trag-edy and glory. Missionaries were twice forced to withdraw from some parts of the country due to looting and rape. The Africans themselves suffered beyond measure. Through it all, Christians were enabled to stand. Leadership arose and developed stature un-der the force of necessity. Hundreds of churches and preaching points throughout Central Congo remained open and even grew in the midst of the strife. For the most part schools remained open, and teachers continued to work, often without pay. Wherever our traveling trio went, we had to listen to the varied versions of this story. It was indeed one of triumph in an atmosphere of travail. Observers could not praise too much those who endured and fought back.

From the center of Elizabethville we ventured out in several di-rections. Northward we went to Mulungwshi. There in a magnificent site was a principal Methodist mission station for Southern Congo where missionaries had pioneered. One of them was now retired Bishop John M. Springer. He and a party of col-leagues walked from east to west across the narrow waist of Africa. The trek took three months, a distance which can now be covered by jet in three hours! In 1912, they were invited to estab-lish a work within the territory of the Lunda chief, "Mwant Yav."

We then had the exciting experience of being flown over great distances in a mission plane. It was a four-seater Cesna 180. Paul Alexander, from Texas, was the pilot, and proud to tell us he had taken flying lessons from Charles Lindbergh. His proficiency was beyond dispute but he was a bit of a cowboy. For example, when coming in for a landing he would sometimes induce a stall. The plane would literally drop; then a sudden infusion of power would cause it to recover for a stable landing. This we could have done without, but Joe of course enjoyed it!

Still, we owe to Paul our lives as we flew over trackless jungle. Occasionally we would find ourselves over savannahs and flood plains where frequently were to be sighted hippos, zebras, bison, antelopes, and elephants. We observed copper mines at Kolwezi and river basins, mountains, and scattered villages. We also viewed the results of the ravages of war. Then, to our relief, we would land on airstrips at out-of-the-way places such as Sandoa, Katurve, Wemba-Nyama, Lodja, Katakakombe, and finally Kindu. Each place is the scene of an array of missionary ventures and heroic tales of the experiences of the Church. At the time of our visit they were very unsettled. Only the presence of U.N. troops guaranteed some semblance of order.

At each place we met with missionaries and their African colleagues. Without exception they showed the marks of suffering and the anxiety of living under conditions of such danger. In spite of it all, we found morale high. Missionaries were filled with admiration for their African associates and vice versa. The Africans had had to advise their counterparts to leave for periods, but they also wanted them back. They had become colleagues. As one African put it, "We had to say 'No' to the missionaries in order to say 'Yes' to the Holy Spirit." This was the avenue to maturity.

In repeated sessions with such people we found their eyes were on the future. While grateful for what had been done, they were focused on what remained to be done. Almost everywhere their insistence was the same: the need for leadership, for training, for scholarships, for fuller engagement in the unparalleled demands and opportunities with which they were confronted. They emphasized always the need for spiritual deepening and commitment. They showed a longing for peace and justice and self-respect. They knew too that the times called for reconciliation and reconstruction on a scale the church could not supply. Therefore, the role of interpreters and advocates for a New Africa was clearly demanded. The need also was constantly to inspire and nurture hope among people who had suffered so sorely and for so long.

While my own role was to listen and encourage, trying to lift morale with church workers, Joe was able to concentrate on other, more basic and long-range matters. He could test his reading against the vast laboratory of Africa itself. For instance, he had recently read a book by a Belgian priest titled *Muntu* that had addressed him deeply. He was once overheard speaking with a young African woman about the term. Her response was, "How did you learn about this word? It is a wonderful word." She spoke of it as something very precious.

We learned that the word in various related forms is used in all of the Bantu languages. On a literal one-to-one basis, in translation *muntu* means "man." Yet it reaches far beyond that: it means person or even personage. It means people – even a whole people. It refers to the individual being a part of a whole people, a clan, a tribe, a nation. Further, it implies human, or humaneness – the importance of being human – a fellow-feeling. It suggests humanity, humankind; and human beings in relation to animals, to trees, to nature, to dancing, to music, to the drums. *Muntu* is a way of life.

Muntu deals with dimensions of life in which Africans excel. The first person plural is more important than the first person singular in most African languages. It is reflected in greetings: "Are you alive?" "Did you sleep well?" "Has your day gone well so far?" One could observe that these notions seem deeply rooted in the African people and the African-American psyche. It is already present in the two most original American musical motifs; namely, the Negro spiritual and jazz in its many forms – both essentially African-American.

Muntu helped Joe articulate the pulsebeat of the continent on our trip, and he referred to it repeatedly for the rest of his life. *Muntu* became a kind of gateway which helped open up for him the keys to other cultures as well.

We hasten on, never forgetting that during our pilgrimage we were progressively becoming more global persons.

The next leg of our travels in the Cessna was our longest uninterrupted flight – more than five hours aloft. We had been well-advised to avoid coffee or tea before we took off. Our route led south, over Lake Nyasa and again through war torn areas, over dark serpentine rivers, over villages and waterfalls, finally to a landing in Ndola, Northern Rhodesia (at present, Zambia). Our stay there was brief, but we did see more copper mines, for Central Africa is richly endowed with this ore. Of special interest was a solemn visit to the site of the crash of Dag Hammarskjöld's plane – a personal tragedy for Africans and the whole world. Significant also was a visit with the Ecumenical Institute at nearby Mindolo, established by the World Council of Churches and the All-Africa Conference of Churches. There we were able to check our views and impressions with those experienced persons who devoted their lives to much research. Joe added their perspective to his Europe tour learnings about lay renewal.

A further two-hour flight in a Viscount aircraft of South African Airways transported us to the city of Livingstone. We visited a small but delightful museum of African arts and craft. We found the weather exceedingly hot, the way Africa is supposed to be. A few miles from Livingstone we crossed over a bridge of the Zambesian Gorge which separated Northern and Southern Rhodesia (now Zimbabwe). We recuperated from our excessive fatigue by a three-day stay in Victoria Falls Hotel. It was something of a period piece, architecturally speaking. This hotel offered fine food and an incomparable setting.

Our first glimpse of the Falls themselves we enjoyed as the pilot flew us over the chasm. From the ground we visited it again and again, gasping at its grandeur from every angle. It surely must rank as one of the most awesome sights of sheer natural wonder the world affords. Dr. David Livingstone, in 1855, was the first European to see it, we were told. A noble statue of this missionary explorer still has his eyes fixed on this great chasm. The Africans called it "The Smoke that Thunders," and so it does.

What struck us was the way the beauty of the unbelievable setting had been maintained intact, in contrast with the commercial and industrial exploitation of, say, Niagara Falls. The Zambesi River at this point is about a mile and a half wide, and the whole torrent plunges into a deep and narrow gorge, a drop of 350 feet! The falls may be observed from the opposite side of this massive cleft in the earth. This was done with great care for no guard rails were in place.

The experience is truly one of awe and wonder. A great cloud of mist, generated by the falling water, lifts about half a mile into the air. The mist condenses and even on a clear day a driving rain envelopes everything. The visitor is simply soaked to the skin. The verdure is wonderful and ebony trees vie with tangles of fern fronds overhanging the edge of the river. Here monkeys and baboons sport, seemingly enjoying the experience as much as their human cousins. The rain forest surrounds everything.

Here it was that young Stan and I observed a sight which in such a setting only angels are supposed to see: there was Uncle Joe – my brother – dancing, Zorba-like, on the very brink of this wondrous chasm! This may properly be called an experience of ecstasy, and it must have been for him, as for us, one of the great moments of his life. The sheer, overwhelming power of Africa had seized him, and for a few moments he was embraced by the force of a whole continent! This is in no small part becoming a global person!

Every such experience must come to an end. We flew on to a short visit to Wankee Game Reserve, then on to Bulowayo, and finally Johannesburg, which is known familiarly as Jo'burg. Our sojourn there was brief but we did glimpse this City of Gold. We thought we were experiencing an earthquake, only to learn that it was merely the settling of cavernous abandoned mines far below the surface of the earth! Again, we felt the earth shake as miners in their compounds danced barefooted with such vigor as to cause the ground to quiver. We saw skyscrapers and we saw *apartheid* (pronounced a-part-hate, with emphasis on the "hate"). As young Stan noted in his diary, "The Africans are not treated well and look very angry. The government is trying to separate the Africans from white people entirely. They have separate restaurants, drinking fountains, park benches, telephone booths. I do not think this is fair. They treat Negroes even worse than we do in the U.S." It would be another thirty years before apartheid collapsed!

Two other memorable experiences we had in Johannesburg: one was a visit – all too short – to the Institute of Race Relations. The very fact that it existed at all was a sign of encouragement. It was to contribute to the great changes which were finally inevitable in South Africa. The other was a museum of African music. Its presence also delighted us as did its director, Dr. Hugh Tracey. Throughout our trek across the continent, a conviction kept growing in our minds. We observed the art forms of Africa: the dance, the music, the drums, the poetry, the sculpture and carvings, the decorative arts on the walls and floors of African huts, and so on. We noted also the relative absence of these arts in the churches that seemed to regard art forms as threats to Christianity, though this

scarcely ran contrary to the main stream of church history. Few
African hymns were sung. Instead the hymns were rather dull and
dingy renderings or translations of familiar Western hymns. This
was in contrast to the rich hymnody in various languages of India.
In Africa, drums and dance were taboo in Christian worship. This
was to continue for some years more.

In Johannesburg we tested our views with Dr. Tracey. We had
concluded that proper recovery of the native arts would lend stability to church and society, undergoing such sweeping change. We
were assured that this viewpoint was valid. In ensuing years it has
been marvelous to witness the arts strengthening rather than weak-
ening the churches in Africa. Worship has become alive and
vibrant. Finally, in the mid-1980s, the use of drums in worship was
sanctioned even in the Roman Catholic Church.

After our rather short and shocking dip into South Africa, it
was with some relief that we returned to Southern Rhodesia (now
Zimbabwe) and to its capital, Salisbury (Harare). This turned out to
be a modern city of about 200,000 people. It was a very important
center for the Methodist Church. The country was beautiful. So
also was the climate, especially in the parts of the country on the
high plateau – three thousand feet and higher. We arrived in Salisbury on the first day of spring, which was actually fall by the
calendar of the Southern Hemisphere.

It was possible to drive by car to all the principle centers within
a few days. The countryside was so underdeveloped that one experienced being in the wilds. Antelope and crocodiles were
frequently seen. Baboons seemed to be everywhere. There were
rivers to be forded, caves and rock-carvings to see, and scattered
primitive villages. We touched such places as Rusape, Nyanazuwe,
Old Umtali (now Old Mutare). We saw schools, farms, hospitals,
and clinics – all part of the missionary work of service. At an especially attractive town in the higher mountains, Nyanga, we visited
Bishop Ralph Dodge, a longtime friend and experienced missionary. He was able to brief us thoroughly on conditions and trends on
the continent. He was also a man of vision – of passion – whose
determination saw to it that scores of able Africans received advanced education to equip them for the leadership roles so sorely

needed across the continent. The whole church is indebted to such persons.

Sooner than we had anticipated it was time to leave this continent which had shown us hospitality for more than a month. We flew to Nairobi, our last city. First, however, two final observations are in order. Both illustrate Joe's reflections on Africans.

The first had to do with how the Gospel may be related to Africa in contemporary terms. He was probably alerted to this approach through his relationship with Professor H. Richard Niebuhr. A hint of this was present in the references made earlier to the term *muntu*. In a word, the Gospel authorizes and empowers us to enter into our full humanhood. More specifically, it relates to what may be called the salvation questions: what are the deep human questions or issues for which the Good News in Christ is the answer?

It may be noted that this perspective is a bit Tertullian in nature. For example, one way of posing the question might be: what is the focus of what might be called the historical memory of a people? This we often tested among the elders of the people we met. With astonishing frequency the answer was an event or experience of deliverance, which can be seen as an Exodus-like event. It may be illustrated by Jesus Christ as deliverer. This is not as fantastic as it might seem at first blush. The Gospel of Mark is often seen as a reinterpretation of the Book of Exodus.

Or again, what does a given culture take for granted? What are the accepted goals or norm of conduct? Is it unity, solidarity, or a sense of the participatory? Insistent probing tends to reveal the forms of "taken-for-granted-ness" elements in a given society. These then are subjected to criticism in the light of Christian revelation: they are first a denial and then an affirmation of the Gospel.

Or, what is the ultimate goal or aspiration of Africa? First replies may be quite superficial. The question may be pushed further and further back. Is it prosperity, security, destiny? Very often one reaches the notion of dignity. This too may be denied under the scrutiny of the Gospel, for dignity is not achieved by human striving. This is first denied and then it is affirmed. It is to be received as a gift.

Partly prompted by such salvation questions, we had occasion to confer quietly and guardedly with some ardent nationalists in Southern Rhodesia. We spoke of Gandhi's weapon of nonviolence – *Satyagraha* – the "power of truth." We found that the Shona equivalent was "Simba re idi." This could become the slogan – the cry for freedom – upon which a nonviolent revolution might be built. It was again a heady experience!

So the time came that when we left Africa we were only partway around the world. Clearly we had been deeply addressed and were never to recover from the experience. The forces at work in Africa were as mighty as they were multiform – mighty like the power of the Congo and Zambesi Rivers. Here was a segment of humanity which we found young (and also ancient), fresh, earthy, open, vital, spontaneous, proud, angry, virile, confused, and powerful. The whole natural setting seemed to resonate to a mighty force. And have I mentioned the clouds? The mighty, lofty cumulus formations seemed to reach unbelievable proportions. At night from a plane the summer lightning seemed to burst out in all directions. It was full of awe. Africa was alive!

One cannot say the rest of our voyage was all downhill. But the main event for us was over. We journeyed on to Bombay (now Mumbai), where twenty-five years before I myself had been introduced to the subcontinent of India. Now was the time to introduce my son and my elder brother to the mystery and magic and majesty of a people who had come to mean so much to me. Here Stan's mother was born; here his maternal grandparents had toiled and brought hope and a positive difference and enrichment to the lives of many. Here I had worked, and here I had served in World War II.

Our paths led on to New Delhi. We were honored to be received by Jawaharlal Nehru, the Prime Minister. He was good enough to inscribe for Stan a copy of his book *Glimpses of World History*. We toured the garden in which Mahatma Gandhi was assassinated. Of course, we could not fail to go by Agra to see the Taj Mahal – without rival as the most beautiful building in the world. In later days one visitor quipped, "There are only two kinds of people in the world: those who have not seen the Taj and those who have." We were now numbered among the latter – and we had seen Victoria Falls, too! Then it was on to Lucknow, my wife's home city; then to Sitapur, the town of her birth. An all-night car ride carried us to Sat Tal (Seven Lakes) in the lower Himalayas where Stan's grandfather, E. Stanley Jones, had established a religious retreat – a Christian Ashram. During the night's journey we had seen deer, a tiger with its kill, and a black leopard on the prowl. Panna (Emerald) Lake at Sat Tal had just lost enough of its chill for us to take a brief plunge into its waters. Another day afforded us an elephant ride through Corbett Park where more of India's flora and fauna were to be seen. At least our small company had a quick look at a great land and a great people.

Much sooner than we could have wished we were off by jet to Hong Kong – a place of grandeur and beauty, but at the same time a strange anachronism, or so it struck us. Of course, we shopped – after all, the home folk would have expected no less of us. We observed some of the creative Christian service rendered in Hong Kong, a place of meeting of the West with the East and the cultural collisions such entails.

We proceeded to Taiwan – "Free China" as it was then called by some. The airport was surrounded not only by verdant rice fields but also antiaircraft guns. A further flight brought us to Tokyo where we landed in a heavy rain storm. For Joe, this completed his first circumnavigation of the globe, for in this vast city he had been stationed with the U.S. Army nearly twenty years before. This time, it was under condition of greater comfort, for much of the ruined city had been rebuilt. We visited friends and institutions and luxuriated in accommodations in an ancient Japanese inn.

After these days we moved on to Honolulu, and then home. Oh, yes, we did enjoy April 10, 1963, twice, as those must who cross the International Date Line from West to East.

We had all three become "global persons." Stan, my 12-year-old son, speaks the last word for all three of us:

> I think this trip has been very worthwhile. I think this trip
> was taken just at the time the world is at the height in politics
> and in beauty for this decade. This trip has shown me the hate in

Leopoldville, the refugees and the homeless in India and Hong Kong, and the good job missionaries are doing all over the world. I will remember this trip all my life, and it will help me in my later years because you can't face the world until you know what the world is facing.

It will be noted that this chapter is based on extensive notes and a diary kept by the writer and by my young son. Many have inquired about a possible journal kept by Joe himself. I have heard that he actually kept such a journal for years and some have reported having seen him writing entries in it. (A diligent search has failed to find any such documents.)

Almost immediately after this journey, Joe manifested the immense inspiration the trip had generated for him. Africa had a large place in his frequent references to Ur images, and his speeches were filled with references to Africa. There can be no doubt that the journey expanded his outlook and helped transform him into the global person he was becoming.

To this chapter a postscript needs to be added. When I was about to give up on the search for his notes on the trip, I came across these words in Joe's characteristic handwriting, entitled "Overall Impressions":

A new force in universal history – the Younger Nations

1. A fresh life force is present in the new peoples of the world, which may already be the spring of action which determines the responses of the older western nations and hence the future of history.

2. An indifference to the East-West struggle, though they will use it to their own ends, is manifest in the new nations as they are busy building their nations in a spirit of creative nationalism.

3. A sense of destiny is evident in these new people as they search for images of their role in world history and for ways and means of contributing their unique gifts to the world.

Here Joe seems to sense the new North-South dynamic, which in later decades came to rival the traditional East-West dynamic – hence, a new force in globality.

10
THE CHICAGO YEARS:
EI, ICA, O:E

The more one becomes acquainted with the Ecumenical Institute (EI) or, to use its subsequent designation, the Institute of Cultural Affairs (ICA), the more remarkable the undertaking seems to become. Already we have recounted its genesis on enlightened university and seminary campuses, where students and faculty took seriously the crisis which confronted both the church and world in the period after World War II. We have explored something of the gestation period of a movement – parallel with similar developments of Christian renewal in many parts of the world – centered in Austin, Texas: the Christian Faith and Life Community. We have followed, in 1962, what was termed the "Great Trek" of seven committed families from Austin to Evanston, Illinois. There the former Institute of Ecumenical Studies, a department of the Church Federation of Greater Chicago, became the Ecumenical Institute: Chicago. In 1964, the Institute relocated on the West Side of Chicago, using the facilities of a former theological seminary of the Church of the Brethren. This was to be EI's primary home for the next eight years. For the record, on December 15, 1971, the Kemper Insurance Company donated its building at 4750 North Sheridan Road in Chicago to the Institute. It proved to be an excellent and versatile facility. It was promptly renovated to suit program needs and rather Spartan living facilities. This greatly facilitated the whole undertaking. For several years both "campuses" were used by EI/ICA.

The remarkable nature of this story is evident in the fact that in 1962 the staff numbered thirteen adults. By July of 1972, the staff had grown to more than 1600 members in the Institute's thirty-six metropolitan centers in North America and in twenty-eight over-seas locations.

For many renewalists it was enough to approach church and society issues in a purely academic fashion. This was a necessary part of the task. The Ecumenical Institute saw as its vocation the actual engagement in renewal activities; that is, to undertake updating the church at every level in as many areas of the world as possible – all for the sake of society.

A 1971 publication describes the staff at the time:

> Professionally, the staff represented a broad cross section of experience and training. Twenty-eight percent of the staff was clergy. In terms of religious heritage, Roman Catholic, Jewish and fourteen Protestant denominations were represented. To expedite their work, the staff adopted a corporate living style. Sufficient numbers were employed outside the Institute to meet the living expenses of the entire staff on a stipend basis, this in collective fashion. Occupations included computer programmers, accountants, lawyers, university faculty members, doctors, nurses, engineers, businessmen, social workers, teachers, auto mechanics and commercial artists. This principle of self-support meant that every penny donated to the Institute went into its programs.

In this writing no effort will be made to recount this whole story in historical sequence and detail. After all, our focus is to tell something of the career of Joseph Wesley Mathews, who was deeply involved in every aspect of the genesis of the movement called EI/ICA. The full account urgently awaits the attention of a skilled and experienced church historian. When that research is finally undertaken, it is my conviction that Joe and this movement will loom large in the history of church renewal undertakings in the 20th century. In addition to a careful historical account of the Institute, I see also the need for a theological-sociological analysis of the total program. Again, no pretence is being made to perform that service here. Already I am in correspondence with scholars who are capable of undertaking these tasks.

"Just what was the Ecumenical Institute and what did it do?" There is no better way to answer these queries than to allow Joe once again to respond in his own words, after moving to the West Side of Chicago:

The program of the Institute is rooted in the new image of the church as mission. We call ourselves "structural revolutionaries" because we are unreservedly dedicated to the principle that the church is renewable from within. The new sense of mission in the church is the context for all our activities.

The local congregation in every situation is the focal point for our work. It is the place where everyday decisions are made, life styles forged and the world most directly and significantly touched.

Today the People of God at the grassroots are the new "elite" in history – from them will come a disciplined body of churchmen. They must become theologically equipped and practically enabled to be the church in word and deed.

These insights and convictions set the stage for answering the question "What does the Ecumenical Institute do?"

Our role is to aid in the renewal of the church for the sake of all civilization. Our strategy is threefold:

1. *Training*

The Ecumenical Institute, founded from a resolution of the Second Assembly of the World Council of Churches, is a comprehensive research and training center. We provide both lay and clergy with the intellectual tools and the practical model building skills which every awakened person needs. Our methods and curricula evoke a latent Christian memory and enable participants to appropriate the contemporary cultural wisdom. Both jobs must be done simultaneously. Over 60,000 persons were touched by the program of the Institute as it was taught by the faculty across the nation and throughout the world.

2. *Community Reformulation*

Our inner city project goes beyond all previous approaches to community reorganization. We are attempting to build a model which will be applicable to every urban area across the world. In a limited geographical area we deal with all of the problems of all of the people. Crucial to this is the depth human problem – the way a man sees himself in the world. In Chicago's West Side ghetto, the resident operates out of a victim image.

Wherever authentic human community is to emerge, new images of human significance must be consciously created and forcefully dramatized. This is what we mean by "imaginal education" – motivating a person to come to terms with his depth human problem. Adequate self-images offer the deep awareness of individual significance, personal integrity, and vocational accomplishment. They endow the human imagination with those pictures that allow a man to appropriate his own unique gift to history.

3. *Research*

The 200 persons who are the faculty of the Institute work as a research team. New curricula, materials and procedures for the training of adults, youth and children are constantly being developed. New models of the family, new forms for public, family and private worship are tested by the faculty, corporately and individually. Bound together under a common covenant, the faculty is an experimental "family order" discovering what it means to be a disciplined body of people for the sake of the mission of the church. By sharing meals and facilities, living costs are cut to a minimum. By living at the center of our mission in the West Side ghetto, we are constantly involved with those with whom we work. By supporting ourselves financially, every penny that is given to the Institute goes directly into the mission. By living in covenant, we are accountable to each other for the particular aspects of the mission.

Our world, secular-scientific-urban, is a radically new historical arena. This brand new world demands a new lifestyle – religious, secular, disciplined, practical, and profoundly human.

That's what we're about at the Ecumenical Institute.

In the preceding chapter our narrative followed Joe and his two companions in his first trip around the world. In this experience he became thoroughly convinced that his summons to participate in the renewal of the church was not merely a local task but a global one. For that reason the flow of the story was interrupted in order to resume its telling in a new key – one of worldwide inclusivity, which characterized his labors for his remaining days.

Two other factors must also be kept in view. The first is the ecumenical movement. It is usually dated from the great missionary conference in Edinburgh, Scotland, in 1910. Here missionary leaders from many lands and many church traditions assembled to consider their common task. Among those present were not only Western church leaders but representatives of so-called mission lands as well – "younger churchmen" they were to be called. Although Orthodox Christians were participants, the Roman Catholic Church, by specific papal choice, was not. The Edinburgh story has been told repeatedly and well. Fortunately, by force of history, Roman Catholic attitudes changed and finally that great Christian body also became involved in the ecumenical venture.

Even as we speak of "globality," the very word "ecumenical" means worldwide, or the "whole inhabited world," and derivatively, "the whole church throughout the whole inhabited world," and further, "the whole task of the whole church throughout the whole inhabited world."

Joe, of course, became awakened to this fully when he was invited by Roman Catholics (and at their expense) to be part of the fourth session of Vatican II. Before that, Joe had been a frequent speaker at Roman Catholic Church renewal sessions, where they came to know that he and they were "on the same wave length." At Vatican II, Joe was accompanied by one of his colleagues, Fred Buss, and by me, his brother, by then a United Methodist bishop.

We stayed at a *pensione* near Vatican City, which had served as the residence of Professor Albert Outler for the four sessions of the Council, when he and Mrs. Outler lived in Rome. Indeed, he made all the arrangements and within a short time "showed us the ropes" of this great event. The plenary sessions were held in St. Peter's, and the large nave was transformed into a kind of football field with bleachers on either side to accommodate the more than two thousand bishops who took part. At the crossing near the famous statue of St. Peter and facing the Bernini altar was a section for observers and guests to take in the whole of the proceedings. Just opposite were similar seats for the cardinals. In front of the altar was a throne for the pope, from which he presided when present; in front of him were six seats from which one of a presidium of cardinals presided in turn during the pontiff's absence. Each day's business began with mass, the pope presiding on one of the days we were there. Proceedings were in Latin. Either Professor Outler or a young American priest would translate for us; our high school Latin was not up to the task. The fact that we had access to the refreshment area of the hierarchs added to the interest and allowed us to mingle with Roman Catholic bishops from many lands, and in some cases to meet old friends from India, Africa, and elsewhere.

While we were at the Council the subject came up concerning the ninety-five theses, which Martin Luther (on October 31, 1517) had nailed to the church door in Wittenberg. The very delicate question of indulgences was discussed. This was not officially one of the *schemata*, and I recall the acute embarrassment that prevailed during this discussion. It was reflected accurately to me by my interpreter. One of the bishops was frank enough to acknowledge on the floor of St. Peter's that this was the focal issue that had triggered the Reformation and that the very basilica in which they were meeting had been built largely from the sale of indulgences. No action was taken by the Council, but elaborate measures were taken to explain this subject to the press and visitors. Monsignor Gregory Baum acknowledged at that time that indulgences symbolized all that Protestants feel about Rome. Responsible intercession by the whole church for its wayward members is what indulgences mean, so said the monsignor.

This was precisely an illustration of why Vatican II was necessary. As Boston's Cardinal Cushing once remarked, "We simply *had* to have the Council." Its aim was *aggiornamente* – updating of the church in the face of the modern world. In sum, Vatican II was a modern miracle – the impossible had happened, the immobile had moved. It was a venture in international adult education *par excellence*. Just imagine what it meant for twenty-five hundred of the top leaders of a great institution to go aside for fourteen week sessions, four years in a row, to come to know one another and to sit at the feet of the greatest minds of the institution. In Rome a new morale was released, a new momentum generated. A new openness characterized the Roman church and a new opportunity confronted her.

Still, it was not so much what Vatican II accomplished that was significant, but what it made possible. Looking back over forty years, to many persons, the Council that was so exciting a generation ago has receded, and for them its aims have not been realized. Theological students today seem strangely unmoved by it, but those of us who experienced it, whether from near or far, knew that it was one of the truly significant happenings of all church history: our generation had seen God manifestly working his will in history with and through his people in an unprecedented way. The rich experience of Vatican II became a firm foundation for many relationships between the Ecumenical Institute: Chicago and Roman Catholic groups.

The second development of great significance that emerged in the 1960s was the civil rights movement. It is not surprising to find that very early Joe's interest was aroused. From boyhood on, he himself had been reared in an atmosphere congenial to racial justice. His continuing commitment to such ends was reflected through his war years and beyond.

The move of the Ecumenical Institute from "comfortable" Evanston to the West Side of Chicago was prompted in considerable measure by the evident necessity of addressing racial issues. If the urban problem in general was to be tackled it had to be done in practical approaches to the most virulent forms of urban ills present in their new West Side setting. (It should be mentioned also that the Brethren Seminary being relocated to suburban Chicago was more than glad not to be seen as deserting the city. It was turning over its property to a group whose aim was to address this urban blight.)

One of the first tasks undertaken was to create a theologically grounded course in racial understanding. This was undertaken largely by the efforts of Joe and his close colleague Gene Marshall. Black members of the Order were also fully engaged. It was understood from the beginning as no mere academic exercise but rather as one leading to a comprehensive and concerted effort at practical ghetto renewal.

Nor was the EI team removed from the action of the movement as it manifested itself under the leadership of Dr. Martin Luther King, Jr., in the South in the spring of 1965. One of Joe's colleagues, Charles Lingo, writes of EI's involvement:

> Joseph Wesley Mathews' involvement with the Civil Rights movement in Chicago began early after their arrival. He and Gene Marshall created a statement made and/or document concerning issues of racial justice, and they created a course that they offered in the spring of 1965, around Easter, when they were already on the west side of the city.
>
> It was this direct involvement in the activities of Selma, Alabama, and all that this meant which led directly to what came to be known as the Fifth City Project.

Lingo continues:

> Joe's investment in the Fifth City Project was his structural approach to racial justice. He believed that the protest approach to legal segregation that had been effective in the South needed a modification toward concrete on-the-ground demonstration of comprehensive change in the structures of local ghetto community living, by the residents who lived in such impoverished circumstances, and who themselves had to experience the transformation of their own victimization by developing leadership among themselves as they step-by-step learned how to create a reformulated community.
>
> Joe advocated the Fifth City Model of Community Reformulation before the U.S. Congress and argued to keep it distinct from other collaborative approaches. EI staff attended and participated in dialogue with other racial justice efforts in Chicago during 1966-68. But JWM's [Joe's] influence toward the developing of a specifically local model for social and racial justice was guided by the intent to serve global priorities of the Church in its various worldwide concerns to alter human suffering in local communities. He followed a path that moved through civil rights concerns toward an approach to universal human rights.

TWO FOUNDATIONAL PROGRAMS

Fifth City Reformulation Project

Instead of attempting a sequential account of EI/ICA, I endeavor to tell of a number of the programs and projects of the Institutes. They are all interrelated, one program built on another; experience gained in one activity feeds into another. The totality of all these activities is startling.

The Ecumenical Institute: Chicago – EI, as it was familiarly called – offered four emphases: study or research, worship, order, and mission. Each element was of great importance. All effort was for the sake of mission and the mission or task was under constant revision. Here was a company of committed scholars and highly motivated persons who found themselves, by circumstance and deliberate choice, in a section of Chicago's West Side which was desperately crying for attention. They all felt under compulsion to "do the necessary deed" – to endeavor to remedy the critical situation. With astounding boldness they began to address the demand before them as the "Fifty City Project."

The question was frequently raised as to how the program got its name. One account is that the section was bounded on its North by Fifth Avenue. Another more likely origin arose from sociological terms: the downtown or center city, the inner city, suburbia, and exurbia (beyond the suburbs and in the instance of "strip cities" linking up with another exurbia of a neighboring city. In addition, within the city were various communities which did not neatly fit those categories and were deemed a fifth dimension of an urban complex – hence, Fifth City.

George Walters, a longtime staff in the Fifth City Human Development Project, contributes the following from his experience:

> The "fifth dimension" was that of "those who care" deeply about their community and have engaged themselves as the "structural revolutionaries" to take responsibility for rebuilding their communities by addressing the needs of the people and institutions in their communities for the humanizing and civilizing tasks in the world today. These communities were a sign of possibility to "those who care" in the rest of the communities of the

world who too could assume this responsibility. This fifth dimension was far more than an ideology, but included developing the transferable methods and practical approaches that other communities could use.

This basic project and program of EI/ICA was really a centerpiece of the efforts of the Institutes. It was always central to Joe's thinking. He showed great pride in it until his dying day.

It has seemed to me proper that another voice should be heard in describing this fundamental venture in pursuit of true humanness in what had been a marginal and exploited part of Chicago. I asked Dr. John Epps, also a close associate of Joe's, to give an account of his recollection of the undertaking. He sent this short note on how Joe operated on a day-to-day basis. This shows Joe's operational style and is followed by a resume of the Fifth City story.

Joe functioned as a hands-on director of projects designed to develop methods that would help the local church in its service to the world.

Joe's style of operating, during the period in which I knew him, was distinctly that of the Dean of the Institute. He operated corporately and by means of consensus, yet it was he who symbolized the decisions that the group had made. Joe operated from a "cubicle," literally, in the midst of other operating functions of the institute. It was always open to anyone who chose to enter into the deliberations and planning that was taking place. Joe arrived at 5 a.m. and met with a small group of those who wished to be present for an hour. During this time, he presented his latest brooding and research into new topics. At 6 a.m., the group adjourned to the "Daily Office," a brief worship service involving Institute staff. He then joined the rest of the staff for breakfast during which a "collegium" took place exploring some topic of concern to the group. Afterwards, people "went to work." Joe completed his day in the cubicle around 2 p.m. and adjourned to his apartment for more solitary study and planning.

The Fifth City Community is a 16-block area in the heart of Chicago's West Side black ghetto. After coming from Texas and sojourning in Evanston, the EI staff moved into the ghetto as residents and helped the community leadership initiate the project.

Fifth City became a laboratory for human development. After extensive interviews and research, Joe and the staff discovered that fundamental problems in the community were not economic, though poverty was rife, but were human/ spiritual. A self-image of being victim to society pervaded the community and effectively negated all attempts at improvement. The Fifth City Project undertook to alter this victim image through a wide variety of programs. The programs included a preschool, after school associations for youth, community celebrations, a 18-foot "Iron Man" statue at the center of the community to symbolize unyielding resolve, community symbols on posters throughout the neighborhood, housing improvement efforts, a health clinic, community cleanup days, songs, tours for residents to other parts of the country and to other countries, a new shopping center, and many other efforts.

Living in Fifth City, Joe and the staff of the Institute experienced the difficulties that go along with ghetto life: regular thefts, occasional muggings, incessant noise, the presence of drugs, including of course alcohol – it was said that the life expectancy of a radio antenna on a car parked in the neighborhood was about an hour before it would become a toy sword in the hands of a neighborhood child.

Nevertheless, remarkable changes were made and were duly celebrated on two occasions by the visit of the Mayor of Chicago, who became an honorary member of the community the first time he came to congratulate residents on their efforts.

Fifth City generated unimaginable spin-offs. In the first instance, it was directly "replicated" by the initiation of Human Development Projects around the world. Secondly, Fifth City was the arena in which Joe and the staff developed participative methods that have now become the "Technology of Participation" that has been taught to more than 30,000 people around the world. Work in the preschool and with teachers in the local schools produced an approach called "Imaginal Education" that built on the work of Kenneth Boulding and provides the possibility of using images to affect the self-image and therefore the behavior of the student.

Notable learnings emerged from the project:

- Success depends on working in a limited geographical area.
- You have to deal with all the people.

- You must deal with all the problems.
- You must identify and address the underlying "spiritual" problem.
- Using symbols are key to success.

These became known throughout the Institute as the "Fifth City Principles." One other less tangible thing learned was the capacity of local citizens to care for and transform their situation. Joe had enduring respect for the people of Fifth City – Tom Washington, Lela Moseley, Ruth Carter, and many others were high on his meditative council.

In fact, Joe retained an enduring love for Fifth City and was interred with a handful of soil from the neighborhood in his urn.

On one occasion, when Mayor Richard J. Daley of Chicago visited the project, on its tenth anniversary, he remarked publicly before community citizens and EI staff:

> Everyone here has accomplished much; that is why I say we thank the Lord and thank you for this fine day. There's no reason why we can't do what you've done in the next ten years and remove every slum and every blight in Chicago.
>
> Congratulations from a grateful city to fine, hardworking people who had a dream. And, Dean Mathews, may we dream and have visions because a country without vision and without dreams would be lost. I think, as you said, at no time in the history of our country have we needed wholesome and good dreams of what the future should be of our cities and our country than we need today.

RS-I (Religious Studies I)

We are sketching some of the many facets of the program of the Ecumenical Institute. RS-I, as it has been known, along with Fifth City, is one of the two things most people know about the Ecumenical Institute: Chicago. It is one of fourteen core courses which emerged over a score of years. Essentially, for Joe, it emerged from raw theological studies at Yale. It was shaped more fully during the Perkins years and then further refined in the fulfillment of the "Austin experiment." It never really ceased to reshape itself as it was taught or led by hundreds of teachers, or "pedagogues."

Basically, RS-I was an intensive forty-four hour weekend study experience. It intermingled lectures on God, Christ, the Holy Spirit, and the Church with worship and meditation, reflection, discussion, meal conversations, and decisions – all focused on what it means to live a fully human life.

A quote from a RS-I prospectus reveals the nature of the undertaking:

> What is life all about? How can I understand myself in this world? How can I genuinely and humanly participate in the activities of life? How can I be and act so that history itself is affected? – these underlying questions determine deep human development. The ultimate aim of RS-I is to understand the meaning of the Christian Gospel for our lives in the 20th century. The course is introductory to the full theological curriculum of EI and is prerequisite to the eight courses of the cultural curriculum.

Joe and EI ransacked contemporary theological literature to find short essays or study papers which shed light on the various facets of the problems of effective living. The four primary study essays for the course were by Rudolf Bultmann, Paul Tillich, Dietrich Bonhoeffer, and H. Richard Niebuhr.

Tens of thousands have been awakened and have become more authentically human by going through RS-I. It is amazing that, as a validated experiment, it is applicable in any culture throughout the earth. It is a new form of evangelism for the 20th century. It was basic to EI involvement and program.

CORPORATE RESEARCH AND STUDY METHODS

It has been constantly emphasized that the basic secret of EI/ICA lay in its corporate nature. The Order:Ecumenical (O:E) was central. Once my brother asked me what I thought held the group together. I replied, "Discipline." He was not displeased with my response, but he would have been more pleased had I said, "Corporateness." Of course corporateness and discipline belong together.

They are in fact a unity, and the combination forged a oneness in the Order. This fact was so integral that Joe did not stand out as the sole leader. Each and every awakened and devoted member realized that he/she was in charge of the whole group. This was the intention and all members sought to make it a reality. To illustrate this I cite wisdom from Lao Tzu in ancient China:

> Leaders are best when people barely know they exist, not so good when people obey and acclaim them, worst when people despise them. Fail to honor people, they fail to honor you. But of good leaders who talk little, when their work is done, their aim fulfilled, people will all say: "We did this ourselves."

A dramatic instance of this was that very early in their experience, when EI determined to take seriously the urban issue, they understood how very little they really knew about the matter. Therefore, they borrowed from libraries in the city almost every available volume which would shed light on the subject. Corporately they read most of the relevant literature. Then participants were assigned to write a one-page précis of the assigned volumes. The total came to about five hundred pages (a little reminiscent in size of a metropolitan yellow pages directory). Then they had repeated seminars for discussion and charting their findings. Thus, corporately, in a short while they had "wrapped themselves around" the formidable topic.

Charting Method

The word "charting" has just been used. This became a fundamental method and lent itself readily to corporate study. Here is a short summary of the method:

> The most important thing about studying a paper or book is to get hold of the patterns and structure that the author uses. This is to move beyond the content to what actually is in the author's mind.
>
> 1. Concentrate on the whole of the paper much as you would a picture. This produces a gestalt for you.

      a.   Scan through the paper (or table of contents, if one). Look for the author's major breaks and subdivisions.

      b.   Run fingers through paragraphs. See what words, enumerations, etc., jump out at you.

      c.   Go through and number the paragraphs. Lay out a chart horizontally on a piece of paper.

      d.   Read the conclusion, and the paragraphs before and after the divisions.

      e.   Circle the important words.

      f.   Find key paragraphs where the structure and/or thesis is laid out.

      g.   As yet you are not interested in content but only the topical headings

2.   Relate the paragraphs and topics.

3.   Read and sum up the paragraphs. Do not start necessarily with the first paragraph, but those that set the topics up and the structure out. Then complete all paragraphs.

4.   Further relate the paragraphs and the topics to refine your structure until a final gestalt comes.

5.   In your own words write a brief proposition stating what is in each paragraph, each section of your structure and finally for the whole paper.

6.   Retitle the paper and topics in your own words.

7.   Relate the final topics and propositions to other writers and your own self-understanding.

8.   Analyze and criticize the author in relation to #7.

Charting should be done from left to right (in our language) in order that your eye may help your mind grasp the structure. The above method and example, which is detailed for illustrative purposes, may look laborious, but actually saves time. With a little practice the summaries can be shortened to what is the important thing in a paragraph or body of work, giving you a memorable holding image for the whole.

Charting reveals the structure of an article or book and permits dialogue with the whole rather than concentration on any part. The method requires one to make decisions about the article at every step and so to enter into a give-and-take relationship rather than a passive reading.

This corporate approach lay at the bottom of every EI program and was one of the secrets of its power. Charting could become elaborate almost to the point of a fine art. It was found that a determined group could chart out almost anything and the procedure resulted in a focus on the heart of a matter. Also, the Institute used "flow-charts" and "mind maps"; "social triangles," as they named them, enabled a group to analyze a complex economic-political-cultural issue effectively.

Corporate Writing

Another aspect of corporate methodology had to do with *corporate writing*. We shall return to this more fully in the discussion of Human Development Projects, but at a more elementary level consider the composition of a speech or short article. This can be illustrated by what was called the "four by four" or "three by three." It involved an analytical approach to any given subject. First of all, the topic was broken down into three or four main points. Then each of these points could be separated into three or four sub-points. All these could be arranged in order. The chart really became an outline for dealing with the subject. Then one merely had to clothe each point and sub-point with appropriate phrases. As complex as that may sound, it was sure to produce clarity of expression. To this can be added rhetorical shadings of force and beauty. Even the most inarticulate member of a group was enabled quickly to become a more effective writer or speaker. This became a thoroughly road tested method of corporate study and action. It was as if every discussion of this group approach could be applied to every program.

PROGRAMS OF INCLUSIVITY

Global Women's Forum

The note of inclusive society has been sounded worldwide in recent decades. It was heard "loud and clear" by EI/ICA and, in turn, it increased the volume on a global scale. This has already been alluded to in discussion of the Austin experiment. Racial inclusivity was at the forefront of the Fifth City Project. As well, inclusivity related to the women's revolution. Joe's wife, Lyn, was deeply involved in this emphasis.

Though integral to many aspects of the Institute's offerings, it was by definition at the heart of what came to be known as Global Women's Forum. I cannot do better than to cite a document of that title which was ten years in the making:

> Women of every nation and circumstance are today part of what has been called the Female Revolution. Self-consciousness about this revolution varies widely; but generally it can be said that there is a gulf between the emergence of a new sense of selfhood resulting from this revolution and authentic modes of engagement in society. Roles also vary greatly within any given society, such as between educated and uneducated or urban and rural women. There are external structural impediments to full social engagement, such as legal restrictions on jobs, property-holding and education. Likewise, there are objective blocks of tradition which associate women solely with home tasks, burden bearing, nursing, subsistence farming or other designated roles. In addition, there are the more internal hindrance perpetuated by women's own image of self-depreciation or by their unwilling-ness to risk taking responsibility for shaping either society or new patterns of womanhood. Obviously, there is pain and pathos for and among women themselves today, as they are denied par-ticipation in the total society, either because of structural injustice or their own decision. But perhaps the more profound tragedy lies in society's cry for leadership to deal with the com-plex social issues while at the same time being denied the unique human creativity of much of the female population of the globe.
>
> Global Woman's Forum is a one-day program designed to maximize women's participation in the 20th century world. It ac-knowledges and affirms the burst of consciousness and creativity present among women everywhere today. Whatever their age or role, pictures of new possibility are offered. This forum is de-signed to enable women across the world to choose priorities for their lives within the context of our total society's needs. It also provides a collegial bond among women of diverse backgrounds and nationalities as they encounter the pressing issues in their own communities and society as a whole. Part of women's cur-rent self-consciousness is related to the creation of stories about

womanhood that go beyond outmoded images of their role. The experience of the forum allows each woman to create that new story and begin to think through positive new directions for her life.

Global Women's Forum does not presuppose the issues or the answers that will be generated during the day. Its methods combine the concerns of the individual with the wisdom of the group. In the morning session, the opening talk provides a framework for each woman to look at her own life with its unique relationships and responsibilities. In the dialogue that follows, major blocks to woman's authentic participation in society are identified. The morning workshop discerns areas of needed social change before small units meet to talk through the direction of present trends. At lunch the conversation centers on the qualities of women from the past who have had an influence on the individual participants. Then the afternoon begins with a contextual talk focusing on 20th century social challenges and responses. The workshop following examines possibilities for employing women's creativity and care. During the plenary session, the group suggests specific and practical steps toward engagement. The forum closes with group reflection on the day.

In sum, the program emphasizes individual authenticity for women and then moves toward the power which is generated corporately and collectively by women who have been awakened. It has often been observed that in race relations when awakened people of color confront their white counterparts, the latter are likewise challenged and prompted to awakenment as well. So too the same dynamic may be seen at work when authentic women confront their male counterparts who are encouraged to experience their own fullest humanity. Thus the whole of humanity benefits. This truth was under constant demonstration in the 1970s and until today.

Groups of women brought together under the aegis of the Global Women's Forum often engaged in odysseys to many parts of the world. Once such a group visited with Indira Gandhi when she was Prime Minister of India. She listened to them intently and then spoke to them with enthusiasm, for she immediately sensed the powerful truth they were expressing. She said, "You know, every man and woman has more to offer then they can possibly imagine, yet they are not called upon to share. You may take it for granted that everyone is waiting to be asked to give themselves away in the service of some real human concern." What an insight and assertion!

The programs of EI/ICA may be seen as experimentation in an array of awakenment and educational endeavors. Every program was a response to some felt need which was not being addressed in society. The Institute took these matters seriously, addressed them with astonishing persistence and intentionality, as well as with an amazing success rate.

An effort will not be made here to pursue the various dimensions in depth. This is illustrative of the need – mentioned repeatedly – that a thorough examination of these matters needs to be undertaken in depth by competent and objective scholars. The raw material for their exploration is abundant.

ASPECTS OF EDUCATION

We shall touch lightly on three aspects which particularly relate to education.

Imaginal Education

Throughout the many efforts at educational renewal which have been undertaken by EI/ICA, there runs a common thread, what they call "imaginal education." This approach was suggested by a seminal work of Kenneth Boulding, *The Image: Life in Knowledge and Society*. He was always given credit for this transforming insight. Stated basically it insists that:

  a. Human beings operate out of images.
  b. These images determine behavior.
  c. These images can change
  d. When images change, behavior changes, and as a result people change.

This may be illustrated in an individual sense by the example of self-worth. If one has low expectations, a cap is placed upon one's achievements. A "can't do" attitude persists. Or this can happen with respect to a community. A village in Egypt, El Bayad, is often cited as typical. It was the accepted reality or image in El Bayad that no water was available from wells; hence, there were no wells. Change the image to "there *may* be water." When they drilled, they found water and new forms of agriculture and health became possible – the community changed. Imaginal education opens the possibility of a new way of seeing. A new world is born. Taken seriously and applied seriously, imaginal education is the result. EI/ICA acted upon this insight as affording universal truth and an effective education method for any situation.

The Institute has employed imaginal education as a basic method for all their religious and social projects and programs. They have developed courses and curricula of imaginal education, and have influenced education globally.

The Global Academy

A comprehensive curriculum, embracing all EI/ICA methodologies gradually emerged. Dr. Marilyn Crocker, an Order:Ecumenical member, describes the offering in these terms:

> The Global Academy was first offered in 1968 as an 8-week program of the Ecumenical Institute. It "packaged" the comprehensive curriculum – the religious and cultural studies courses plus methods courses (intellectual, social and spirit methods) – as an intensive, residential leadership training program. The Academy was always a "work in progress." Its construct and content were revised on an ongoing basis to incorporate the most recent theoretical and practical research. Eventually the Academy was offered three times a year: winter, spring and fall. The work of the summer Research Assemblies as well as the Institute's demonstration programs – originally Fifth City and later the Human Development Projects – significantly influenced the Academy curriculum during the '70s and early '80s. A further influence was the participant pool itself, initially comprised of North American lay and clergy in the late '60s. By the early '80s, men, women, and students from as many as twenty nations and many different religious orientations participated.
>
> As an example, participant statistics from the Report of the 35th Global Academy (spring 1982) documents 110 people par-

ticipated, representing 19 nations, on 6 continents, and 4 major religions: Buddhism, Islam, Hinduism and Christianity; 59 women, 51 men; 4 from Phase I (20 years and younger); 77 from Phase II (21-40 years); 20 from Phase III (41-60 years); 7 from Phase IV (over 60 years); 54% from the U.S., 46% from other countries. Participants included a young Muslim scholar from Egypt concerned with rural village development; a retired Anglican pastor from New England with years of inner city experience; a recent high school graduate and several college students; a Roman Catholic nun; a Sri Lankan Buddhist pre-school teacher; a New York business executive; a Boy Scout Master; the principal of a theological college in the Pacific Basin; a consultant from Mozambique; a teacher from Korea, and many others.

A total of sixteen modules were included into the curriculum. It is a bold and transformational pedagogical training experience.

University 13

Under the canopy of imaginal education, University 13 is an astonishing concept. A scholar speaking of the 20th century asserted, "A rough and ready description of a college education is to seek the truth." Everybody needs a college education but everyone cannot go to college. Would it be possible to make up for this educational deficit for those who possess the latent intellectual ability? EI/ICA responded affirmatively and developed a program to achieve this end.

Sometimes it is said that a college education is the residue remaining for a college graduate when he/she has forgotten everything ever learned. Aside from specific professional skills, there appears to be a kind of deposit or cultural formulation that may be grasped in the intellectual and social life of the university. This is the focus of University 13—thirteen weeks of concentrated and selective educational experience for mature persons—a project which endeavors to supply this "deposit." As stated by the Institute:

All who are intellectually capable, not some, must be equipped to engage authentically in the determination of the future because the future of us all is their future. They must be privy to the social memory, to the current wisdom, and to the operating patterns of our society so that they may effectively participate on a variety of levels in the decision making processes that determine their destiny. They must be given the real opportunity to share in the general models of 20th century thinking, to recognize the overarching issues that face humankind today, and to possess the broad tools that enable one to release his/her thrust into the determination of the drama of humanity.

The thirteen week course was in fact devised and road-tested. It aimed at conveying the "essence" of many disciplines. One could wish that organized labor would put its weight behind such a proposal. If this experience of intellectual growth could be added to vocational training, the society at large would benefit immensely.

PROGRAMS USING THE INDICATIVE PLANNING METHOD

By "indicative planning" EI/ICA meant building out of the real stuff of one's situation rather than planning by theoretical objectives. What is the early education indicative in a village of 150? Trained village mothers to help lead the preschool program, not accredited teachers from outside the village. That is a "good idea" that will probably not be implemented by the basically poor residents. The following programs – HDP Consult, LENS, and Town Meeting – are examples of the Institute planning method used by thousands around the world to help them help themselves, whether they be villages, organizations, or urban communities.

Human Development Project Consult

We have already described in some detail the innovative program of community reformulation in Fifth City, Chicago. This venture came to be seen as a paradigm that could be pursued anywhere. So it was that EI/ICA went about replicating the Fifth City model, initially in twenty-four communities – one in each of the twenty-four time zones around the world. The symbolic force of such a program was nothing less than colossal. Every hour was "high noon" in some human development project around the globe.

One might hastily conclude that this would be possible only by ignoring cultural differences and in fact demonstrate cultural imperialism. Not so! In truth, the cultural stamp of each project maintained its unique character. The methodology for devising the program was found to be universally applicable, but the resulting program was *sui generis*. In other words, no program was imposed on any community. The content was entirely local, though the methodology was universal.

> Human Development Projects demonstrate that local socio-economic development is possible with grassroots engagement. Indeed, without that engagement, it is not. Each project began with a 5-day "consult" in which a strategic 5-year plan was developed by the community. Participation by a large segment of the community was assured by interviews and public meetings so that the project gained ownership by those who would benefit from it directly. There was also participation by outside professionals who, at their own expense, traveled to remote villages and urban areas to contribute their expertise to the development of the community. This proved immensely beneficial, not only to the communities, but also to the professionals from all sectors of society who found this a way to act on their care for the world. Many stayed in touch with the communities they had advised and provided ongoing assistance to the programs.

This writer was a participant in the emergence of one such Human Development Project (HDP) in the town of Pace in the Mississippi Delta country. It was a memorable experience for all who took part. I also had the privilege of visiting several other projects: Maliwada in India; Termine in Italy; the Isle of Dogs in London; Kawangware in Nairobi; and one in Hokkaido, Japan. Each encounter was a unique and thrilling experience for the observer and a transforming one for the communities involved.

Human Development Projects were reflections of Fifth City but completely adapted to the various cultural settings in which they were located.

At the five-day consult, typically about two hundred persons were involved using the indicative planning methodology. The work was intense and full involvement was insisted upon. The first day was devoted to determining the *practical vision* or collective dream of the community. Every one in the community was canvassed. Their various suggestions were tabulated in a "brainstorm" manner. The data – often up to two or three hundred items – were then gestalted, that is, the varied items were scanned to relate those data similar in nature, using some symbol (i.e., a star, a circle, a square). Grouped data were marked by a common symbol and written into paragraphs. No item was lost. The result was an essay which embodied the collective vision of the community's future. Every participant could claim ownership and the results were invariably startling, for participants see an articulation of their common hopes and dreams.

The second day dealt with the question: Why is our future vision not being realized? What is standing in the way? A careful examination of the various blocks was tabulated in detail. These "rocks in the middle of the road" were numerous – some economic, some political, some social, some due to pure lethargy or stubbornness, some by entrenched customs, and so on. This step was always highly revealing of the nature of their local problems. Looking at these data, the participants were asked to look at them as a whole and give names for the *underlying contradictions*, the deep structural reasons why their vision was not coming to be. These data were also tabulated and written up. This was experienced as a heavy day, the community confessing what is restraining it.

The third day concentrated on *strategic proposals* to remove the roadblocks. This was usually a very awakening experience, because local people were surprised at their own ability to do creative thinking. As they began to "see light at the end of the tunnel," their spirits rose.

Nevertheless, a proposal is merely a good idea and its mere statement accomplishes little. The fourth day was therefore crucial. The task was "to put legs on the proposals," to translate them into tactics – doable activities – which could bring about what those gathered proposed. These were formulated into *tactical systems*. Now the dynamic of the procedure began to be evident. The tactics – all performed together – set the proposals in motion which in

turn gradually worked through the roadblocks so that their collective vision might be realized. This day was also devoted to
organizing programs that included, of course, personnel to perform
the tactics to seek the necessary funds – either locally or outside
resources.

On the fifth day, while the staff and auxiliary created the five-
year plan booklet, the participants cleaned up the community and
set the stage –literally – and dressed up for a special initiating
celebration, which recognized their common accomplishments and
hosted and listened to dignitaries who were crucial to implementation. The five-year plan book was presented to each participant or
family. A community story, song, and symbol were presented, with
the help of the children of the community, who often were part of a
newly initiated preschool program that week, if none had existed
before. All present were deeply moved during the celebration,
whether they lived there, had been there for the week, or were
there for only the closing celebration.

The Institute staff were experienced in the methods and helping
facilitate those gathered to consense on their best intuitive wisdom
about their past, present, and future to organize their thinking into
practical form for implementation. John Epps states some of the
practical principles at work:

Regard the local community as an isolated economic entity.
1.   Bring money in.
2.   Close the "exit" routes through which money would
     be drained immediately from the community.
3.   Circulate it rapidly within the community.
4.   Relate to the larger economy from a position of ad-
     vantage.

Community organization also played a large part in each
project. Residents were offered the opportunity to participate in
various "guilds" that undertook the projects that were proposed
in their consultation. Residents were also organized into "stakes"
that were geographically delineated and provided a system for
caring for each resident.

Joe was addressed in India when, after visiting a successful
project, a government official said to him, "Anyone can do one

village project. I have 5,000 villages to care for." This challenge led Joe to initiate a "replication" scheme that involved 232 villages in the state of Maharashtra, India. It was a comprehensive scheme involving extensive training of local residents in basic methods of local development, assisting them to conduct village consultations and initiate local improvements. A subsequent replication scheme was undertaken in Kenya. Indonesia practiced a modified version involving clusters of villages around central projects. Finally, probably nobody knows how many Human Development Projects have been initiated by the Institute.

The HDP model of sociological analysis and planning is highly adaptable to many uses. This writer has seen it applied to agricultural projects in Zimbabwe and evangelistic endeavors in the United States. We will touch briefly on two other adaptations, namely, the LENS and Town Meeting programs.

LENS

LENS, the second program using the indicative planning method, is an acronym for Living Effectively in the New Society. (Sometimes this was interpreted as Leadership Effectiveness and New Strategies.) The HDP approach presupposes a basic religious orientation, termed Religious Studies I, which EI taught to church-related groups. LENS can be seen as resting upon what could be termed a secular base, but which nevertheless recognizes universal religious overtones and could use local religious insights.

John Epps states the essence of the LENS method:

> During the early 70s, Joe began the search to extend the impact of the Institute. A huge audience was not being reached by the Religious Studies I course that EI taught to church-related groups. LENS was the result.
> This 44-hour workshop is designed for 100 people at a time and focuses on assisting people to grasp their responsibility for the societal issues they face. It is a multi-pronged workshop that has people working in teams on various tasks, including analyses of the economic, political, and cultural realms of society. It helps participants develop a shared vision of the future; identify social contradictions that are blocking the vision; develop strategies

and action plans for implementing renewal; create a story that captures the meaning of the times, a song that celebrates the group's resolve, and a symbol that expresses the commitment of the group.

Joe led a large team of people, including Institute staff and volunteers from the private sector, in developing this course. While it is impossible to specify just when the research began – since it drew from insights gained in the Fifth City project and built heavily on the Social Process analyses begun in 1971 by the Institute – it was clear that Joe demanded nothing less than excellence in its design and packaging. Numerous weekends were spent in concentrated task forces developing segments of the course. More weekends were spent in rehearsing and refining the design.

LENS workshops involved groups in team efforts that contributed to a total group output through workshops, discussions, celebrations, and talks. There was always input from the course leaders, but the products of the deliberations were the creation of participants.

One insight of the work on LENS was that people, when seriously involved in effective work on caring for society, experienced a profound dimension of life that had been concealed. Joe often spoke of this as a "religious" seminar, contrasting it to Religious Studies I as a "secular" course. What he meant was that in LENS people come to realize the profound dimension to ordinary experience and find ways to symbolize it. In RS-1, people discover the practical, secular meaning of the Gospel.

Joe supervised the creation of materials for LENS courses. They involved extensive decor packages, exquisite participant workbooks, and poster worksheets for teams. In this creation, Joe never compromised on quality, and the course actually did provide an experience of excellence for participants.

Once LENS was ready, Joe initiated a series of treks conducting the course in various locations around the world. After each trek, the team returned and held extensive debriefings. The course was modified and refined and sent out again.

The move to LENS marked a period of "turn to the world" in the life of the Institute. Prior to 1973, the work of the Ecumenical Institute/Institute of Cultural Affairs was primarily through the church with the aim of discovering ways for the church better

to serve the world. In 1973, Joe led the Institute in making a shift
– doing an "end run," as he called it – in which ICA would develop signs of effective societal care through its network or
movement, with the expectation that they might become labora-
tories and models for the church to follow. LENS represented
that care in and for the primary sector. The HDP's represented
that care in and for the local sector.

Town Meeting

In 1976, as the Bicentennial of the United States was approaching,
ICA developed another program which used its methods with considerable effectiveness. It was called Town Meeting. Basically it
was a program of social awakening. Of course, the Town Meeting
was an approach used historically in American history for planning
and implementing plans for community betterment.

In format, Town Meeting, created by the ICA in a wide-
reaching use of its indicative planning method, was a one-day
workshop which used the basic methodology underlying HDP consults and LENS. A community discerned their vision, roadblocks,
and proposals. They also created a story, song, and symbol for the
closing celebration.

An effort was made to hold a town meeting in at least every
county in the U.S.A. Essentially this goal was more than met.
Same for Canada. In all, well over 5,000 such gatherings, called by
different names, were facilitated by the ICA network globally. Collectively, the impact was profound. The follow-up varied from
place to place. At the very least this was a social demonstration of
great potential and pointed the way for any community bent on social transformation, showing immense possibilities generated by
ordinary people who yearn for community transformation.

In this chapter we have reviewed only a few of the courses and
programs of EI/ICA. Originally, Ecumenical Institute programs
were directed toward persons and groups dedicated to the renewal
of the Church for the renewal of the world. Members of the Or-
der:Ecumenical, the core group of the EI, saw under Joe's
leadership that they did not necessarily need to wait for the church

to become aroused to its mission of awaking humanness every-where. Therefore, EI developed a secular arm called the Institute of Cultural Affairs (ICA), which was free to directly address this lar-ger mission.

The Other World in This World

Let me mention one last endeavor of the many the Institute created and shared globally. This one pointed the way toward the "recov-ery of the other world." Joe nearly always said that he simply stumbled on to this "discovery-invention." As long ago as 1942, in *Theology Today,* Professor H. Richard Niebuhr wrote an essay in which he stated that humankind lives in two worlds, and whenever we attempt to reduce life to either one alone, something goes seri-ously wrong. During the first half of the 20th century, things clearly went seriously wrong, particularly for Western peoples. It was simple enough in the name of the scientific worldviews to dump the myths which enlivened humanity for centuries, but a costly price was to be paid. People live at one ordinary, everyday level, but religious insights and their accompanying stories point to a depth level where the meaning of human significance abides or is rooted. From time to time human consciousness is illuminated so that the "deeps of life" are glimpsed. Then significant existence is realized and life is expressed in all its fullness and authenticity. It was this phenomenon that EI/ICA explored in great detail under the insistent probing and prodding of Brother Joe. (See "Recovery of the Other World," a talk given by Joe in *Bending History.*)

As I write I look up to a picture frame of four parts: a some-what barren and isolated landscape; a winding river; a rugged mountain; a tossed yet tranquil sea. These are elements of a topog-raphy of "The Other World in the midst of this world." These come to be metaphors for the profound experiences in the human journey in search of authentic depths, awakening in

1. *The Land of Mystery*: awesome wonder
2. *The River of Consciousness*: radical freedom
3. *The Mountain of Care*: profound love
4. *The Sea of Tranquility*: unspeakable fulfillment

In the Order:Ecumenical and the ICA, these four elements were analyzed, divided, and then divided again into identifiable states of being. They afforded a means of articulating the total experience of profound humanness. They could be described accurately as a New Religious Mode, which when applied to the societal task afforded a New Social Vehicle. This discovery offers immense power and possibility for people as individuals and groups throughout the world. It becomes yet another way in which the Institutes were empowered for effective mission themselves, and another way for them to be empowering agents in the world.

Joe saw to it that O:E, EI, and ICA were and are a corporate adventure. He was more than happy to have it so. Behind it all was the sometimes bleeding body of Brother Joe, who was willing to give his all – to become a nobody – on behalf of all humankind.

11
JOURNEY'S END

It may seem to the reader that the preceding chapter was a kind of *excursus* from the story of Joe Mathews's journey. But, not so! O:E/EI/ICA were clearly the lengthened shadow of Joe. This is nowhere more evident than in the 2005 book *Bending History: Selected Talks by Joseph W. Mathews,* a compilation of some thirty of Joe's addresses or "talks," as he preferred to call them. Few speakers have more completely or consistently pulled back the curtain and allowed others to examine his inner life. The story of the Order and the Institutes is Joe's story as well.

Personal Life during the Chicago Years

Joe had a personal life to live. He was married to Lyn and increasingly she became his colleague and almost his alter-ego. Recall how her letters during war years revealed how much she yearned for more learning. Well, it happened and she grew in intellectual and spiritual stature, so that she could play the role of master teacher in the Institute's courses. Later on, after Joe's death, she became a kind of the prioress of the continuing Order:Ecumenical. As a leader she found a way of being her own person. Through the years, under conditions that externally seemed impossible, these two built a marriage and a family.

They were parents of three sons. A volume could be written about children of the Order. Very often Joe was castigated about this very matter. No doubt some children were damaged by their experience. In many respects, however, they were privileged to have the advantages of cross-cultural living. Some naturally adjusted better than others. When I have asked young Joe and Jim, their two living sons, about this, they have ordinarily responded affirmatively: though life was hard, life was good in the Order. It is certain that father Joe was there for them in crises. Like every parent he could recount the many times that he had to snatch them back from the brink, so to speak. I have seen him set aside other demands while he taught them to fly a kite, to play a game, to just be with them. I know the agony he went through when he learned of the tragic death of their youngest son, John. I was with Joe at the time in Utrecht in the Netherlands. I heard repeatedly his agonizing cry in the night: "Oh, John." Yes, he had his own painful life to live and death to die.

There were other wrenching family losses along the way. After decades in the family of which he was a part, without a death, on November 9, 1961, his own father died. Joe has told the story on the finest piece of writing he ever penned: "The Time My Father Died." First published in *Motive* magazine, it has been reprinted many times. Elizabeth Kübler-Ross praised it greatly. Though he was gifted with a clear, bold script, writing was not his forte. Public speaking was the medium in which he was at home and at liberty. This article about his father was an exception. He wrote it with vividness, with conviction, with power. Would you like to read Joe's autobiography? Then here it is: the account of his father's death was also the story of Joe's life. Joe often noted that we all, without exception, at a funeral or memorial service, have reflected on our own life and death as well as that of the deceased.

Then on February 1, 1966, Joe's older brother, Don, died. It was Ash Wednesday. I have before me Joe's list of twenty-five brief reflections about this event. They speak of empathy, guilt, pain, longing, love, of deep indebtedness, of need to embrace, of parting; on Don's part to pick up the mystery of death, and the survivors' part to continue in the mystery of life; of fond remembrances. It was all there – uttered from the depths.

Then, in the autumn of 1967 came the death of Mama. I was abroad when Papa died, so Joe "spoke words" over him. Joe was abroad when Mama died and it fell to me to "do the needful." Ever afterwards, Joe spoke of Mama with great tenderness and unfailing respect and love.

Next came the death of Elizabeth. Lyn, years later, sent me a note she found among Joe's papers.

I saw Elizabeth today. It was for the last time. She was in her
death. Ever since the plane landed I have oscillated between
nameless despair and indefinable elation. It is like hot and cold
chills. I want at one moment to joke and laugh and be gay. It is
elation. And then I want to be alone and brood and be miserable.
Only once did I feel like crying and then only for a flash of a
fraction of a second. I have experienced a strange sense of comradeship with her. There has been no feeling of remorse or guilt
as there has been with others in death – just comradeship. What
makes this strange is that outwardly in the missional sense we
were not comrades. I have remembered that we who remain are
only five. Could it be the fellowship of death? Perhaps. Or ties of
family? Maybe. Or is it the deeply hidden spirit relation of mys-
tics?

During the Chicago years, Joe had a life to live and there were
deaths to die.

Public Life during the Chicago Years

Another dimension of Joe's ministry was his speaking and preaching. The demand was incredible as his itineration was wide-
ranging. As the years passed the pace intensified. Joe's longtime
(and long-suffering) voluntary secretary and administrative assistant, Betty Pesek, has compiled a list of his many speaking
engagements. They were mostly before college, university, seminary, and church audiences. He spoke to Protestants of every
stripe, to Roman Catholics, and very often to Jewish groups.
Sometimes he addressed civic clubs and business organizations.
Often his addresses were to church assemblies, conferences, or
ecumenical gatherings. Several times he talked before the Penta-
gon and Congressional Committees or other governmental bodies.
He never lacked for subject matter, for his work was largely of a
research nature, and a continuous stream of material was generated. He always spoke with great energy and force, often
deliberately provocative. Almost invariably people were changed
after exposure to his speaking.

Of course, his engagements for public addresses occasioned extensive travel – mostly in the United States and then beyond. As a boy he was immensely pleased to be a part of an expanding world through his journeys that carried him to the ends of the world. It began with his travel around the world with this writer and a nephew, already narrated in some detail. In another journey we traveled together to Vatican II. There were many other instances in which we two brothers itinerated together, often accompanied by some member of the Order:Ecumenical.

The trip to the Fourth Assembly of the World Council of Churches convened in Uppsala, Sweden, came during the summer of 1968. (We also visited the Fifth Assembly in 1975 in Nairobi.) In going to Scandinavia, we tarried briefly in the Soviet Union, our first venture behind the Iron Curtain. We observed the sights of Moscow, the Kremlin, cathedrals, churches, even found tickets to the Bolshoi. In our visit to some of the churches we noted the predominance of elderly women worshipping there. We were greatly stirred by the architectural wonders of Leningrad (now, once more, St. Petersburg.) We were even fortunate enough to see "Swan Lake" in the famous Kirov ballet theater. Fortunately, we were able to visit the Russian Orthodox seminary in the city.

The World Council Assembly was held in the ancient university town of Uppsala, July 4-19, 1968. It was during the Biafra War. Some 2000 representatives of more than two hundred denominations were present. Among the United Methodist delegates were Senator George McGovern of South Dakota and Congressman John Brademas of Indiana. We benefited by extensive conversations with them. They were a part of the greatly increased number of lay persons among the delegates. The presence of many more women, people of color, and Third World participants was noteworthy.

The King of Sweden graced one of the sections by his presence. Greetings from Ecumenical Patriarch Athenagoras, from Pope Paul VI, and Cardinal Bea were all most welcome. Notable addresses were given by President Kenneth Kaunda of Zambia and by Lady Jackson (Barbara Ward), who spoke eloquently on "Rich and Poor Nations." Lord Caradon and novelist James Baldwin spoke against racism. "Pete" Seeger entertained the delegates at night with his music. Roman Catholic presence and participation was noteworthy. Martin Luther King, Jr., had been asked to deliver the principal sermon. His tragic assassination in April 1968 cast something of a pall over the occasion. Sri Lankan Methodist D.T. Niles acquitted himself well as he substituted in the high pulpit as preacher. Quite appropriately the worldwide scourge of racism was placed in sharp focus. The Assembly's theme was "All Things New" – and not a moment too soon!

During the Assembly, Joe absented himself for three days to journey alone by train from Uppsala to the "Land of the Midnight Sun." He always referred to this experience in later years as awe inspiring in the extreme. Just imagine, there was no night there!

The following year, Joe was able to realize a long held dream of participating in one of the prominent church renewal events of postwar Europe, the fourteenth Kirchentag, meeting in Stuttgart, July 16-20, 1969. Joe and I, together with a young pastor from Maine, the Reverend Peter Misner, and Father Robert Quinn, a Paulist priest from Boston, were invited to this session. More than thirty thousand persons attended, including a thousand visitors from overseas. A certain amount of turmoil was evident at the sessions, occasioned by a quite vocal youth protest. In 1969, Richard von Weizsacker, later West Germany's president, presided over the Kirchentag and observed sympathetically that the younger generation did not want to leave the church in the hands of the older generation, but "claims its own place in the church." All four of our small company were deeply addressed by the spirit and thrust of Kirchentag, and Peter Misner found that it greatly empowered his future ministry. We also discovered that a visit to Hans Küng in his chalet at nearby Tübingen was a lasting benefit to us. He was brimming over with hope and enthusiasm that the church might be fully renewed in our time. This visit opened the door to a larger acquaintance with the Eastern Orthodox world.

On several journeys, Joe and I were in touch with leaders of Pre-Chalcedonian Churches – Armenian, Coptic, Ethiopian, and Syrian Orthodox. One trip in 1972 took us to Cairo where we visited the highly gifted Pope Shenuda III of the Coptic Orthodox

Church (regarded as the 117th successor to St. Mark the Evangelist as Patriarch and Pope of Alexandria), and with one of his associates, Bishop Samuel, who was later killed in the terrorist attack when President Anwar Sadat was assassinated. The same tour took us to Addis Ababa to meet the Patriarch of the newly constituted Ethiopian Orthodox Church, Abuna Theophilos. One of his younger associates also later became a Bishop Samuel. He too was killed by communists. Of great interest was a circuit we had around Ethiopia. It carried us to Lalibela, a fabulous town of ancient churches, to Aksum; thence to Lake Tana – source of the Blue Nile – and its old church on an island; then back to the capital city. Later in this trip we met with one of the two Catholici of the Armenian Church, this one near Beruit, Lebanon; and the Patriarch of Antioch in Damascus. We stopped in Istanbul to pay respects to the Ecumenical Patriarch, Athenagoras I, but he was ill. These were not merely courtesy visits. They were intended to open doors – and they did – for further association with the program of the Ecumenical Institute.

Mention must be made of our invitation to Rome on the occasion of the canonization by Pope Paul VI of Elizabeth Ann Bayley Seton, the first American-born citizen to be elevated to sainthood. Some fifteen thousand Americans and thousands of others thronged St. Peter's Square for the outdoors ceremony on a sun-drenched day. The service itself was of exceeding interest. The invited Protestant clergy, including Episcopal Bishop David Leighton of Baltimore (for Mother Seton had been a convert from the Episcopal Church), were welcomed and entertained by Roman Catholic bishops. Cardinal Dearden of Detroit was gracious enough to remark, "You cannot know how much your presence means to us." The visitors were impressed and discussed how necessary saints are for the whole human family – exemplary figures through whom God "sets wrong right." If the church does not acknowledge saints, then the secular world will try to do so. Of course God makes saints; it remains for the church to identify and acknowledge them. All branches of Christendom – including Protestants – have found ways of doing this.

The recollections of "journeys with Joe" do not nearly exhaust the record showing that during the last decade of his life (1967-1977), between programs requiring his presence in Chicago, he was almost constantly on the road. This included repeated visits to every inhabited continent, not to mention islands of the sea. He led countless study groups, made contact with secular and religious leaders, sought locations for Human Development Projects, and held consults for the establishment of the same. In addition, he made repeated nurturing visits to these many demonstration centers. One who reads of these strenuous activities is almost exhausted by the experience. Joe must have empathized with St. Paul who spoke of "journeyings oft."

In 1972, I finally established the often postponed practice of keeping a daily journal, a routine followed for the ensuing thirty years. Of course, there is a record of every instance of being together with Brother Joe. The real reason for writing this biography at all has been to discharge the obligation I have long accrued, which is due to him. We were exceedingly close through the years, mutually indebted to each other, intimate, and completely open in our reciprocal relationship. There was nothing that either of us was not willing to do for the other, and this we continued until his death.

Recently I came across these words by a famous linguist: "Many of us, I believe, are guilty of letting our life, or large parts of it, slip away unlived." Not true of Joe! Once awakened, he lived life to the hilt. He knew himself to be under obligation to every last and even least human being. He truly knew that as a Christian his task was worldwide and lifelong – yea, history long – in its demand. For him, the mandate to love neighbors and even enemies was in force as long as life and health endured. He knew himself to be under a kind of life sentence. He was, I believe, a religious genius, but he would have reflected, "I am still an unprofitable servant."

Critique and Evaluation

I have made bold assertions about Brother Joe. Let me balance this by stating that I am fully aware that I am not a person who can claim unbiased judgment about my brother and the movement which he led for at least two decades. Along the way he and the Order were almost constantly under a barrage of negative criticism. On the other hand, from many quarters, including the academic fraternity, there was a good measure of affirmation. Again, Joe chose not to answer his negative critics but must have been sustained in considerable degree by those who were supportive of the endeavors.

It would be a well-deserved tribute to the people of Maliwada Village in Maharashtra to begin with their attitude toward Joe and his work. "Joe was loved by the villagers of Maliwada, and people who met him anywhere respected him because he walked the journey of humankind. People could literally feel it, as he came amongst them." Upon learning of his death a Hindu responded: "A bright star has gone out in the sky today." A Muslim: "The sun has set for a wise man, and it is a very dark time for all of us now." The imagery itself is significant. One recalls in connection with the astronomical metaphor that a critic of George Whitfield was answered by a defender: "The sun has its spots; shall we therefore try to put out the sun?"

It was often said of Joe that one loved him or hated him. There was no middle ground. In candor, I must say that from time to time I felt that he came on too strongly, but I was in a position to observe that his life, his manner, was characterized by deep earnestness. His close colleagues tell of how his directness was embarrassing, even when on visits for soliciting support. More often than not, however, the person being solicited seemed to appreciate his directness and candor. He sought not merely a donor's material aid but demonstrated a genuine interest in the donor. St. Paul says somewhere, "I sought not yours but you."

Then, there was the matter of Joe's language, which would from time to time turn to profanity. This he seemed to feel was warranted. He felt some folk needed to be shocked. Martin Luther often proved that he was not above employing quite earthy language. Tempted to feel that he would in his zeal go too far, it would dawn on me rather forcefully that his drive was for nothing less than the renewal of the church. This too was the aim of the amiable and no less earnest Pope John XXIII and his focus on *aggiornamente* – "updating" of the Roman Catholic Church. Though Vatican II went a long way in this task, it was by no means completed. Even as I write these words, news has come of the death of Pope Paul II, prompting many liberal Roman Catholic theologians to observe that renewal is still incomplete.

Sometimes there emerged the mean-spirited suggestion that the Institute promoted communist or Marxist ideology. It is true that the Order sometimes referred to themselves as constructive revolutionaries, but I have noted from various government reports that the communist label was not at all warranted or even suggested. After all, it was stated of early church leaders that they were intent on "turning the world upside down." Yet they regarded the world already to be upside down and to turn it over was merely to make it right side up!

The boldness with which the programs of the Institute moved into various parts of the world was sure to evoke criticism from various quarters on transcultural grounds. Representatives of many countries had already journeyed to Chicago or wherever programs were. They were deeply committed to the Institute methods. These persons, in turn, would help to spearhead the consultations through which various Human Development Projects were to be established. Their methodology was to use a virtually contentless approach, which imposed no specific elements upon local people. Rather, the details were drawn from local participants, who in turn dictated the detailed plans, using a maximum of local insights and resources.

Nevertheless, occasional charges were directed toward the Institute, for example from Japan, that their procedures were insensitive to cultural differences. In fact, unusual attention to and respect for the uniqueness of varied cultures was a characteristic of the studies of the Institute. Accusations of rigidity, one-sidedness, and provincialism were made. Yet, Japan, in particular, from the mid-19th century onwards, has welcomed outside influence and Western methodology. At the same time that critics of the Institute made their complaints, the Japanese invited other Western experts who were surely far less sensitive to cultural uniqueness.

Also, some complaints arose within some Roman Catholic religious orders. At first, the fear was expressed that Human Development Projects in India were "too American." Actually they found that far from being dominated by Americans, six nationalities were represented at the primary India project. The Catholic superior charged with investigating the Maharashtra initiative admitted that in advance he was quite anti-American, but after exhaustive examination, gave the program a complete bill of health. His report stated,

> I feel that the Maharashtra Project of the ICA has so many new elements in it – which I have never seen put to use by any other agency which I have read about in a whole bibliography on theories on development – brought together and put to application simultaneously, that I find this approach is worthwhile being known and that it is certainly worthy of every support.

A similar evaluation was made by Eric H. Biddle, Jr., of a Human Development Project in Mississippi:

> The Pace (Mississippi) HDP, for example, where ICA has been the catalyst in developing the agricultural and economic infrastructure in a poverty stricken Delta backwater, is a dramatic example of how well ICA's comprehensive approach can work. It is perhaps the best example I saw of community development in nine years of inspecting federally supported poverty and volunteer projects (in a special report on examination of EI/ICA, July 17, 1980). [*]

Not infrequently EI/ICA was charged with being a cult. This conclusion appears to be without merit and entirely unsubstantiated. Of all the slurs that might be leveled on Brother Joe, this seems to be the one with the least warrant. He made every effort to be a nothing. He may at times have had the limelight, but did not seek it. A cult, almost by definition, is focused upon securing large

---

[*] The writer was a participant in the consultation in Pace which formulated this project. In November 2005, with his wife, he revisited the site and discovered much evidence of its lasting transformation.

sums in support of what usually was a lavish lifestyle for its leaders. The members of the Order:Ecumenical lived under a vow of poverty and to an astonishing degree identified themselves with the poor.

Fortunately, well-informed persons who knew the facts answered such allegations. One letter, dated May 9, 1980, written by Dr. Joseph D. Quillian, Jr., Dean of Perkins School of Theology, is quoted in its entirety:

To Whom It May Concern:

I address you as above since I am moved to make a statement to you and to any others with whom you wish to share it.

It has come to my attention, with no little amazement, that the Order of the Ecumenical Institute and Institute of Cultural Affairs has been characterized as a "*cult.*" The implication is that the Order exercises close control of its members and forbids and prevents anyone's withdrawing from the Order once in it. What disturbs me is that this would seem to identify the Order of the Ecumenical Institute with various suspect cults of current notoriety.

If the above characterization were without possible harm, I would count it simply as an uninformed opinion that is downright laughable and therefore not to be taken seriously by any responsible person. However, because of my own concern with regard to some several cults that I do consider dangerous, I feel an obligation to say that it is totally erroneous to call any part of the Ecumenical Institute a cult, or to associate the Ecumenical Institute even vaguely with such company.

I would describe the Order of the Ecumenical Institute as a voluntary community of an exceptional degree of personal commitment for Christian service and living. I have known well at least twenty members of the Institute.

Joe Mathews and I were in graduate study at Yale together in the late 1940's and were with each other almost every week across a period of two or three years. In 1951, I invited him to come as dean to the small college in Tennessee, which I served as president, but he declined. In 1954, I came to the faculty of Perkins School of Theology where he already then was serving. Our offices were next door to each other. I visited him in Austin and in Chicago. I saw the Ecumenical Institute at work in those places, and in a chapter of the Institute in Dallas. In fact, we had a group of students in Perkins School of Theology in the 1960's who were related to the Ecumenical Institute and who held family worship services each afternoon at 5:00 p.m. in the building in which my office was and is.

The worldwide work of the Ecumenical Institute has been carried on with an exceptional degree of creativity and devotion, and always in full loyalty to the nature and mission of the Church. I have always felt that the Ecumenical Institute performs a notable service to the Church in venturing on ahead in sensitive and effective mission that is difficult for the larger church to undertake directly and immediately.

It is apparent that I have high regard for the Ecumenical Institute, its work and personnel. Any diminishing of the Ecumenical Institute is, in my opinion, a loss to the Church.

A similar letter was written on May 19, 1980, by Dr. W. Jack Lewis, then serving as a chaplain at Cornell University. With respect to the allegation that the Order:Ecumenical (and the Institute) is a cult, "I believe such charges are absurd." He speaks more at length about Joe and his colleagues and their work in Austin, and later on in Chicago:

I have been astounded that the vision of a worldwide mission which Mr. Mathews and others shared when we all were in Austin together has begun to materialize as they have established centers, houses, and communities on every continent. From time to time they have invited me to join them in their mission, but for family and personal reasons I have declined. They live under a self-imposed discipline as the Order:Ecumenical which enables them to do their work with a singleness of mind and heart known to few outside religious orders.

Joe Mathews, as Dean and Director of E.I. and I.C.A., was a powerful person of great conviction and brilliance. He was a Methodist through and through, which helps to account for such discernable "method" in his development on a worldwide scale. His understanding of the Christian gospel was both personal and social. The social impact of his vision and that of his colleagues can be seen in the Institute of Cultural Affairs. The I.C.A. is literally global as it utilizes lay people of many professions and skills to help village folk and ghetto dwellers to make new self-discoveries and to develop self-reliance, which stimulate life and growth and fulfillment.

The personnel and projects of I.C.A. are closely related to established churches on the various continents where they are working, especially in Africa and Latin America. I feel certain that religious leaders of different traditions are prepared to support and encourage the work of I.C.A. in their midst.

I have no doubt that the Order:Ecumenical calls for dedication and discipline and discipleship far beyond the demands of most conventional parish churches. Not everyone is prepared for such commitment any more than at the height of the missionary movement in the days of John R. Mott and Robert E. Speer when they sought to win the world for Christ in one generation. But to label what they did or what the Order:Ecumenical does today as a cult in the pseudo-religious sense characterized above is indeed preposterous, in my judgment.

Other colleagues speak of Joe's influence on their lives and beyond. John P. Cock accompanied Joe and me on a trip to Rome to visit heads of the Roman Catholic Church in 1974. He is now a writer. He sent this note with a quote from one of his books:

When I think of Joe, I remember that point in my life as a minister when the Christian symbols were not making much sense to me. I contemplated leaving the ministry. After my wife and I attended a Parish Leadership Colloquy in Virginia – and a month later attended an RS-I weekend with about fifteen laypersons from our church – our lives were changed. From that point on, the Christian symbols of God, Christ, Spirit, and Church have made profound sense to me.

The following quote is at the heart of Joe's message:

I had a chance to love the Aboriginal people in Australia. I wrote a bit of poetry – terrible poetry – but it spoke to them about the meaning of their past, including the brutality of the white man. It painted a new possibility of the future of black people across the world. It laid out the meaning of the present in terms of their real demands. That's what I mean by divine love. That's all Jesus did. He opened the future, made new the past, and filled the present full of meaning. And that's our vocation.

John Cock continues:

Years later I wrote a book about Christology (*The Transparent Event*, 2001), interpreting theologians whose Christ images make sense to me, and of course Joe is at the top of the list of some great theologians: Kierkegaard, Tillich, Bultmann, H. R. Niebuhr, Gogarten, Ogden, Sobrino, and Segundo, and others. In that book I wrote,

> *[Joe] was a revolutionary churchman who was pushing the limits of his and our self-understandings till the day he died in 1977, relentlessly trying to articulate and communicate what the two thousand years of Christianity had to do with the meaning and mission of authentic self-hood and global community. . . . I have read [Joe's]* **The Christ of History** *dozens of times and find a new insight at each reading. I have taught from it and have seen lives begin the transformative process as a result of its power. . . . [It will] continue to speak to the deeps.*

A comment about Joe's transparent style of living, from a letter from F. Nelson Stover, on the Board of ICA International, reads

> Joe saw through the particulars of life to the Universal; he embodied transparent living. Most people, at some time or another, see through the veil of the mundane and experience themselves at one with the enlivening energy of the Universe. A few of these people savor this experience and are empowered by it. A few of these people know how to make this mode of living the dominant characteristic of their lives. A few of these people know how to teach others to touch the wild Mystery of life. And, finally, a very few of these people know how to sustain those who have seen the wonder and to catalyze them into giving contemporary form to the universal presence. Joe was in this final, select, and rare group. Joe was able to convey his journey to the center of being in a language that could be understood by people of all religious persuasions. Joe made religion transparent.

When religious strife is rampant, and the religious alternative – unbridled consumerism – is
wreaking havoc on the environment and providing
little of the anticipated fulfillment to the human soul,
Joe's understandings and practices for embodying
transparent living take on a significance beyond their
time.

To conclude this section I quote from two more colleagues who
were also associated with Joe for extended periods. This is part of
a letter from Gene W. Marshall (Realistic Living, Bonham, Texas),
who worked and studied with Joe at Austin and was an early leader
with the Institute in Chicago:

I became a loyal supporter of Joe's work at the Christian
Faith and life Community in Austin, Texas. There, I attended
Joe's early version of the course which was eventually taught to
thousands under the unassuming title "Religious Studies I." The
effectiveness of this carefully crafted weekend witnessed to Joe's
genius. . . .

In 1962, this journey eventuated in a fateful choice on my
part to join, along with my wife and children, with Joe and his
family and the other families in Evanston, Illinois, to begin a
Christian family order. For the next 14 years, I lived in close
proximity to an amazing flow of Joe Mathews' creative innovations. I remember most of these innovations as mountain peaks
of transformation in my own life. For me, the highlights of this
period were (1) the methods of being a lecturer, seminar teacher,
conversation leader; (2) Joe's lecture for the Cultural Studies
course on the shift in religious metaphors from the traditional
two-story to a one-story form of religious thinking; (3) the audacity of living in a black Chicago ghetto in the 60's, with
profound respect for another race and with profound respect for
living in considerable danger; (4) Joe's lectures and charts on
Prayer, Meditation, and Contemplation, later expanded into nine
charts Joe called "The New Religious Mode"; (5) the invention
of powerful methods of reading and discussing the Bible – the
first three Gospels, and later John and the Psalms; (6) the creation of the Social Process Triangles and the whole idea of
creating a social ideology based on the spirit recovery of radical

Christianity; (7) the careful description of the dynamics of awe and the artful delineation of 64 separate states of being organized under the major headings of Mystery, Freedom, Care, and Tranquility; (8) the objectification of the methods of social planning – methods that were used in community reformulation in the Chicago ghetto and later in town meetings and community projects across the world; (9) Joe's lectures on the Ur-images – those basic "life quests" of the various cultural and religious traditions of the planet; (10) Joe's lectures on the contentless Christ, a complete de-Westernization of the New Testament breakthrough; and (11) the family order itself – here Joe led the rest of us in continually maturing our thinking on the communal and missional dynamics of movemental Christianity, studying the religious orders of traditional Christianity and redesigning the dynamics of communal life and common religious action performed by our order, a group of families that grew from seven families to hundreds of people of many backgrounds living in all parts of the planet. All these amazing things profoundly addressed my life. And I have only described the highlights. . . .

He was continually leaping out into vastly fresh, theoretical and practical directions. Most of these wild leaps had to do with giving practical form to some dimension of profound spirit. Religious Studies I was such a form. The methods of religious practice, the styles of communal life, the missional programs – all were forms created to contain and express profound spirit. Beneath Joe's restless, innovative style was his philosophy about what it means to give embodiment to spirit. Joe remarked that spirit was continually crying out, "Give me form! Give me form!" And then he explained that spirit cannot be held in any of the forms we invent to contain it. It drives on, demanding further formations. . . .

The outward forms we give to profound spirit always have a certain fragility. . . . So to be true to Joe's legacy means neither clinging to his original ways of doing things nor launching innovations that have nothing to do with giving embodiment to authentic spirit – that restless spirit which is always responding to Reality's onward march. Joe's legacy is not some residue of stable organization or some set way of doing something. And his legacy is not doing novelties that have no profound meaning. His obvious and deepest legacy is his example of audacity: being people who clearly discern the profound spirit moving in this moment of history and who in obedience to that spirit risk everything to give this spirit appropriate form. Such form will indeed be fragile, but if it gives form to profound spirit, it will shake up the lives of another generation of people and alter significantly the destiny of this planet. . . .

Joe's greatness, I believe, is most present in his theological and spirit constructions. His passion to give these constructs ethical and social realization is also part of his greatness. . . . He knew that a new form of Christianity was knocking at the door. This is perhaps the most crucial place for us to pick up his legacy and move forward. . . . This task, I believe, was the centrality of what Joe Mathews was doing with his life. . . .

The last citation comes from Dr. John Silber, a former dean of the University of Texas and later President of Boston University.

I met Joseph Mathews shortly after I left Yale to join the faculty of the University of Texas at Austin. As I recall, he and I both arrived in Austin in 1955 and were "new boys" to the campus. As a churchman, Joe had no official faculty position at the University of Texas. It was a secular institution with no department of religion and no university chaplains. Rather, it was a largely secular campus of about 25,000 students. There were several churches situated around the campus or not too distant from it. The Presbyterian church and the Methodist church were located immediately adjacent to the campus. The Episcopal church was only a block or so away, and about a quarter of a mile from the campus was the First Baptist church. Despite the proximity of these churches and the fine quality of many of the ministers who led them, none had any dramatic impact on the campus of the University. It wasn't long, however, before Joe Mathews created something of a religious revival. It wasn't a tub-thumping revival or one to be associated with evangelism or, in today's terminology, the religious right. It was, rather, a spiritual and intellectual revival as he invited students to a recognition of a religious dimension to their lives, and in a sense he pushed them to new depths of intellectual search and spiritual awareness. He shocked the congregation of the First Baptist Church by throwing the large pulpit Bible to the floor. He then reminded them that we do not worship objects of leather and paper and that to do so is idolatry.

He abhorred disciples, but he had eager followers. A spiritual pied piper, he attracted students to him who simply thirsted after the knowledge and spiritual insight he offered. It is hard to imagine that in only two or three years he created the Christian Faith and Life Community. He purchased a large house on 19th Street, as a residence for students and also as a venue for the programs he developed.

I became aware of his work because students in my classes would tell me about him. It was clear that many of my students were also students of his, and I was delighted to discover that he was assigning very fine and difficult reading. He assigned them books and essays by Reinhold and Richard Niebuhr and by Kierkegaard, authors whose works I thought were important for students, particularly in an age that was increasingly secular in orientation. His courses were as demanding and rigorous as any taught at the University. If those who participated in his program did not wish to study hard and complete writing and seminar responsibilities, they could not survive. But their thirst was sufficient to prompt their seeking for several years the enlightenment his program offered.

He and I in our separate ways, I in philosophy and he in the Christian Faith and Life Community, became increasingly visible on campus and increasingly interesting to our student body. The student YMCA immediately adjacent to the campus was a center for lectures on current issues. The Y invited Joe Mathews and me to debate one another. The assumption was that I would be the voice of secularism and he the voice of Christianity. Indeed, that is how it was interpreted by then-Dean of the Graduate School, Professor Brogan, and by the Chancellor of the University, Logan Wilson. Subsequent to our debate, I was asked by Wilson, "Why, if you had to preach atheism, did you do it at the Y?" The formulation of his question deeply offended me, because as a matter of fact I had defended a more traditional interpretation of Christianity that was perhaps less meaningful to the students than the existentialist version of Christianity presented by Mathews. Since the question was formulated that way, I offered a response much in the Joe Mathews mode. Why, if I had to teach atheism, did I do it at the Y? I responded, "They were the only ones who asked me."

Sometimes the shock approach seemed to be the only approach by which to get people to think, and Joe Mathews was certainly willing to take the risks that go with that approach. At the debate at the University Y, he presented Christianity as the answer to an existential question. As a Christian, one could stand at the brink of nothingness and find acceptance and courage without despairing. My response was that standing at the brink of nothingness, Christians could find in the incarnation of God in Jesus Christ a bridge across that chasm and the spiritual assurances that went with it. I suspect my reference to the traditional Christian view was far less interesting or acceptable to the students. It required a belief or faith they did not have; and Joe Mathews met them in the midst of their disbelief, where they lived, and through the educational programs of the Christian Faith and Life Community, he led many of them to develop their own faith. He was so successful that a very large number of students entered religious careers and several followed him when he moved to Chicago to develop his program there.

If the Methodist Church or Protestantism as a whole had had the structure and rigor of the Roman Catholic Church, Joe Mathews would probably have been treated first with hostility, as was Saint Francis, and then, after he was judged by the fruits of his efforts, admitted into the fold as one of the great contributors to and encouragers of the spiritual life. Joe Mathews was a man of integrity and character, possessed of a faith that drove him incessantly to bring spiritual enlightenment to as many as possible. I never knew personally a more deeply committed and intellectually honest spiritual leader and teacher.

To this might I add the short tribute of Monsignor John J. Egan, a long-time Roman Catholic friend of Brother Joe:

What did Joe Mathews give to me? He loaned me himself – not to keep, but to listen to, to be nourished by his thought and spirit, to learn from his accumulated wisdom, but more than anything else, to be inspired by his love of God and his respect for the little people of our planet.

Joe's Final Confession

The pace at which Joe lived increased at the end. He surely knew that his remaining days were few. He often spoke to his colleagues about "taking care of themselves." Then he failed to apply that care to himself. Rather, he cared for others. He cared completely and he cared to the end.

Among his last words of good counsel to his associates were these:

> Finally, guard against *irrational conflict.* Maybe I can plead a personal statement. I am extremely grateful to all of my colleagues over the last twenty-five years who have put up with all my stupidities, my personal flaws, my personal mistakes, my wickednesses, my stumblings, my down-right sinfulness. In case I never get a chance to do it, I express my deepest gratitude to you. It has occurred to me that if you could put up with my flaws, stupidities, and mistakes, through all these years, you ought to be able to forgive the mistakes and the flaws and the stupidities of each other. (*Bending History*, p. 238)

These words also are among the last that he uttered publicly. They seem to be an adequate valedictory. They are not a "paean of self-praise." He was willing to allow the strands of his weaknesses as well as his strength to be used in the weaving of the tapestry that was his life.

*****

This biography of my brother Joe is fulfillment of a promise I made many years ago. As I finish it, but more than ever now, almost thirty years after his death, I feel that church and society have to hear about Joe and his historic work. For, as I said in my words over Joe at his death, "he did perform the Christian's job of constantly turning matter into spirit!" Maybe to go full circle, the reader might return to the beginning of the book and read again the words from Brother Joe's last rites.

~J.K.M.

Postscript

Many observers have raised the question of what happened to Lyn, Joe's faithful partner in creating his legacy, and his legacy itself. In the following sections the reader will find the current story of O:E/EI/ICA and the full text from Lyn's Memorial Service in 1998 (containing comments regarding her role with Joe and following his death).

EI, ICA, O:E Since 1977

By William and Nancy Grow, members and staff of the O:E/EI/ICA (Nancy, a former missionary to Korea)

Brother Joe saw the ghettoes, the gulf between rich and poor, and the spiritual malaise of society at mid 20th century and decided to do something about it all. His practical vision and determination attracted people looking to make a difference in the world. He was instrumental in forming a worldwide organization, community, and movement whose impact continue today.

At the time of Joe's death, the Institute of Cultural Affairs (ICA) was established in 47 countries. It was operated by an international community of families consisting of over 2,000 persons bonded in an experimental secular- religious order. This Order was also the core of a movement of over 100,000 colleagues across the world inspired by courses and academies taught earlier by the Chicago-based Ecumenical Institute, sister organization of the ICA.

From 1977 to the global conference in Oaxtepec, Mexico, in 1988, the ICA, the Order, and the Movement fulfilled most of the programmatic efforts begun under Joe's leadership. In 1979, an office was established in Brussels to support the international growth. By 1980, as part of a mass awakening campaign, over 5,000 U.S. Bicentennial Town Meeting planning events had been facilitated in the U.S. and hundreds more conducted in other nations under the banner of Global Community Forum. As of 1981, participatory strategic planning workshops (LENS) had been facilitated for organizations in 93 locations around the world.

By 1982, over 50 International Training Institutes for laity and clergy had graduated a new generation of ecumenical church leadership in Latin America, Africa, Asia, India, Australia, and Europe. An audacious plan to demonstrate the possibility of grassroots community revitalization in rural villages and urban neighborhoods catalyzed an explosion of self-help Human Development Projects in 43 nations. Modeled on their mother project, the Fifth City Community Reformulation Project (now in its 40th year), this work became a network on which "the sun never set." The results were celebrated in 1984 with the International Exposition of Rural Development held in India.

The Oaxtepec conference signaled the de-formalization of the Order:Ecumenical and initiated a transition from an all-volunteer movement to a paid staff in autonomous operating locations. Most polity decisions in the ICA shifted to the local level. The Order's Global Assignment Committee was taken out of being, leaving every member family with the responsibility of redeciding its own relationship to the ICA. Staff in many ICA locations decided to continue operating as before through a variety of corporate and individual financial support mechanisms. Some staff gradually "reassigned" themselves to launch full-time ICA offices in other locations, while some left the ICA to become established independently and then, in some cases, to continue as ICA volunteers. The Order as a structural form survived for several years in many of these new relationships. The Order as a spirit remnant continues to exist among current veteran ICA staff members and as an informal network of missional colleagues inside and outside of the ICA, linked together by memory, internet, and occasional meetings.

Since 1988, the ICA in the United States has experienced several reconfigurations. It began as a loosely related entity based in three different areas of the country, East, Heartland, and West, with three different financial systems, and linked mainly through the national ICA Board and an annual national financial audit. Each area contained remnants of older ICA offices, which gradually disappeared or whose staff coalesced into program centers that began to specialize in particular types of programs. For example, in

the West, Seattle staff developed creative programs in children and
youth development that grew out of the Order's earlier work with
its own families' children. Phoenix staff standardized and docu-
mented the Technology of Participation (ToP) methods, built on
extensive network of ToP trainers, and created the International
Technology of Participation Training of Trainers. As a result of
these efforts, the revolutionary legacy of participatory group methods forged under Joe's inspiration has permeated the private,
public, and volunteer sectors of many nations. In the Heartland, the
ICA in Chicago inherited the responsibility for maintaining an historical building in Uptown donated to the Ecumenical Institute by
the Kemper Insurance Company in 1972. The ICA staff transformed this building into an International Conference Center and a
Community Resource Center (CRC). Today, the CRC is the largest
one-stop social service center in the nation, serving over 1,000 cli-
ents per week in tenant partnerships offering a large range of
health, social and financial services, including refugee aid societies
for twelve nationalities. In the East, a network of smaller field offices focused on entry- level job training, environmental justice,
and community revitalization through public engagement. An example is the development in Colquitt, Georgia, of a unique form of
community performance called *Swamp Gravy,* a story-based folk
life play which has been replicated within Georgia and in seven
other states and Brazil.

By 1998, a growing need to create a more unified public face
for ICA in the U.S.A. led to its eventual reorganization into a single national entity with four program teams and an infrastructure
support team. The four program teams were called Community
Revitalization, a Culture of Participation, Transformative Learning, and Community & Youth Leadership. In addition, an
experiment in participatory executive governance was initiated
with the National Leadership Team, composed of a representative
from each of the five teams. Much of the work of the program
teams is conducted in partnership modes with other not-for-profit
organizations.

Joe's legacy of global responsibility has continued to flourish.
Most ICAs which began prior to 1988 have continued to develop

into strong independent national organizations with indigenous leadership and linked through ICA International in Brussels. Examples include Australia, Belgium, Canada, Egypt, Guatemala, India, Japan, Kenya, Malaysia, Nigeria, Taiwan, the United Kingdom, the United States, and Zambia. Since 1988, several promising ICAs have been started up in the face of adverse social and political situations. They include Bangladesh, Benin, Ghana, Nepal, South Africa, Tanzania, Tajikistan, and Zimbabwe. In other nations there continue to exist incorporated ICAs in various states of staffing and activity, such as Bosnia, Brazil, Chile, Cote d'Ivoire, Croatia, Germany, Peru, Spain, The Netherlands, Uganda, and Venezuela.

Beginning with the publication of *Winning Through Participation* in 1989, there has been a proliferation of books and newsletters about the history, methods, and activities of the Institutes produced by various ICA offices and taskforces, and by individual ICA staff members, former and active. The most recent publication is *Bending History*, an anthology of writings of Joseph Mathews. More information on available publications is accessible at _www.ica-usa.org_.

In terms of the future of Joe's legacy, another significant part of the story is the outgrowth of creativity from the seeds that were scattered as a result of the decisions made at Oaxtepec. This is the contemporary permeation of the Institutes' methods in global society by hundreds of former ICA staff and board members. Examples range from Project Vida in El Paso, Texas, to an HIV/Aids Prevention Initiative in Africa; from staff members in the U.N. Development Programme to Habitat for Humanity in Costa Rica; from the founders of "Food for All" in California to facilitators of Viva Rio in Brazil; from the international business Kanbay to the International Association of Facilitators (IAF). From this creativity, the vision of Joe Mathews can be found across the world in educational institutions, church bodies, government agencies, environmental and civil society organizations, business, health and legal systems, professional societies, and more. The emerging face of the new global civilization is being formed with the help of an "invisible college" of persons, methods, and ideas that originated directly or indirectly from the Spirit Movement that "Brother Joe" shepherded.

The Memorial Service for Evelyn Johnston Mathews Edwards

The Memorial Service for Evelyn Johnston Mathews Edwards (Lyn) was held by her colleagues in Chicago, June 4, 1998. The following are texts from the service. The gathered community sang some of Lyn's favorite songs at the beginning of the service. Following the reading of the Obituary, the community sang together the "Fifth City Love Song," maybe Lyn's favorite song. Then a prayer was offered in gratitude for her persona that so impacted all who knew her. The Eulogy and the Sendout recounted dimensions of her profound contribution to history.

The Obituary

Let there be gatherings around the planet earth to celebrate the life force of Evelyn Johnston Mathews Edwards, who has traveled on to a world of pure and eternal spirit. She was born Evelyn Clara Johnston to Carolyn Myrtle Wilson Johnston and Samuel Howard Johnston in Wilmington, Delaware, on June 19, 1917, and peacefully departed, surrounded by family, on June 4, 1998, in Chicago, Illinois.

Evelyn was a wife, mother and sister. Married to Joseph Wesley Mathews, who died in 1977, she gave life to three sons: Joseph, James, and John (who died in 1972). She was also a matriarchal presence and role model to her daughters-in-law, Nancy and Teresa, and a loving grandmother to Melisa, Juan, Brent, and Amber. Later in life she enjoyed a second marriage to Clifford William Edwards, who preceded her in death. She is survived by her sister, Eleanore Johnston Peterson.

Although formally educated at Maryville College in Tennessee and Stanford University in California, Evelyn spent her life's journey being tutored by the pain of the Great Depression, World War

II, the Civil Rights Movement, and the innocent human suffering of the disenfranchised. Her destiny was significantly shaped as well through her participation in the missions of the Christian Faith and Life Community in Austin Texas, the Order:Ecumenical, the Ecumenical Institute, and the Institute of Cultural Affairs in Chicago, Illinois. Yet, in the end, history itself mediated her intellectual and spiritual development as no person or institution could have. Not one to measure her worth by material standards, she creatively expended the power of her knowledge and the wealth of her spirit in a relentless drive to create a safe, caring and just world.

Evelyn was, and will continue to be, a member of her family, a friend, a colleague, and a mentor to many people of diverse cultures, races and spiritual orientations. She has now come full circle and will be deeply missed but never forgotten.

The Fifth City Love Song

(Tune: "And I Love You So")

> And I love you so, that people ask me how,
> How I've lived till now, I tell them I don't know.
> People say I've changed, that they don't understand,
> Ever since the day, the day I took your hand.

> [*First refrain*]
> And yes, I know how lonely life can be.
> The shadows follow me, and night won't set me free.
> But I don't let the evening get me down,
> Now that you're around me.

> And you love me too; your thoughts are just for me.
> You make my heart alive and set my spirit free.
> The book of life is brief, but once a page is read
> All of love is there; this is my belief.
> [*Repeat first refrain*]

> You are City Five, Chicago's Old West Side,
> Where Iron Man first was born to build a global sign.

Oh, yes, I know you've changed, and some do not believe
This world has a new day since courage set you free.

[*Second refrain*]
    And yes, we've known this world's great agony,
    The billions still denied their hopes and destiny.
    But we will go wherever they may be,
    'Till all communities live free.

I've lived with you so long; no other love have I,
Your pain is all my own; your buildings, streets and cries.
Soon I may pass away, but love will still remain,
The Iron Man standing tall, that all the world may gain.
[*Repeat second refrain*]

The Prayer

    We pray in gratitude for the life of Evelyn:
for her affirmation of life in a time of negativity;
for her boundless curiosity that was not curbed by fear of the
    new;
for her care that was wide and deep, directing itself to those most
    of us forgot, and played out in large and small ways;
for her purity of heart, and the innocence that made the most
    jaded amongst us reconsider our lives;
for her willingness to do whatever was needed, whether it was
    speaking words before hundreds or washing the dishes;
for being slow to anger in an age that needs this reaction for the
    sake of its survival;
for living out of forgiveness and never holding a grudge;
for being a lady and making it possible for us to know one;
for her eagerness for life when many her age have retired in
    every way;
for all the times she showed up where no one expected her to go
    and
for the love she showed the youngest and the oldest of the lives
    around her;
for her mind that loved the majesty of the universe and gave it to
    others;

for the sadness we feel that tells us something marvelous is over.

We pray in gratitude to the creator of us all for the wonder that
was Evelyn.
Amen.

The Eulogy: Lyn, A Profound Contribution to History

By Raymond Spencer, CEO of Kanbay International, Inc.

Lyn was a lady. Elegant, caring.
Lyn was a wife and a mother. Loving, sharing, nurturing.
Lyn was a friend. Doing all of the "little things" that enliven and
refresh relationships.
Lyn was a colleague. Challenging people to live their commit-
ments.
Lyn was a profound spirit person, a symbol in the best sense of
that word.

One of her most cherished ways of looking at the deeps of spirit
life is called the Other World, a four-part description of the topog-
raphy of the life of spirit. It is, therefore, altogether fitting and
proper that the Other World is used to describe the greatness of
Lyn's life in the dimensions of mystery, consciousness, care, and
tranquility.

First is Mystery.

Lyn was elegant enigma. The elegant part is obvious. It had to do
with a style that defined gracious presence. Whatever she was doing, she did it with the passion and intensity that convinced you of
its significance – whether it was addressing a meeting in an Indian
village like Maliwada, or acting in a play at the Admiral, or keeping books in Chicago, or producing the Kanbay newsletter. If Lyn
was doing it, you knew it was worth doing. But there was more. In
the midst of whatever she did, there was a twinkle, a note that indicated more, something hidden, another dimension, a mysterious
quality that defied specification. Lyn could cling stubbornly to values many of us considered passé, but she was also relentlessly

open to the new, however many sacred cows it demolished. No matter how committed she was to a project, you always knew her real commitment went further. The twinkle proved it. She was in awe of life and life was in awe of her.

One never, I think, really knew Lyn. It wasn't just that she kept her own conscience, although she did that with care. It was rather that the better you knew Lyn, the more aware you became of Mystery. While she was an accessible person, you could never be quite sure what she would say or do. Perhaps that was one of her greatest gifts to us who were her friends and colleagues: translucence to the Mystery. *Lyn was mystery.*

Second is Consciousness.

Lyn was actively aware. Always reading new, "edge" books on the world and spirit, she continually engaged life. She intentionally gleaned meaning from the many situations life presented her. In recent years Lyn hosted the "Wild Women's Book Club," a sign of her interest in lifelong learning and interest in creating and being a part of a conscious community. In her late seventies she attended two Vipassana meditation retreats. She declared that those ten days of silent meditation were the most difficult thing she had done in her life. Yet she kept coming back for more. While deeply rooted in the historical church, she had a profound understanding of the oneness of humankind. An elder in one of the villages her organization was assisting was asked if these foreigners were religious. He replied, "Oh no, they're too holy to be religious." Lyn was a true holy person. *Lyn was consciousness.*

Third is Care.

Lyn was boundless love. She cared deeply for her family, friends, and colleagues. She knew most clearly when a colleague or friend needed a word or intervention, and she never shrunk from delivering that word in a caring, direct fashion. She worked tirelessly at figuring out how to assist people through difficult situations and often chose to help them see the importance of what they were doing as a way to give them courage to deal with their own challenges.

She was sustained by possibility. She was clear that at the heart of things there is hope and possibility. What a grand demonstration her life was. Although she was sensitive and responsive to the needs of others, her care exceeded feeling. She deeply loved Fifth City and its struggles for socio-economic change and justice. And she felt a wonderful affinity to the people of that Chicago neighborhood where she lived and worked. She was a woman who believed she could do anything and would do most anything. In her lifetime she was a financial person, a fund-raiser, a teacher, an archivist, a historian – telling her story and collecting other stories. In recent years while working on projects like the archives, the redoing of the Religious Studies I course, and the Stories Project, she focused on mining the wisdom of the past, bringing forth the gems that could reflect and possibly influence the future. What she did not know she set about learning. Lyn poured her care into particular projects passionately. She could cook you a personal dinner or be a leader at an international conference. *Lyn was care.*

Finally is Tranquility.

She looked upon life with a sense of gaiety and freedom. She took the vicissitudes of life in stride, appropriating them in a joyful manner. In one of her most memorable public speeches, she declared, "I am stuffed with effulgence!" While it might seem effulgence means unspeakable joy, it also means radiance or light. Lyn is the embodiment of radiance; her radiance illuminated the lives of all of us who have gathered here to celebrate her completed life. *Lyn was and is endless tranquility.*

Lyn both lived the Other World and delivered it most powerfully and empoweringly to those around her. She was a demonstration of living one's life fully at every age. She will be missed. We are privileged to have shared her journey. And she remains for us as the symbol she was while alive: a symbol of a profoundly human life. May there be those raised up who might carry that life posture forward.

The Sendout

By Bishop James K. Mathews

Just now I walked around the table upon which Lyn's ashes lie. Was this some archaic ritual? In reality, I was "walking around the boundaries," to help define the *sacred space* which gives meaning to our gathering. Whenever God's people gather, there occurs a fresh definition of sacred space – or we could say that the Church happens all over again, even in this beautiful sanctuary.

This has become sacred space for us because here and now the earthly part of Evelyn Johnston Mathews Edwards made its final entrance. We all stood as one to acknowledge the honor we hold for her.

It became sacred space because Lyn's life has touched each and all of us significantly in so many ways which have made all the difference for us.

Because here we have sung the Songs of the Spirit – songs she and we have come to love – and to hear words which in their very sacredness make this a more sacred space too.

Because here words have been spoken which have made clear our love for Lyn, words too long left unspoken in the past.

Because here Lyn finally received her very own "4 by 4" in the tribute given by Raymond Spencer. In fact, she lived her way into it. In a rare way she embodied the *Mystery*. She progressed through the years from a relatively casual approach to life to an acute sense of *Awareness* or *Consciousness*. Surely her *Care* extended to all. And through vicissitudes which would have overwhelmed most of us, she was the very model of *Tranquility*. I cannot help thinking that Lyn is even now laughing a little at the rest of us, for she possessed a sly sense of humor. Here we are, still puzzled about mystery and meaning while she now knows the answer.

Let me say more about sacred space. It is a good thing that we meet in a rather large church, for a great multitude needed to be accommodated. Nevertheless, this church has proved to be not nearly large enough. From where I stand the invisible ones who are present far outnumber those we can see.

We rather piously confess from time to time that we believe in the "Communion of the Saints," as if we knew what we were talking about. We must mean something by the phrase. Could it be that whenever we gather in solemn and sacred assembly, somehow all those who *believe* – of whatever time or place – are present with us? So you see why a great deal of sacred space is needed.

Thus it is that
Abraham and Sarah are here;
and Isaac and Rebekah;
and Leah, Rachel, and Jacob;
and Joseph and Moses and Aaron and Miriam;
They too are here.
And what of King David? – though "kinging" has more or less
   gone out of style.
Present too are the prophets. Isn't it great to have Isaiah here,
   and Jeremiah, and Ezekiel and Daniel and all the Minor
   Prophets too?
And Ruth and Naomi together with all the faithful men and
   women of old?
Then the Apostles are here and Mary and Mary Magdalene and
   Jesus, especially Jesus, who promised that where two or
   three are gathered together in his name, he would be in their
   midst.
In the number is also Paul, for this is St. Paul's Church. He has
   to be a very busy Apostle to get around to all the churches
   which bear his name!
Then there is St. Augustine and St. Cyprian and St. Tertullian,
   (although the Church never got around to calling him a saint,
   he who said that "the soul is naturally Christian" – sort of
   like Lyn).
Then there is St. Francis, St. Thomas, St. Martin Luther, Sts.
   John Wesley and John Calvin.
And St. Martin Luther King, Jr., and St. Mother Teresa and that
   other St. Teresa, and Mahatma Gandhi.

They're all here! And a host of others, too. This is indeed sacred
    space!

But this is supposed to be a *sendout*. Well, it is – with extended
remarks! These ashes are not Evelyn, for she was separated from
them days ago. We send her out because she has been called out of
God into the Great Venture which lies ahead of us all. She is not
alone on her journey, for others have gone before: like her son
John; her parents; Joe; Bill. But above all has gone before her the
One who conquered the last enemy, *death*, and called it what it is!
Nothing!
    And we send out all the others gathered here to go out and be
the scattered people of God, doing unendingly the "necessary
deed" which brings life to all.
    We sang a moment ago "Those who wait on the Lord." Some
of us recall that those words were sung around Joe's deathbed
while he, with his last strength, tried with his lips to shape the syl-
lables. Not a bad way to die! Not a bad way to live!
    Lyn was a Global Person. Therefore, I give the benediction in
Marathi, the language the people of Maliwada speak; then in
Shona, of Zimbabwe, where Joe long ago danced like Zorba on the
rim of the chasm of Victoria Falls. And then in English:

The Grace of the Lord Jesus Christ;
Which is the Love of God the Father;
Made real and present right here and right now by the Holy Spirit;
Be with us all, now and all along the way. *Amen.*

List of References

Bonhoeffer, Dietrich. "Freedom," *Ethics*. New York: Macmillan, 1965.

Boulding, Kenneth. *The Image: Knowledge in Life and Society*. Ann Arbor: University of Michigan, 1971.

Bultmann, Rudolf. "The Crisis of Faith," *Rudolf Bultmann: Interpreting Faith for the Modern Era*, ed., Roger Johnson. London: Collins Liturgical, 1987.

Cock, John P. *The Transparent Event: Post-modern Christ Images*. Greensboro: tranScribe books, 2001.

Jenkins, Jon and Maureen. *The Other World . . . In the Midst of Our World*. Gröningen, NL: Imaginal Training, 1997.

Kierkegaard, Søren. *Fear and Trembling* and *The Sickness Unto Death*, trans. Walter Lowrie. New York: Doubleday, 1954.

Marshall, Gene W. *The Call of the Awe: Rediscovering Christian Profundity in an Interreligious Era*. New York: Writers Club Press, 2003.

Mathews, James K. *A Global Odyssey: The Autobiography of James K. Mathews*. Nashville: Abington Press, 2000.

——. *The Matchless Weapon: Satyagraha*. Bombay: Bharatiya Bidya Bhavan, 1989.

Mathews, Joseph W. *Bending History: Selected Talks of Joseph W. Mathews*, ed. John L. Epps, *et al*. Tampa: Resurgence Publishing, 2005.

——. *The Christ of History*. Chicago: *Image: Journal of the Ecumenical Institute: Chicago*, Number 7, June 1969.

——. "The Time My Father Died," *Motive* magazine of the Methodist Student Movement of the Methodist Church, January-February Issue, 1964; *i.e.* (newsletter), Ecumenical Institute: Chicago, August 1964.

Niebuhr, H. Richard. "The Responsibility of the Church for Society," *The Gospel, the Church and the World*, ed. Kenneth Scott Latourette. New York: Harper & Brothers, 1946.

——. "Toward a New Other-Worldliness," *Theology Today*, April 1944, Vol. 1, No. 1.

Otto, Rudolf. *The Idea of the Holy*. New York: Galaxy, 1958.

Pesek, Betty C., ed., *et al*. *The Circle of Life: Stories of Ordinary People and the Gift of Spirit*. Chicago: Institute of Cultural Affairs, 2000.

Spencer, Laura. *Winning Through Participation: Meeting the Challenge of Corporate Change with the Technology of Participation (ToP)*. Dubuque: Kendall/Hunt, 1989.

Stanfield, R. Brian. *The Courage to Lead: Transform Self, Transform Society*. Gabriola Island, BC, Canada: New Society, 2000.

——. *The Art of Focused Conversation*, ed. R.B.S. Toronto: ICA Canada, 1997.

——. *The Workshop Book*. Gabriola Island, BC, Canada: New Society, 2002.

Tillich, Paul. "You Are Accepted," *The Shaking of the Foundations*. New York: Scribner's, 1948.

[ICA books: go to http://www.ica-usa.org Online Store >Books.]

Index of Proper Names

A

A Global Odyssey, viii, x, 231
Addis Ababa, 202
Africa, Bulowayo, 160
AGAPE Community, 139
aggiornamente, 172, 205
Alexander, Paul, 156
Asbury College, 60
Athenagoras, Ecumenical Patriarch, 200
Austin Experiment, 133

B

Bainton, Roland, 106
Baldwin, James, 200
Barbieri, Bishop S. Uberto, 145
Barnes, Roswell, 138
Barot, Madeleine, 139
Barth, Karl, 111
Baum, Monsignor Gregory, 172
Bea, Cardinal, 200
Beers, Jesse L., 50
Belgian Congo, 152
Bending History, 195, 197, 216, 220, 231, 240
Berea College, 59
Beruit, 202
Bethany Biblical Seminary, 147
Biblical Seminary, 63, 64, 65, 147
Biddle, Jr, Eric H., 206
Bissman Company, 53
Bonhoeffer, Dietrich, 117, 179
Bossey, 137, 139, 140, 144
Boston, x, 15, 16, 142, 144, 172, 201, 213
Boston University, x, 142, 213
Boulding, Kenneth, 177, 185
Brademas, Congressman John, 200
Broadway Temple Methodist Church, 65
Brogan, Professor, 214
Brokaw, Tom, 84
Brooklyn, 88
Bultmann, Rudolf, 117, 179, 231

Bunyan, John, 91
Buss, Fred and Sarah, ix, 146, 171
Butler, Bishop, 111

C

Calhoun, Robert, 106
Calvin, John, 45, 228
Camp Rucker, 82
Canary Islands, 151
Caradon, Lord, 200
Carter, Ruth, 178
Centenary College, 117
Central Texas Presbytery, 130
Chateau Bossey, 139
Chicago, ix, xii, 17, 25, 26, 31, 41, 43, 63, 68, 105, 121, 144, 145, 146, 147, 167, 169, 170, 173, 174, 175, 176, 177, 178, 188, 197, 199, 203, 205, 207, 208, 211, 215, 217, 219, 221, 222, 224, 226, 231
Christ Church (Methodist), 65
Christian Faith and Life Community, x, 130, 131, 132, 133, 134, 135, 136, 139, 142, 143, 144, 147, 167, 214, 215, 222
Church Federation of Greater Chicago, 145, 167
Church Missionary Society, 134
Church of the Brethren, 147, 167
Clark, Don, ix
Clemons, James T., x, 122
Cleveland Playhouse, 54
Cock, John P., x, 209, 239, 240
Colgate University, 101, 117, 118, 119
Columbia University, 116
Congo Polytechnic Institute, 150, 155
Congo-Brazzaville, 154
Congo-Leopoldville, 154
Connecticut, New Haven, 66, 76, 78, 80, 82, 106, 117
Connecticut, Sharon, 66, 76, 78, 79, 80, 82
Connecticut, Stamford, 117
Cooper, Gary, 48
Coptic Orthodox Church, 202
Corpus Christi, 62, 149

233

I

Ibiam, Sir Francis, 152
ICA, x, xii, 167, 168, 175, 176, 179,
    182, 185, 186, 187, 188, 194, 195,
    196, 197, 206, 210, 217, 218, 219,
    220, 232, 239, 240, 241
Illinois, Evanston, 144, 146, 147, 167,
    173, 176, 211
Illinois, Forest Park, 26
Imaginal Education, 177, 185
India, Maharashtra, 192, 204, 206
India, Maliwada, 68, 189, 204, 224,
    229
Institute of Cultural Affairs, x, 167,
    193, 195, 207, 208, 217, 222, 231,
    239
Iona Community, 140
Italy, Termine, 189

J

Japan, Hokkaido, 189
Japan, Okinawa, 67, 83, 84, 85, 97, 98,
    149
Japan, Tokyo, 98, 164
Joan of Arc, 91
Johannesburg, 160, 161
Johns, Benjamin, 76
Jones, E. Stanley, viii, 36, 164

K

Kagawa, Toyohiko, 98
Katakakombe, 157
Katurve, 157
Kawangware, 189
Kemper Building, ix, 17, 18, 68
Kemper Insurance Company, 167, 219
Kentucky, 59, 60
Kiely, Harry C., x, 125
Kierkegaard, Søren, 22, 124
Kimpese, 155
Kindu, 157
King, Jr, Martin Luther, 174, 201, 228
Kirchentag, 201
Kolwezi, 156
Kraemer, Hendrik, 137, 139
Kramer, Stanley, 137
Kübler-Ross, Elizabeth, 198

Küng, Hans, 201

L

Lagos, 154
Lake Nyasa, 158
Lambarene, 154
Lamumba, Patrice, 155
Lao Tzu, 180
Latourette, Kenneth Scott, 106, 231
Lawrence, William, x
Leibrecht, Walter, 144
Leiden University, 137
Leighton, Bishop David, 202
Lenningrad, 200
Leopoldville, 154, 165
Lewis, Edwin, 64, 65, 108
Lewis, W. Jack, x, 130, 131, 208
Lincoln Memorial University, 58, 59,
    60, 130
Lindbergh, Charles, 156
Lingo, Charles, ix, 174
Linz, Manfred, 138
Living Effectively in the New Society,
    192
Livingstone, 159
Livingstone, David, 159
Lodja, 157
Luccock, Halford, 106
Luce, Henry, 86
Luther, Martin, 106, 172, 174, 201,
    204, 228
Lutheran World Federation, 145

M

MacArthur, General Douglas, 83
Makin Atoll, 85
Marshall Islands, Majuro, 85
Marshall, Gene W., x, 124, 211
Martin College, 121
Maryville College, 87, 221
Mathews, Eunice Jones, viii, 88
Mathews, James Davenport, 7, 27, 30
Mathews, James Johnston, 117
Mathews, John Donaldson, 120
Mathews, Laura Mae Wilson, 27, 67
Mathews, Margaret Davenport, 30
Mathews, Rebecca Donaldson, 27, 28,
    30

Mathews, Stanley, 24, 26
Mathews, William, 28
McCleskey, David, x
McCord, James I., 138
McDermott, Tara, 6
McGovern, Senator George, 200
McLeod, George, 131
Metropolitan Art Museum, 64
Metropolitan Opera, 64
Michalson, Carl, 66
Miller, Joaquin, 55
Miller, Samuel H., 138
Mindolo, 158
Misner, Peter, 201
Mississippi, Pace, 189, 206
Monrovia, 151
Moore, Bishop Arthur J., 57
Morrill, Justin, ix
Moseley, Lela, 178
Mott, John R., 209
Mulungwshi, 156
muntu, 158, 162
Murphy, Russell, 51
Mussolini, Benito, 83
Mutare, 161

N

Nairobi, 162, 189, 200
National Council of Churches, 137
Ndola, 158
Nehru, Jawaharlal, 163
Neill, Alice Mathews, ix, xiii
Neill, Bishop Stephen, 138
Netherlands, Utrecht, 198
New York Public Library, 64
New York Theological Seminary, 63
New York Times, The, 64
New York, Hamilton, 28, 41, 118, 119, 120
New York, Norwich, 118, 119
New York, Oneida, 117
Niebuhr, H. Richard, 105, 106, 112, 115, 117, 124, 129, 162, 179, 195
Niebuhr, Reinhold, 66, 108, 112
Niles, D.T., 201
Norris, Edwin, 55
Nyanazuwe, 161
Nyanga, 161

O

Oden, Bishop William B., viii
O-E, xii, 167, 179, 196, 197, 217, 239, 240, 241
Ohio Northern University, 32, 33, 35, 42, 46
Ohio, Ada, 22, 28, 30, 32, 37, 41, 42, 43, 47, 48, 50
Ohio, Delphos, 29, 33
Ohio, Hammondsville, 37
Ohio, Huntersville, 30
Ohio, Mansfield, xiii, 41, 49, 50, 51, 52, 53, 62
Ohio, Richland County, 49
Ohio, Upper Sandusky, 37
Ohio, Wellsville, 37, 38
Old Umtali, 161
Olympic Games, 57
Order-Ecumenical, 17, 18, 23, 143, 146, 179, 186, 194, 196, 197, 200, 207, 208, 209, 218, 222
Outler, Albert, 106, 121, 171

P

Pacific Palisades, 57
Palo Alto Methodist Church, 88
Pennsylvania, Breezewood, 22, 27, 37
Pennsylvania, Lancaster, x
Pesek, Betty C. (Mrs. Martin), ix
Peterson, Eleanore, x
Pierce, Carol (Mrs. Joseph), ix
Pope John XXIII, 205
Pope Paul VI, 200, 202
Pope Shenuda III, 201
Pope, Liston, 106
Prince Henry the Navigator, 150

Q

Quillian, Jr., Joseph D., x, 207
Quinn, Father Robert, 201

R

Reisner, Christian F., 65
Richter, Dr. Julius T., 64
Rockne, Knute, 51

Roosevelt, Franklin D., 105
Ross, Roy, 138
RS-I, 125, 178, 179, 209
Ruedi-Weber, Hans, 138
Russia, St. Petersburg, 200

S

Sadat, Anwar, 202
Saipan, 85, 86, 89, 94, 96
Samuel, Bishop, 202
Satyagraha, viii, 163, 231
Schweitzer, Albert, 154
Selma, 174
Sendwe, Jason, 155
Seton, Elizabeth Ann Bayley, 202
Shaw, George Bernard, 56
Sheridan, William Brinsley, 51
Sherrill, Bishop Henry Knox, 145
Shute, Nevil, 137
Slater, Bishop Eugene, x, 127
Slicker, Joe and Anne, 146
Smith, Ben, 46
Smith, General Ralph C., 86
Snodgrass, Henry, 43
Southwest Texas Conference, 130
Speer, Robert E., 209
Spencer, Raymond, ix, 224, 227
Spike, Robert, 138
Springer, Bishop John M., 156
St. Andrews University, 131
St. George's Castle, 150
St. Patrick's Cathedral, 64
Stanford University, 88, 221
Stanley, Henry M., 155
Stover, F. Nelson, x, 210
Stromsem, Janice, ix
Stuart, Marvin, 88
Syria, Damascus, 202

T

Taj Mahal, 163
Taylor University, 32
Taylor, Bishop Prince A., 154
Temple, William, 111
Tennessee, Harrogate, 58
Tennessee, Lafollette, 60
Tennessee, Pulaski, 121
Tennessee, Tipperell, 59

Texas, Austin, x, 22, 41, 125, 130, 131,
133, 134, 135, 136, 137, 138, 139,
142, 143, 144, 145, 146, 147, 167,
178, 182, 207, 208, 211, 213, 222
Texas, Langtree, 55, 56, 57
Tillich, Paul, 66, 108, 117, 145, 179
Titus, Carol, 88
Tojo, General, 83
Town Meeting, 188, 192, 194, 217
Townley, Kay, ix
Tracey, Hugh, 160
Tracy, Spencer, 64
Troelsch, Ernst, 114
Trueblood, D. Elton, 88, 138

U

Union Theological Seminary, 66, 105
University 13, 187
University of Texas, x, 131, 142, 213
Uppsala, 200, 201

V

Valparaiso University, 32
Vassar College, 118
Vatican II, 145, 171, 172, 173, 200,
205
Vayhinger, John M., x
Victoria Falls, 22, 152, 159, 164, 229
Virginia, Lee County, 61
Virginia, Robbins Chapel, 62
Virginia, St. Charles, 61, 62

W

Wagers, Herndon, 113
Walters, M. George, ix, 175, 239, 240
Warren, Canon Max, 134
Warren, Don and Beverly, 146
Washington, D.C., x, 27, 58, 122
Washington, Fort Lawton, 98
Washington, Tom, 178
Webber, George W., 138
Wedel, Theodore, 138
Weizsacker, Richard von, 201
Wellesley College, x
Wendelin, Rudolph, 6, xi
Wesley Theological Seminary, 122

Resurgence Publishing

Resurgence Publishing Corporation is a not-for-profit corporation founded in the state of Florida by M. George Walters, John P. Cock, and Betty C. Pesek. Its primary purpose is to promote the utilization of the archives of Joseph Wesley Mathews for further research and publications that further the spiritual and social tasks that are Joe's legacy. RPC activities are coordinated by its founders and the Editorial Guild to promote publications. All copyrights are solely for the protection of the intellectual property rights of the Joseph Wesley Mathews family heirs.

The Archives

Joe felt that his efforts to give shape to the resurgence of the Spirit in his time might be a contribution to others who had a similar passion – love for the church, deep faith in God, and gratitude for the presence of the *word* in their lives. His legacy is far greater than the eighteen file cabinets filled with his papers, writings, talks, reflections, tapes, and other pieces of research. These file cabinets, however, stand as a symbol of his life's work that affected so many people in so many places.

Betty Pesek maintained Joe's personal files from 1967 to 1977. At the time of his death in 1977, he asked his wife, Lyn Mathews, and Betty Pesek to protect these works and keep them separate from the Ecumenical Institute and Institute of Cultural Affairs archives that were maintained by others. His papers and works were personal. Many documents that he had a hand in creating for O:E, EI, and ICA are also in these files and have his personal notes and asides handwritten in the margins. Joe left instructions that whenever anyone wanted to borrow his papers, immediately duplicate a copy and save the original to allow for future borrowers.

During Joe's life we did not have the advantages of modern technologies for maintaining documents and images. It is mind-boggling that the entire room filled with the file cabinets, plus nu-

239

merous additional materials in the personal possession of others, can today be contained on a single DVD Rom Drive. The *Resurgence Publishing Corporation* editorial guild has actually begun this process, digitizing and OCR processing the many papers and resources needed to publish this book and the previous publication, *Bending History*. This may be the secret to finally finding an institution to host these works, since entire libraries are now managed this way for online research.

Joe had an intuition that his collected works might be helpful and wanted them to be available to others to further the efforts to which he had dedicated his life. Lyn and Betty have had numerous conversations with Bishop James K. Mathews, his brother, and approached several institutions. Conversations continue.

The Editorial Guild

The Editorial Guild was formed by Resurgence Publishing Corporation to provide editorial consultation to those who wish to contribute publications that utilize materials from the Joseph Wesley Mathews Archives. They work directly with the authors and external editors of those works and engage many volunteers who also want to contribute to the efforts. Current members include:

M. George Walters: IT professional, programmer, knowledge management for maritime and banking industries. Served with EI/ICA/O:E in USA, India, Malaysia, Philippines, Ethiopia, and Belgium. Resides in Florida, USA.

John P. Cock: writer, spirit journey guide and blogger, earth guardian. Served with EI/ICA/O:E in USA, Australia, Indonesia-Malaysia, and India. Author of seven books. Resides in North Carolina, USA.

Betty C. Pesek: human relations. Archivist of the Joseph W. Mathews files. 1967-77 assistant to Dean Mathews. Former English teacher and speech therapist. Editor of book on EI/ICA/O:E stories. Resides in Illinois, USA.

John L. Epps: writer, consultant, teacher. Founding member of Int'l. Assoc. of Facilitators and Malaysia Facilitator Network. Ph.D. in systematic theology from SMU. Served with EI/ICA/O:E in USA and Malaysia. Resides in Kuala Lumpur, Malaysia.

George R. Holcombe: pastor, consultant. Seminarian where J. W. Mathews taught. Served with EI/ICA/O:E in USA, Australia, India, Malaysia, Hong Kong, Korea, Marshall Islands. Professor Emeritus, Wesley Seminary, Philippines. Resides in Austin Texas, USA.

Printed in the United States
51344LVS00005B/1-102